ON THE EDGE OF GENRE

handwritten: 180

The Contemporary
Canadian Long Poem

The long poem represents a significant body of work by some of Canada's best-known contemporary poets. Eli Mandel, Daphne Marlatt, bpNichol, George Bowering, Michael Ondaatje, Dennis Cooley, Frank Davey, and Robert Kroetsch have all produced work in this form. Smaro Kamboureli looks at these works individually and collectively to determine the extent to which they form a new genre.

She begins by placing the Canadian long poem in its historical context, following its roots from the nineteenth century, through the twentieth, and up to the present day. Drawing on the work of such theorists as Derrida and Kristeva, she offers an acute critical reading of the theories that link the long poem to the epic, lyric, and documentary genres. Each of the poems is then analysed within this theoretical context.

Kamboureli concludes that the contemporary Canadian long poem both demands and defies generic definition and is in fact 'at the edge of genre.' Her work breaks new ground in applying theory to what many critics consider the single most significant form of modernist and postmodernist literature.

SMARO KAMBOURELI is Assistant Professor of English at the University of Victoria.

THEORY / CULTURE

General editors:
Linda Hutcheon and Paul Perron

On the Edge of Genre

The Contemporary Canadian Long Poem

Smaro Kamboureli

UNIVERSITY OF TORONTO PRESS

Toronto Buffalo London

© University of Toronto Press 1991
Toronto Buffalo London
Printed in Canada

ISBN 0-8020-5908-2 (cloth)
ISBN 0-8020-6848-0 (paper)

Printed on acid-free paper

Theory/Culture Series 5

Canadian Cataloguing in Publication Data

Kamboureli, Smaro
  On the edge of genre

  (Theory/culture)   1000784942
  Includes bibliographical references and index.
  ISBN 0-8020-5908-2 (bound)   ISBN 0-8020-6848-0 (pbk.)

  1. Canadian poetry (English) – 20th century – History
and criticism.*   2. Literary form.   3. Literature –
History and criticism – Theory, etc.   I. Title.
II. Series.

  PS8155.K35 1991   C811'.5409   C91-093794-X
  PR9190.5.K35 1991

This book has been published with the help of a grant from the
Canadian Federation for the Humanities, using funds provided by
the Social Sciences and Humanities Research Council of Canada.

in memory of bpNichol
and for rbt –

> Listen. Speech is the prudence of the aged
> And time is a passionate sculptor of men
> And the sun stands over it, a beast of hope
> And you, closer to it, embrace a love
> With a bitter taste of tempest on your lips.
>
> Odysseus Elytis, 'Marina of the Rocks'

Contents

viii   Contents

Acknowledgments

This book could not have become what it is now without the questions and insights of teachers, colleagues, and friends who often helped in ways they were not always aware of.

bpNichol and George Bowering listened attentively and patiently to my many queries about their long poems; Daphne Marlatt gave me access to unpublished material; Douglas Barbour let me read his forthcoming monograph on Daphne Marlatt and, together with his wife, Sharon, offered moral support.

This book has gone through a number of revisions. I am indebted to Kevin Kennedy, my research assistant, who double-checked the quotations for accuracy and assisted me, as did my colleague Stephen Scobie, in the final stages of research and proofreading, to Diana Rutherford who typed the final manuscript, to Margaret Allen for her scrupulous copy-editing, and to the graduate students at the University of Victoria who participated in my seminar on the Canadian long poem in the spring of 1989. Any oversights or other errors in this study are solely my responsibility.

Special and deep thanks go to the numerous friends who offered their understanding, support, and intellectual stimulation: Joan (Peterson) Doherty and Ken Probert from my Winnipeg days; Shirley Neuman, Fred Wah, Pauline Butling, Roy Miki, and Linda Hutcheon whenever I met them in my comings and goings within Canada; Evelyn Cobley, Lola Lemire Tostevin, Jane (Kroetsch) Vigano, and Phyllis Webb who, with unfailing generosity of spirit, saw me through the various difficulties I encountered in the final stages of preparing this book. I am grateful, too, to David Thatcher for his gift of six jasmine plants, which he planted outside my study window on a special day, for the readiness with which he responded to my numerous technical queries, and for his assistance with proofreading.

A special debt of gratitude is also due to Robert Kroetsch, who helped me to clarify and refine many of my ideas during the different stages of this study.

Thanks are due also to Frank Davey, Eli Mandel, and the late Ann Munton, organizers of the 1984 conference on the long poem at York University, and to Arnold Davidson, chairman of the 1985 MLA session on Canadian literature, for giving me the opportunity to have my ideas challenged by stimulating dialogue. I am grateful to Clive Thomson, organizer of the October 1983 international conference on Mikhail Bakhtin at Queen's University, for accepting my contribution to the conference – the paper in which I first presented my ideas on the long poem. Bakhtin no longer figures in the book as the 'critical' influence that he was at the time, but what he had to say about genre has ir-revocably altered my way of reading the long poem. I would also like to thank the School of Criticism and Theory for offering me a fel-lowship that allowed me to exchange ideas on genre theories with participants in its 1986 session. A T.E. Glendenning grant from the Special Collections, Elizabeth Dafoe Library, University of Manitoba, allowed me to examine Eli Mandel's and Dorothy Livesay's papers. A travel grant from the University of Victoria also permitted me to study George Bowering's papers in the National Library in Ottawa.

The support of Gerald Hallowell, my editor at University of To-ronto Press, provided me with the encouragement I needed to con-tinue and complete this book.

I wish to express my thanks to the authors who have granted me permission to quote from the following works: Margaret Atwood, *The Journals of Susanna Moodie* (Toronto: Oxford UP 1970); Douglas Bar-bour, *A Poem as Long as the Highway* (Kingston, Ont.: Quarry 1971), *Visions of My Grandfather* (Ottawa: The Golden Dog Press 1977), and *He & She &* (Ottawa: The Golden Dog Press 1974); Robin Blaser, *Image-Nations 1–12 and the Stadium of the Mirror* (London: Ferry 1974); George Bowering, *Allophanes* (Toronto: Coach House 1976), *Kerrisdale Elegies* (Toronto: Coach House 1984), and excerpts from his papers collected at the National Library; Dennis Cooley, *Bloody Jack* (Winnipeg: Turn-stone 1984); Frank Davey, *King of Swords* (Vancouver: Talonbooks 1972); Don Gutteridge, *God's Geography* (Ilderton, Ont.: Brick 1982), and *Te-cumseh* (Toronto: Oberon 1976); D.G. Jones, *Under the Thunder the Flow-*

ers Light Up the Earth (Toronto: Coach House 1977); Lionel Kearns, *Convergences* (Toronto: Coach House 1984); Robert Kroetsch, *Completed Field Notes* (Toronto: McClelland and Stewart 1989); Dorothy Livesay, *The Documentaries* (Toronto: Ryerson 1968), and excerpts from her papers collected at the University of Manitoba; Eli Mandel, *Out of Place* (Toronto and Victoria: Porcépic 1977); Daphne Marlatt, *Steveston* (Vancouver: Talonbooks 1974; rpt Edmonton: Longspoon 1984); Michael Ondaatje, *The Collected Works of Billy the Kid* (Toronto: Anansi 1970); Stephen Scobie, *McAlmon's Chinese Opera* (Dunvegan, Ont.: Quadrant 1980), and *The Ballad of Isabel Gunn* (Kingston, Ont.: Quarry 1987); Lola Lemire Tostevin, *Gyno-Text* (Toronto: Underwhich 1986), *Double Standards* (Edmonton: Longspoon 1985), and *'sophie* (Toronto: Coach House 1988); Fred Wah, *Breathin' My Name with a Sigh* (Vancouver: Talonbooks 1981), and *Music at the Heart of Thinking* (Red Deer, Alta.: Red Deer College P 1987); and Jon Whyte, *Homage: Henry Kelsey* (Winnipeg: Turnstone 1981).

Mrs Ellie Nichol has granted me permission to reprint passages from bpNichol's *The Martyrology* (Toronto: Coach House 1972–87); the publishers of Porcépic have granted me permission to reprint passages from Frank Davey's *The Abbotsford Guide to India* (Victoria and Toronto: Porcépic 1986); and University of Toronto Press has granted me permission to reprint passages from *The Complete Poems of E.J. Pratt* (Toronto: U of Toronto P 1989).

Chapters three, four, and five include extended or altered versions of essays that appeared in *Open Letter* (1985), *Canadian Literature* (1987), *Sagetrieb* (1988), and *Tracing the Paths: Reading and Writing the Martyrology* (1988). Also, a summary version of my theoretical argument was presented at ACUTE (1987).

Victoria, 1990

I write because I can't sing   I am the book exiled
from my voice in search of a melody ...

Lola Lemire Tostevin, *'sophie*

Preface

On the Edge of Genre: The Contemporary Canadian Long Poem is a study suggestive of the perplexing questions the contemporary long poem raises when we attempt to read it generically. It began as an attempt to define this poetic form, a form reflecting many of the aesthetic and ideological shifts in the twentieth century, but also marking the colonial beginnings of nineteenth-century Canadian literature. As it evolved, it became not only a book about the long poem in Canada, but also a book about reading genre, about understanding the impact of colonialism on literary forms, and ultimately about locating meaning in a discourse of contradictions. The definition I have reached is tentative, a non-definition, one might wish to argue, for the long poem as I read it finds its energy in its incorporation of various genres and its simultaneous resistance to generic labels. Although I don't quite agree with the differing reasons Dorothy Livesay and M.L. Rosenthal and Sally M. Gall give for calling the long poem a *new* genre, I too call it 'new,' new in quotation marks, for newness or originality is a relative and suspect term, especially when applied to such contemporary literary texts as the long poem.

The long poem has been read as a lyric, as an epic, as a discursive narrative, as a postmodern text. But these readings, although partly invited by the long poem itself, are, I argue here, already misreadings based on the generic fallacy that a literary text, no matter how complex, tends to privilege one genre among the many it might borrow from. The long poem cannot be read as if it were an extended lyric, a strange epic – strange because of our unheroic times – or as if it were a narrative poem; it may share the emotive tonalities of the lyric, but it doesn't sanction the lyric's brevity; it may share the epic's intent to 'sing' of national matters and anxieties – 'O Canada' – but it does so in ways that parody the epic ethos. And when it tries to tell a story, it gets sidetracked and tells instead a story about the telling of the promised story.

These contradictions, this breach of promise, are what this study focuses on. It is not my desire to resolve or reconcile these contradictions; rather, my intention is to understand the generic restlessness of the long poem, why and how it engages itself with disparate elements only to subvert their functions and ideologies.

A number of critics, such as Eli Mandel, Frank Davey, Robert Kroetsch, Michael Bernstein, and Joseph Riddel, to mention only a few, have already addressed the difficulty of describing the long poem from a generic point of view. What I have attempted to do here is to show that it is precisely this difficulty, this resistance to generic definition, that characterizes the long poem as a 'new' genre. At the same time that it tempts us with a lyric, epic, or documentary reading, it breaks free from their specifications; it lies within and beyond the grammar of the various genres it includes. The 'law' of the long poem as a 'new' genre is its lawlessness. Its ungrammaticality results in the thematization of its formal elements and in its treatment as formal elements of its major themes, namely locality, the self, and the idea of discourse. This series of reversals is accomplished in the present tense, a marker of the long poem's desire to reside on the edge of things, within the limits of genres, between the reflexivity of its language and the referentiality of its ideology. The long poem, then, makes itself felt through its discontinuities, its absences, and its deferrals by foregrounding both its writing process and our reading act. While it is interested in the materiality of language, it is also concerned with the unreadability of the world's textuality.

This is why I begin my study with the Canadian long poem's archaeology – attempting to establish not its origins but rather its genealogy, the patterns posited by its ideological and aesthetic ground as they are revealed through readings of nineteenth- and early twentieth-century texts. More specifically, the first chapter looks at the cultural and literary dynamics that made the long poem a form *appropriate* to the colonial conditions and the subject matter of nineteenth-century poets. My reading of how imported forms and ideologies were *appropriated* by the long poem in the nineteenth century takes me to E.J. Pratt's poetry, especially *Brébeuf and His Brethren*, and to Dorothy Livesay's *The Documentaries*. Appropriation in this context signals the poets' moment of recognition, be it conscious or unconscious, that the long-valued and imported forms are at odds with their indigenous material and experience. To appropriate, then, a form that has already been deemed to be appropriate marks also the artist's moment of artistic and ideological empowerment. Even the contemporary long poem, distant as it is from such colonial manifestations, is characterized by this desire to make its own what it so liberally borrows from various genres.

The consistency with which generic and thematic contradictions recur in the long poem becomes the focus of the second chapter. Here I deal with the major critical approaches to the long poem – those of Michael Bernstein, M.L. Rosenthal and Sally M. Gall, Eli Mandel, and Frank Davey, among others. The tension among the disparate generic elements of the long poem, its length and anticipatory devices, its use of documents, and its intertextuality are some of the issues discussed here in the context of contemporary long poems. The three remaining chapters are detailed readings of the treatment of locality, the self, and discourse in the long poems of Robert Kroetsch, Eli Mandel, Daphne Marlatt, bpNichol, George Bowering, Dennis Cooley, and Michael Ondaatje.

What explains and sustains the generic ambivalence of these long poems is the use of the present tense. By dealing with locality, the self, and discourse in the present tense, the writers of these contemporary Canadian long poems construct a literary form that, paradoxically, defines itself by resisting definition.

ON THE EDGE OF GENRE

1

An Archaeology
of the Canadian Long Poem

Archaeology is random, snow castles
are alright for lyric poems.

George Bowering, *Allophanes*

The long poem recurs in the tradition of Canadian poetry in ways that echo Rosalie L. Colie's notion that literary kinds function as metaphors of certain cultural dispositions (6). Some of these cultural dispositions are immediately recognizable: the nineteenth-century poet wanted to define an identity, whereas the contemporary poet often and resolutely resists the proposition that there is such a thing as identity; the older poet wrote out of a belief in the truthfulness of history, while the poet of today sets out to unwrite or rewrite history by deliberately suspending its purported objectivity and inclusiveness; place, the locus of equally strong anxiety and astonishment in the previous century, is rendered now as a palimpsest of geographical and textual layers that the poet has to sift through; even more importantly, the nineteenth-century poet composed in a language and form that were imported tools certain to confer intentionality while suppressing ideological complicity – an intentionality called into question, if not sometimes entirely shunned, by the twentieth-century poet, who tends to write against tradition's grain.

These discrepancies, far from limiting any attempt at generic comparisons, point to a common archaeological field. My intention in this opening chapter is not to suggest that there is an unqualified continuity from poems like *Acadia* and *The Emigrant* to *The Martyrology* and *Al-*

lophanes, for example, but rather to trace the elusive and still debatable origins of a genre. What follows, however, is not a relentless pursuit of an unequivocal origin. I examine the unfolding of this genre in Canada chronologically not because I anticipate finding in linearity what characterizes the contemporary long poem but because alongside the pronounced differences of nineteenth- and twentieth-century long poems there resides a sameness that reveals the ideology informing this poetic form. Despite the apparent consistency of formal and thematic elements in the nineteenth-century long poem, we find many instances where unity is interrupted, a signal not of a wilful undoing of conventions but rather of an absence of artistic security. Contradictory impulses of this kind point to the making of the long poem as genre.

In his 1946 essay 'The Narrative Tradition in English-Canadian Poetry,' Northrop Frye observes that '[i]n looking over the best poems of our best poets, while of course the great majority are lyrical, we are surprised to find how often the narrative poem has been attempted, and attempted with uneven but frequently remarkable success' (1971, 149). Frye reads Canada's poetic past here, but towards the end of the essay he ventures to read its future as well; in the genial and inciting tone we have learned to expect from him, he admonishes modern Canadian poets to 'maintain an interest in the traditional narrative form' (154–5).

Forty years after the appearance of this seminal essay, Barbara Godard donned the mask of Cassandra in order to write 'Epi(pro)logue: In Pursuit of the Long Poem,' her response to the 'Long-liners Conference' at York University, Toronto (1985), a conference that confirmed, while rigorously questioning, the prophetic import of Frye's words. She, like Frye, performs a *pas de deux* by consciously engaging in both prophecy and archaeology: she writes that the 'clash [at the conference] occurred between those who defined the text as a fixed entity, the genre as an isolatable phenomenon, and those who understood the text to be a particular economy of competing desires and discourses'; but she also reminds her readers that 'Toronto is the home of Northrop Frye and recall[s] the famous double bind of Frygian theory, that an aesthetic object cannot be both Canadian and generic'(302).

The paradox that Godard outlines is at the heart of Frye's admonition. The narrative poem in its contemporary manifestations has indeed become a form as commonly used as the lyric. But Frye's emphasis on *traditional* poetic narratives has proven to be a matter of archaeology. In his essay Frye refers, among other poems, to Oliver Goldsmith's *The Rising Village* (1834), Charles Heavysege's *The Revolt of Tartarus* (1855), Charles Sangster's *The St. Lawrence and the Saguenay* (1856), Joseph Howe's *Acadia* (1874), Isabella Valancy Crawford's *Malcolm's Katie* (1884), and E.J. Pratt's *The Titanic* (1935) and *Brébeuf and His Brethren* (1940) – calling the latter Pratt poem 'not only the greatest but the most complete Canadian narrative' (153). The aesthetic completion and the thematic plenitude that Frye has in mind, while they might still be recognized with some qualifications by many readers,[1] reveal why the 'traditional narrative form' is largely a thing of the past. As we will see, this is as much a problem of tradition and its development as it is a matter of genre and ideology. Frye's terms of praise, as his essay testifies, depend on his alignment, within a humanistic literary context, of the thematic treatment of archetypal narrative patterns and genre.

Frye's observation brings into focus the long poem not only as a relatively popular poetic form in nineteenth-century Canada but also as a form organic to the ethos of the period. The latter is stressed, Frye implies, by a tendency readers of Canadian poetry have always recognized to some degree – the tendency of the Canadian poet to choose the long poetic form.[2] Soon after Frye remarked the significance of the frequency of the long poem, more narrative poems appeared: for example, Pratt's *Towards the Last Spike* (1952), Louis Dudek's *Europe* (1954), Earle Birney's *The Damnation of Vancouver* (1957), James Reaney's *A Suit of Nettles* (1958), and Dorothy Livesay's *The Documentaries* (1968). In spite of their differences, the length of these poems affirms that the long poem of the period Frye examines was far from being an isolated or dying form. And he is not alone in noticing the import of this phenomenon.

In 1959, Milton Wilson wrote that 'the discontinuous long poem, the cyclical short poem and the cycle of lyrics have always been the most fruitful cluster of genres in our poetic history' (199). But Wilson was not merely documenting this phenomenon. Echoing Frye's earlier claim, he remarks that Pratt 'writes narratives no doubt, but discontinuous narratives which are always turning, on the one side, into documents, letters and jokes, and on the other, into pure lyrics ... The point at which Pratt's genres meet is worth calling the center of Canadian poetry' (200). This statement not only acknowledges the role the long poem has played in the development of Canadian poetry but also prefigures the poetics of the Canadian long poem. Nevertheless when Wilson argues that 'the measure of Canadianism in poetry is the image,' an image 'designed abroad' (200), again, this time in the form of nationalism, the narrative treatment of theme still remains the overriding principle defining this genre.

A year later, Paul West remarked that '[t]he whole process [of Canadian poetry] tends toward an attempt at modern epic' (212). By limiting Wilson's large categories of poetic genres, West relates the long poem to the ethos encoded in the epic, an important but problematic qualification, as we will see later. In 1969, Dorothy Livesay, while confirming the tendency towards the long form, argued that '[a]lthough this tradition has been somewhat loosely termed "narrative," I propose to show that in our literary context it is more than that: it is a new genre neither epic nor narrative, but *documentary*' (1971, 267). What is interesting about Livesay's statement is not her affirmation of the recurrence of the long poem, but rather her recognition that the long poem ought to be viewed as a 'new genre' and her readiness to define it.

Frye, Wilson, West, and Livesay are concerned with the emergence and subsequent recurrence of the long poetic form as well as with the place it claims in the tradition of Canadian poetry. Their diverse use of literary terms illustrates the generic nature of their concerns while inadvertently marking the fluidity of this form. They attempt to define the Canadian long poem from a structural perspective, and also from a perspective revealing their awareness that they deal with the gradual formation of a literary kind intricately engaged with Canadian literary experience, a kind that takes its shape responsively. With the exception of Livesay's bolder attempt at defining this phenomenon as 'new,' these critics' hermeneutic task involves the recognition of conventions (Frye's narrative poetic form, Wilson's cyclical short poem) and the imperative to modify inherited generic terms in order to accommodate disparity (West's modern epic, Wilson's discontinuous long poem, as opposed to Frye's narrative poem). Although all interpretation relies on intertextual and cultural codes, there is a difference, as Jonathan Culler observes, between interpretation that uses these codes to reach another level of meaning and interpretation that treats a literary 'figure as primarily a reference or allusion' to these codes (1981, 95–6). Frye, Wilson, and West's interpretative moves follow this second route. These critics see genre as a system of aesthetic codes prior to the production of a text and operating within it, a system that guides our response to it. That system, they seem to imply, is not without cultural relevance: culture permeates and in part determines a text's genre. The cultural trait most prominent in their approaches is their desire to observe the continuity of valorized poetic genres *in* the Canadian context. But while Frye, Wilson, and West delight in their identification of familiar structures, Livesay, in contrast, takes delight in identifying a genre peculiar to Canadian literature; where they find discrepancy, and therefore the need to modify existing conventions, she finds a 'new' genre. In both cases, these critics' emphasis on the Canadian context suggests that Canadian culture seems to function as an ideological institution that is amenable to the production of the long poem as genre.

The large number of long poems and the responses they have elicited raise the question of the appropriateness of the long poetic form to the development of Canadian literature. Frye was again the first to address this:

[I]t is at least possible that some of the poetic forms employed in the earlier centuries of English literature would have been more *appropriate* for the expression of Canadian themes and moods than the nineteenth-century romantic lyric or its twentieth-century metaphysical successor. It is inevitable that Canadian poetry should have been cast in the conventional forms of our own day; but though the bulk of it is lyrical in form, a great deal of it is not lyrical in spirit, and when a Canadian poem has failed to achieve adequate expression, this may often be the reason ... [I]t occasionally happens that a successful Canadian poem has owed its success to its coincidence, deliberate or otherwise, with one of the forms of pre-Chaucerian literature. (1971, 148–9; my emphasis)

While Frye acknowledges that Canadian poetry was destined to develop synchronically within the lyric tradition, his primary interest lies in the diachronic implication of this movement. Although he states that Canadian poets employ forms current to their day, he also postulates the obverse, namely that they depart from current generic usage by, wilfully or unwilfully, dipping into the depository of seemingly obsolete forms. This pendulous movement merges synchrony (that is to say, viewing a 'text within a literary continuum') and diachrony ('placing an otherwise unrelated set of events in a linear sequence' [Stock 191]). In Frye's case diachrony marks the extent to which genre and culture correspond to each other discursively.

In tracing the correspondences between literary kinds and cultural traits, Frye plays the role of cultural historian. Old genres bear the marks of their cultural and physical geography. For example, the epic hero's many visits, including an obligatory visit to the underworld, where he tests his prowess and virtue, are an imperative of the epic genre, but owe a great deal to the seascape of clustered islands and to the cultural mythology of Odysseus' Greece. Similarly, Frye emphasizes the importance of Anglo-Saxon alliterative verse – set in a rugged northern landscape and stressing the need for physical strength and personal courage – for pioneering Canada. One of the reasons why the literary kinds cited by Frye were appropriate for the nineteenth-century Canadian poet was that, at a time when there was an absence of literary tradition, they could name Canadian experience in a manner that gave it literary credibility and a place in the continuity of long-established genres.

The diachronic use of genre in the nineteenth century took place alongside a recurring critical anxiety about the uncertain direction of Canadian literature. Archibald Lampman, for example, in his lecture on the poetry of Sir Charles G.D. Roberts and George Frederick Cameron (1891), both articulates and exposes this anxiety. 'A good deal is being said about Canadian literature,' he writes, 'and most of it takes the form of question and answer as to whether a Canadian literature exists. Of course it does not. It will probably be a full generation or two before we can present a body of work of sufficient excellence as measured by the severest standards, and sufficiently marked with local colour, to enable us to call it a Canadian literature' (1962, 27). Lampman, of course, was unaware that the very question he addressed was to become the Canadian aporia *par excellence* that thematizes the 'local colour' of Canadian literature and criticism. Our continuous questioning of Canadian identity, no matter how tentative, might to a large extent constitute the very essence of our literary sensibility.

Lampman provides a number of answers to his question, but the one most pertinent here is that unless poets develop certain 'peculiarities of mind and character' that will affect 'literary expression,' there will be no Canadian literature (27). His study of Roberts and Cameron reveals in part the cause that delays the shaping of an autochthonous literature. His recurring points of reference are models outside Canada: the poetry of Tennyson, Byron, Shelley, Arnold, and Dante Gabriel Rossetti characterizes the traditions within which he locates and studies the work of Roberts and Cameron. These British predecessors function not only as models but as points of origin that author(ize) a beginning for the nineteenth-century Canadian poet. Such a start is, however, a pseudo-beginning, for we can trace it back to a past that, although culturally familiar, is not indigenous but imported.

Even before the moment that marks what we rather arbitrarily call Confederation poetry, long poems written by such poets as Oliver Goldsmith, Joseph Howe, William Kirby, Alexander McLachlan, and Charles Sangster reflect a progression of Canadian literature, but a progression under suspension because, although their poetry progresses chronologically, it regresses generically. The scene in Howe's unfinished *Acadia* (1874) where the young son of a fisherman

> ... with wonder, reads
> Of Crusoe's hairbreadth 'scapes and daring deeds,
> And as strange scenes his infant thoughts beguile,
> Half wishes he were cast on Crusoe's Isle (37)

shows how the nineteenth-century Canadian poet misread the ideological import of his displacement. The geographical gap, which has in the first place occasioned this poetry, is already fictionalized and romanticized. Both writing mode and reading act, together with the response they elicit, are imported. The Crusoe dream of Howe's paradigmatic young reader inscribes him both inside and outside colonialism, for the Crusoe he reads about has become emblematic of British culture by virtue of a radical displacement from it. This moment of quiet repose in *Acadia* reveals that, to borrow J. Hillis Miller's words, 'the author and the reader are the same' (15).

Howe's elevated but monotonous discourse writes a double poem: one declaring his unmitigated allegiance to the Empire, the other affirming his love and hope for Acadia.

> ... bless the feeling, for it ever leads
> To sacred thoughts and high and daring deeds;
> 'Twas that illumed his eye when Nelson fell,
> 'Twas that which urged the unerring shaft of Tell,
> Inspired the plaintive and the patriot strains
> That Burns pour'd freely o'er his native plains,
> And breathes the influence of its sacred fire
> O'er many a chord of Moore's seraphic lyre.

With daring hand that feeling bids me now
Twine a rude wreath around my Country's brow,
And tho' the flowers wild and simple be,
Take, my Acadia, those I twine for thee.   (6)

Although the poet can 'find no trace' in Acadia of 'dark Tradition's stores, or History's page' (31), he himself, against the odds of, and (one would think) humbled by, his raw material ('wild' and 'simple'), inserts the absent traces in the textual landscape he creates. He shows us that, despite his desire to recreate the missing origin, the origin is defined by the very traces with which he supplements its absence. As Jacques Derrida states, '[t]he trace is not only the disappearance of origin ... it means that the origin did not even disappear, that it was never constituted except reciprocally by a nonorigin, the trace, which thus becomes the origin of the origin ...' (1974, 61). In contrast to the colonial signature in Howe's poem, Acadia is perceived as a margin that paradoxically seeks to deny its own marginality – the margin become an extension of the centre, a 'supplement [that] supplements,' that 'adds only to replace' (145).[3] Filled with deconstructive gestures informed by nostalgia, *Acadia* shows that '[i]n form as in diction,' as M.G. Parks puts it, 'Howe was markedly backward-looking' (Howe xxiii).

This double ideology illustrates the extent to which poets like Howe employ genres appropriate to their work but are reluctant, or even fail, to recontextualize them in the light of their Canadian material. By creating a narrative about the history of Canadian literature through their diachronic – one might even call it anachronistic – imitation of British models, they paradoxically create a contradiction of origins. They practise a writing that, in its attempt *not* to cause a disunity between the beginning of their literature and their British antecedents, contaminates the concept of origin.

The 'reality that an authentic literary tradition must ideally reveal – the mark of its originality,' as Homi Bhabha argues, 'can hardly be written in a language and literature of colonial imposition' (95). The long poems of nineteenth-century Canada mark the beginning of a literature that is linear exactly because it transfers the British tradition without necessarily adapting it to the colonized country. As a result, these long poems express an aesthetic and an ideology extraneous to Canadian experience. This ideology – primarily informed by the memory of an abandoned reality – articulates a Canadian cultural vision by reducing and idealizing its complexity: its inauthenticity refers to the cultural and historical gaps.[4] Whereas at this point in Canadian literary history the genre of the long poem operates interpretively by means of mimesis, its mimetic mode discloses what it fails to represent. In this, the ubiquitous dialogue of presence and absence in these poems is almost always measured against the colonizing source.

Oliver Goldsmith's *The Rising Village: A Poem* (1825), written in response to his great-uncle's *The Deserted Village* (1770), provides an example of that dialogue. Goldsmith opens his poem with an apostrophe to his brother Henry that formally dramatizes the relationship between the Canadian and British traditions. In a cheerful and hopeful manner, the poet proceeds to suggest that 'happier prospects rise, / Beneath the sternness of Acadian skies' (23) – happier, that is, than those his great-uncle describes in *The Deserted Village*. But the alternate society that Goldsmith envisions is not entirely free from the problems and anxieties that plagued the 'deserted village' of the mother country. What accounts for this irony, in a telling way, is Goldsmith's own family and literary tradition. Early in his poem he acknowledges his debt to the 'genius [that] formed the glory of our name,' namely the elder Oliver Goldsmith, as well as his efforts to 'emulate his fame' (23). But although the young poet intends to set his great-uncle straight – in his *Autobiography* he accuses the poet of *The Deserted Village* of having '*pathetically* displayed the Anguish of his Countrymen' (11; my emphasis) – the elder Goldsmith's literary influence on the younger poet is apparent and includes the latter's choice of genre.[5]

That same influence of genre, which we should extend to encompass the elder Goldsmith's own British literary milieu, prescribes the culturally accommodating vision of *The Rising Village*. The 'blessings' of Goldsmith's Scotia are far from being entirely its own.

These are thy blessings, Scotia, and for these,
For wealth, for freedom, happiness, and ease,
Thy grateful thanks to Britain's care are due,
Her power protects, her smiles past hopes renew,
Her valour guards thee, and her councils guide,
Then, may thy *parent* ever be thy pride!
Happy Britannia! though thy history's page
In darkest ignorance shrouds thine infant age ...
Matur'd and strong, thou shin'st in manhood's prime,
The first and brightest star of Europe's clime.

The nurse of science, and the seat of arts,
The home of fairest forms and gentlest hearts;
The land of heroes, generous, free, and brave,
The noblest conquerors of the field and wave;
Thy flag, on every sea and shore unfurled,
Has spread thy glory, and thy thunder hurled ...
Then blest Acadia! ever may thy name,
Like hers, be graven on the rolls of fame;
May all thy sons, *like hers*, be brave and free,
Possessors of *her laws and liberty*;
Heirs of her splendour, science, power, and skill,
And through succeeding years *her children still.*   (41–2; my emphases)

The poetic vision here delineates the extent to which the genre of the colonial long poem functions according to the same imperatives that subordinate the colony to the colonizing country. Goldsmith's discourse and genre enunciate more than he intends to say. The inception of his vision in *The Rising Village* reveals that for him, as for many of his contemporaries, a prosperous life in the New World is unimaginable and inoperative if envisioned outside the authority of the immigrant's past. The nineteenth-century Canadian long poem, more conscious of what its subject matter lacks than of what establishes its difference, cannot afford to be subversive. Hence its manifold figures of contradiction. Thus Kirby in *The U.E.: A Tale of Upper Canada* vacillates between the 'lone Canadian woods' – 'Let others far for foreign grandeurs roam, / Dearer to me the loveliness of home' (83) – and the 'native land' of his 'poor Emigrant' who never ceases to 'bear the seeds of Empire o'er the seas; / In farthest lands, plant Britain's mighty name, / [and] Spread her dominion, and exalt her fame' (94). Such poems bear the signs of both colonized and colonialist texts because their 'system of ideological representation' fully acknowledges the double bind they are in; they both 'reproduce and foreclose colonialist structures' (Parry 32, 39).

Choice of this genre, incorporating as it does long narrative accounts of nature, whether pastoral or not, and idylls such as those of Albert and Flora in *The Rising Village* or Jeannie and Willie in Sangster's *The St. Lawrence and the Saguenay*, embodies the signature of the literary 'empire' by prescription. The interplay of presence and absence becomes the metonymic rendering of the tensions between the Old World and the New, between an established literary tradition and a new literature that wants to be seen both as a continuation of continental traditions and as an independent literature.

The passionate recognition of the speaker in McLachlan's *The Emigrant* that 'Poetry is everywhere' –

> Why seek in a foreign land
> For the theme that's close at hand;
> Human nature can be seen
> Here within the forest green   (117)

– does not cancel out, as it proposes to do, the lines uttered immediately above it:

> Thou art not a land of story;
> Thou art not a land of glory;
> No tradition, tale, nor song
> To thine ancient woods belong;
> No long line of bards and sages
> Looking to us down the ages;
> No old heroes sweeping by
> In their warlike panoply.   (116)

The absence depicted by the use of negatives and the repetition of syntactical patterns only reinforces the reasons why the immigrant has to borrow the form of his tale from elsewhere. Mimesis here functions ironically, for it is accomplished by the very absence that the interpretive mode thematizes. In fact, absence operates as an enabling power. What justifies literary loans betrays the ideological reasons that allow McLachlan to read Canada as a cultural non-text. Whereas the unreadability[6] of the new land exposes his own blindness as reader – another exemplary moment in the nineteenth-century long poem reminiscent of Howe's Crusoe – his continental humanism, in contrast, enables him to encounter 'Human nature' in this cultural wilderness through universalization and the device of pathetic fallacy. The fact that he sees Canada as 'The promised land of liberty' (122), while painfully admitting that '"Old England is eaten by knaves"' (123), does not make Canada any more readable. Conveniently, during the obligatory 'Indian Battle,' the defeated

> [Mohawks and] Hurons stood at bay,
> Bore their slaughtered chief away,
> Far unto the woods they bore,
> And were seen and heard no more.   (147)

Unreadability, together with the generic loan it necessitates, is accounted for by an almost blind faith in one's own familiar tradition. The speaker and his fellow immigrants can read and sing only what they have been taught to see and hear. 'Human nature,' the all-encompassing grand theme of the nineteenth-century long poem, eradicates any signs that might reveal a cultural narrative different from, and therefore threatening to, the status quo of imported cultural values. The ideological power of familiarity, however, is humorously undercut when early in the battle our attention is drawn to Bill: 'There was fighting Bill, from Kent, / (Bill was in his element)' (144). Bill's expertise does not deter him from exclaiming, 'Why left I my country?' (150). What is psychologically revealed emphasizes the concepts of colony and wilderness that are fostered by imperial ideology.[7]

   If we observe a hiatus with regard to the stories told in these poems and the genre in which they are told, there is certainly no hiatus as to the social, political, and cultural factors that necessitated these poets' choice of form. Contrary to Carl F. Klinck's disclaimer in *Literary History of Canada* that '[t]he theme of exile or homesickness for the Old Land was not as common in Canadian colonial writing as one has been taught to believe' (136), self-consciousness about one's immigrant condition is often a state of mind that allows for the privileged position from which the speaker is able to assess the prospects and drawbacks of the new country. Edward Hartley Dewart, in his 'Introductory Essay' to the first Canadian poetry anthology, *Selections from Canadian Poets, 1864,* clearly states the dilemma of the nineteenth-century poet:

Our colonial position, whatever may be its political advantages, is not favorable to the growth of an indigenous literature. Not only are our mental wants supplied by the brain of the Mother Country, under circumstances that utterly preclude competition; but the majority of persons of taste and education in Canada are emigrants from the Old Country, whose tenderest affections cling around the land they have left. (xiv)

As Kirby echoes, 'the sons of Britain's Isle' move to the 'fertile West,'

Where England's manly speech is only heard;
Her laws transcribed and her names transferred,
Which her proud Colonists, on every hand,
Plant as memorials of their native land.   (104)

Even when this condition is not represented directly as theme, it is
thematized in the employment of genre and in the typological use of
certain thematic elements: the calling upon the muse for assistance in
writing in a culturally barren landscape; description of the uncouth
new land; a preoccupation with the sublime (often as a corrective to
the foreignness of the landscape); exhortations to the settlers on labour; battles with Indians; love interludes (occasionally allegorical);
and certainly praise of England. These sentiments often occur in the
form of digression from the Canadian material, and almost invariably
in reference to the Old World.

As Kirby and Dewart illustrate, the old forms and what lies on the
other side of the Atlantic still remain the primary vehicle of comparison and experience.

When the poets of other countries sing of the birds and flowers ... of those
lands, whose history is starred with deathless names ... every reference to those
immortal types of beauty or grandeur commands sympathy and admiration.
But let any Canadian bard presume to think that the wild-flowers which formed
the garlands of his sunny childhood ... are as worthy of being enshrined in
lyric numbers, and capable of awaking memories of days as bright ... as ever
was sung by hoary harper of the olden time, and he is more likely to secure
contempt than sympathy or admiration. Things that are hoary with age, and
dim in their distance, from us, are more likely to win veneration and approval,
while whatever is near and familiar loses in interest and attraction. (Dewart
xiv–xv)

Dewart, of course, lays the burden on the demands of audience, but
many of the poems in his *Selections* and other texts of that period claim
a share of it. Susanna Moodie's well-known account of the sickly and
unruly Irish immigrants discloses a certain class consciousness ema-
nating from colonialism. Similarly, these poets write, more often than
not, from a colonizer's point of view. It is left to their textual products
to represent their ambivalent condition and thus suspend the dialectical hierarchy of colonizer/colonized. This initiates the process 'of

othering' (Parry 33) that will gradually lead to the genre and ideology of the contemporary long poem.

It is within this frame – one not very different in its ideological and canonical underpinnings from the fairly recently devised categories of ethnic literature and the writing of visible minorities – that the nineteenth-century immigrant condition, together with the discourse it elicits, has to be understood. Even when not explicitly addressed, issues pertinent to immigrant consciousness are made manifest. They disrupt the seemingly unified grammar of nineteenth-century long poems by the use of genre and discourse, both functioning as double referents: the diachronically employed generic conventions and the psychological longing for the old order of things come to signify the very elements that comprise the poet's present condition.

Paradoxically, it is the apparent absence of a unified sense of a Canadian literary institution that grants these nineteenth-century works their Canadian signature. This is a signature that, while still in its early stages of inscription, generates the conditions necessary for the beginning of another tradition, an indigenous one, determined by the very elements that mark its absence. A poet's colonial condition is reflected in her or his work as a sign whose unity, according to Homi Bhabha, is 'constructed,' and whose 'stability' is 'ironic,' relying as it does on 'its repression of discontinuity and difference,' the very 'modes of meaning that we call realism and historicism' (97). In other words, although we recognize the landscape described in *The Rising Village* as Acadian, we notice that another level of referentiality is encoded in its representation, one that affirms the unity of Britain as a sign authorizing Goldsmith's 'local pride.' Yet the nineteenth-century poet's 'local pride' is different from Williams's concept, which has influenced a number of contemporary long poems, such as Robert Kroetsch's *Seed Catalogue* (1977), Eli Mandel's *Out of Place* (1977), and Dennis Cooley's *Fielding* (1983). Goldsmith's version is imbricated with a pervasive longing for Britain that grants *The Rising Village* a stability perpetuated by the generic conventions of the British tradition.

> Happy Acadia! though around thy shore
> Is heard the stormy wind's terrific roar;
> Though round thee Winter binds his icy chain,
> And his rude tempests sweep along thy plain,
> Still Summer comes, and decorates thy land
> With fruits and flowers from her luxuriant hand;

Still Autumn's gifts repay the labourer's toil
With richest products from thy fertile soil;
With bounteous store his varied wants supply,
And scarce the plants of other suns deny.
How pleasing, and how glowing with delight
Are now thy budding hopes! How sweetly bright
They rise to view! How full of joy appear
The expectations of each future year!   (39)

These lines, although meant to sing Acadia's virtues, can claim no Acadian signature whatsoever. We might, in fact, read them as minuscule condensations of another very British narrative poem, James Thomson's *The Seasons*, or as the convention of seasonal patterns, condensed into 'Summer' and 'Winter' in J. Mackay's two-part poem *Quebec Hill* (1797). The use of conventional rhetoric, instead of speaking of things Acadian, speaks of what stabilizes the signified, the signified here being beholden not only to the generic conventions established in Britain, but ultimately to Britain itself. The lack of any qualities that might differentiate Acadia from what Goldsmith presents as her 'matur'd and strong' origins contradicts the poet's intention to celebrate Acadia.

The contradictions inherent in colonial poetry rupture the unity of the literary work and expose its arbitrariness; the artistic uniformity that ensues from the colonial Canadian signature is deceptive. The relation between Canadian poetry as a signifier and British poetry as a signified, besides its enabling possibilities, can also be a crippling one with regard to the discourse of Canadian experience. In deferring to the given tradition of the imperial country, the long poem of the nineteenth-century colony loses sight of its immediate world. Although a poetry of representation, it embraces a reality that does not intend to enunciate, in fact fails to acknowledge, an indigenous Canadian aesthetic. In many of these poems the marriage of Britain and language functions as an allegory paradigmatic of the imported ideology. The enabling power of the Old World refracts the silence that a poet in the 'lone Canadian woods' might fall into, but at the same time threatens the emerging literature with overdetermination. From being a cultural non-text, the colony gradually becomes a museum preserving the feats and values of Britain. As a repository of monuments, the nineteenth-century long poem posits itself as a literary institution; if it is ideologically inert from our contemporary viewpoint, it is so because it spells out the paradox of a story that wants to be told in a genre that still has to be radically appropriated.

Unwittingly, the colonial poet creates a body of work whose literary devices tend to resist and even deflect the experience of the writing subject. Even Sangster's *The St. Lawrence and the Saguenay*, which successfully maps out the named territory, is written in 'manly speech' badly echoing Romantic discourse.

> Mild Evening, like a pensive Vestal Nun,
> Sits veiled, lamenting for the truant Hours;
> The Day has sprung to heaven to seek the Sun,
> And left her weeping on her couch of flowers;
> Heaven's Angels, bearing moonlight to the bowers
> Where True Love dwells, and Virtue sits enthroned,
> In golden urns collect the pearly showers,
> Singing sweet idyls, low and silver-toned,
> Till the enameled tears some cherub brow have zoned.   (52)

This kind of discourse exposes these long narratives' slippage between what Thomas Cary says 'Habit forms ... taste, gesture, action, thought' (*Abram's Plains* 41) and the lack of an individualistic ideology in the poets' art.

From a generic perspective, such works function in a linear fashion, continuing, that is, the Western tradition. From an ideological and pragmatic perspective, the spatial and temporal context within which they are located is supposed to be represented realistically, but the artistic rendering of its realism questions the appropriateness of the imported genre to which they answer. Genre as something elastic and constantly redefined functions as a historical determinant that exercises influence on the literary representation of a culture's reality. The cultural and historical specificity of genre tends to deconstruct the discourse of given models that belie the experience of the emerging culture. The deployment of genres appropriate to a recipient environment often results in unitary works that feed, and in some cases even inflate, the colonial imagination. Thus the early Canadian long poem is enunciated in a borrowed discourse that neutralizes the problems and concepts inherent in the Canadian context. The discourse of the mother country, in its new-found and conquered milieu, fakes an innocence that refuses to acknowledge the close rapport that tradition tells us ought to exist between genre and culture.

A notable exception to this pattern of a culture's instead of a genre's appropriation is Levi Adams's *The Charivari; or Canadian Poetics: A Tale, after the Manner of* Beppo (1824). Its alternative title points to the degree of the poet's self-consciousness about the writing act, a self-consciousness that departs markedly from the period's conventions. Adams locates himself firmly in Canada: his statement, 'I like thee Canada' (92), in its rhetorical simplicity and straightforward tone proposes to annul the ideological marriage between Britain and Canada. Here too we find descriptions of Canada's climate, dress code, and customs – among them the charivari – only this time they are unequivocally mimetic. Adams uses a particularly Canadian vocabulary (for instance, 'And, oh, those curs'd *cahots*,' with *cahots* footnoted [109]) without feeling apologetic about it; nothing in his poem registers any uneasiness about the ways in which Adams performs his writerly role. His literary indebtedness to Byron's *Beppo* is overtly inscribed in *The Charivari*, but Adams does not merely borrow a genre or appropriate Byron's Venetian carnival. The rendering of *Beppo* is clearly parodic: the excessive digressions, the numerous apostrophes to the 'gentle reader,' the recurring self-reflexive prolations on such rhetorical figures as similes and story-making all suggest not only his troping from his period's conventions but also his appropriation of Byron himself, a poet he clearly admires. Adams is conscious of his role as speaker and author:

> ... it is not that my story
> May prove much better than the lays I scan,
> But 'tis a story, and as stories chime
> In verse more fluent – I've begun in rhyme.   (91)

Yet he also thematizes his use of genre. He shuns the sublime mode – 'Truly pathetic – ultra wrought sublime' (90) – and announces that the muses 'of late have caus'd suspension':

> Indeed 'twere vain to dwell enumerating
> All, who before a self imagin'd shrine,
> On humble knee, their various forms prostrating,
> Would fain that some one might an ear incline,
> Whilst they but shew (their joys or sorrows stating,)
> How faint the sparks of wit which in them shine;
> Therefore I'll leave them plodding ode, and sonnet,
> And turning to my theme – begin upon it.   (91)

The discourse of Adams's poem shares little with the colonial discourse of its contemporary texts. It embraces contemporary reality as is, thus positing itself as a long poem where the othering process has begun to take place. *The Charivari*'s referential markers locate the mother country in Canada, not in Britain. It is this localization, its 'Canadian poetics,' that makes Adams's long poem stand out for its ideological daring of discourse and genre.

If the 'mother country' is the geographical and psychological locus where the Western literary tradition has partly originated, and if it still fosters the imagination of its 'offspring' who have gone away, then a return to its spatial and temporal boundaries could be seen in Freudian terms as a regression to the oneiric *chora* of the mother.[8] Eli Mandel, in his essay 'The Death of the Long Poem,' speaks too of the Freudian journey backwards in poetry, but the itinerary he maps out takes him to a different, in fact opposite, destination.

Mandel chooses to follow the Bloomian line of 'strong poets' and their revisionary movement, their persistence in wrestling with their strong predecessors (Bloom 5). He says that,

In Harold Bloom's paradox, the poet begins by rebelling against death, and his acute anxiety emerges from the fear of two deaths, physical death and poetic death. The threat to the absolute freedom and priority of the self (priority over nature) and the struggle with one's precursors. The poet's desire is to be not only his own father and to displace his 'real' father, but to be the parent of those who gave birth to him in what Bloom, echoing Freud, calls the Primal Scene of Instruction, the moment of election-love when the poet is called and answers. (13)

In adopting Bloom's theory of the 'anxiety of influence,' Mandel fitfully 'misreads' the forces at work in Canada, especially those of the nineteenth century: there are virtually no Bloomian 'strong poets' in that period, and we have yet to discover evidence that those poets 'transform[ed] their blindness towards their precursors into the revisionary insights of their own work' (13) – the process at the heart of Bloom's theory (Bloom 10). Mandel, in a deliberate gesture of erasure, does not mention the complex 'case' of the 'colonial poet' when he discusses the origins of the long poem. His Freudian / Bloomian recourse leads him to the colonial poet's literary 'fathers' without acknowledging the role that the 'mother' country played in this 'family romance.'⁹

Indeed, when talking about theories of genre and origins, we cannot afford to ignore the colonial poet's regression into the oneiric *chora* of the 'mother.' Such a regression functions as a double signifier: it points to the unsatisfying reality of the colonial poet caught at the crossroads of the present (new) and the absent (past, old) worlds; and it reveals one of the regressive but dynamic qualities of the poetic imagination, that of nostalgia. The fantasy of a beginning – which is, paradoxically, always in process – is carried, according to Paul Ricoeur's interpretation of Freud, by two opposed vectors: 'a regressive vector which subjects the fantasy to the past, and a progressive vector which makes it an indicator of meaning' (539). The colonial poet's creativity or initial literary production is activated by this nostalgic regression. The poet at first works with the *symbolism* ingrained in the mother country while ignoring the *semiosis* of the new country.¹⁰ I take the *symbolism* of the mother country to refer to the overdetermination of meaning that culturally fixed codes inscribe on literary tradition. That meaning owes its success of continuity to the homogeneity it attributes to its referential relations. It is precisely this correlation of continuity and homogeneity that necessitates a gaze fixed on the past in order to authenticate, and authorize, the codes of the present. In contrast, the *semiosis* of the new country, lacking as it does any fixed codes, offers the potential to produce a writing that occurs exactly within the gaps marking meaning; such a writing dislodges the totalizing codes and images of the mother country and enunciates the colonial poet's dislocation.

As a result, the colonial subject loses itself in the archaeology of its consciousness, reverses its course, and relocates its present in the past. In the process of unravelling the narrative of its experiences, the colonial subject displaces, to use Ricoeur's words, 'the birthplace of meaning' – especially the established meanings of the old world – thus unlocking its silence and releasing its desire (422). Desire inspires the immigrant or colonial poet's nostalgic movement, and this same desire and the discourse it entails, as we will see in the chapters to follow, become part of the ethos of the long poem. Desire is indeed what enables the poet to deconstruct the preconstituted meanings she or he imports from the mother country by ceasing to see the new country in colonial terms and consciously participating in its literary signifying process.

The colonial poet's nostalgia accounts in part for the frequent pref-
erence for the epic form in early Canadian literature, although there
are many long poems in the nineteenth century that, strictly speaking,
are not epic. Their intent, however, evokes it. Their emphasis lies not
so much in imitating the features of the classical, medieval, Renaissance, and later forms of epic as in attempting to emulate the epic
ethos. Adam Hood Burwell's *Talbot Road: A Poem* (1818), 'the first of
the pioneer epics of Upper Canada,' as Klinck says (Burwell v), hardly
shares any of the conventions of the traditional epic, yet its ethos is
recognizably epic. It is at this point that we move from considering
what makes certain forms appropriate in the Canadian literary context
to seeing how they are appropriated. The epic ethos manifests itself
in accordance with the ecological and cultural milieu of nineteenth-
century Canada.[11]

One of the earliest instances critically articulating this nostalgic ethos
occurs in W.D. Lighthall's introduction to *Songs of the Great Dominion*,
1889. 'Existing English Canada,' he writes, 'is the result of simply the
noblest epic migration the world has ever seen – more loftily epic than
the retirement of Pius Aeneas from Ilion – the withdrawal, namely,
out of the rebel Colonies, of the thirty-five thousand United Empire
Loyalists after the War of the Revolution' (19). Lighthall's language
of superlatives bears the marks of his anxiety (an anxiety similar to
Lampman's) and of his urgent desire to establish a lofty ground for
the beginning of Canadian literature. A.J.M. Smith is partly right when
he says that 'Lighthall's introduction is a kind of Canadian echo of
Whitman's Preface to *Leaves of Grass* (ix). But Whitman's vision does
not get blinded by the traditional epic ethos; quite the contrary, it is
specifically against this ethos, deeply and anciently European, that he
directs his readers' attention, for he is aware of the dangers involved
in the (almost intuitively) mimetic act of colonialism:

[T]he expression of the American poet is to be transcendent and new. It is
to be *indirect and not direct or descriptive or epic*. Its quality goes through these
to much more. Let the age and wars of other nations be chanted and their
eras and characters be illustrated and that finish the verse. Not so the great
psalm of the republic. Here the theme is creative and has vista. Here comes
one among the wellbeloved stonecutters and plans with decision and science
and sees the solid and beautiful forms of the *future* where there are now no
solid forms. (8; my emphases)

Without being concerned about the form and signs of lofty origins outside his own culture, Whitman creates a poem epic in its proportions. His vision is grounded in the reality that surrounds him and in its differences from other countries, not in models inspired in another place and time, by another tradition. He is concerned with the process of American poetry, its future; he delights in the plurality of the American identity and in the immense possibilities of literary form that the American material may create.

Whatever Whitman's practice, the epic as genre, according to Paul Merchant, goes beyond realism and might have originated in the need for established and continuous history (1–4). And it is surely telling that Lighthall's statement is informed exactly by this need. As if in confirmation of the organic correlation that a number of critics have been tempted to make between the physical size of Canada and the length of the epic poem, Lighthall's imagination is captured by the epic ethos in its entirety. He finds a myth appropriate in his mind for the expression of the Canadian experience, but he also appropriates this myth to the extent of denying its mythic origins and universality: '[e]xisting English Canada is the result of *simply the noblest epic migration the world has ever seen* – more loftily epic than the retirement of Pius Aeneas from Ilion' (my emphasis). He measures reality by myth, and in doing so he goes so far as implicitly to deny it is his nostalgic desire that shapes his vision of Canadian literature. The rhetoric and the historical facts that inspire him relocate his desire on a seemingly realistic ground, that of his present world, a world, however, informed by a heroic and mythic past. Constructed as it is out of rhetoric, idealism, a need for a tradition of cohesiveness, and the foregrounding of epic *mythos*, it is also a world that deconstructs Lighthall's own mimetic assumptions as soon as he states them. By evoking a reality he himself creates, he moves away from realism and towards the poetics of the long poem. Where he sees absence he locates an origin of his own invention.

But Lighthall's self-deluding rhetoric should not be taken as the rule designating all appropriations of the epic genre. The diverse deployment of genre in the early long poems marks the cultural code of Canada while, at the same time, it anticipates the heterogeneous form of the contemporary long poem. The simultaneous presence of diverse genres – such as the narrative or epic poem, cycles of lyrics, and dramas in verse – becomes a means of ordering Canadian experience. As a result, a grid of familiar generic codes is superimposed on the sense of estrangement that the Canadian poet feels in her or his new physical environment and previously uninscribed literary milieu.

The appearance of such long poems as Isabella Valancy Crawford's *Malcolm's Katie: A Love Story* (1884) and Lampman's *The City of the End of Things* (1899) and *The Story of an Affinity* (1894) (only recently published in its entirety) shows these writers to be considerably more accomplished in their poetic techniques than their Canadian predecessors, and also more liberated from the strictures of established generic conventions. Richard's vision in *The Story of an Affinity*, which Lampman called 'a small novel in blank verse' (xi), takes the form of a book, a book he cannot read but that the woman he is to marry, Margaret, can. Here, however, the unreadability of one's own vision is truly enabling, for Richard sets out on a ten-year quest for scholarly and spiritual knowledge that is meant to reformalize his uncouth existence. Indeed, references to Richard's 'strange' (4) and 'wild intelligence' (9), to his 'wild light' (13) and 'blind passion' (20), and to 'the mute purpose of his soul' (26) illustrate both his inarticulateness and the fact that his quest is for a form and discourse appropriate to the fulfilment of his vision. Despite his innocent blindness, Richard succeeds in reading his future in a text he does not know how to read. Thus his ultimate discovery is of 'A book more rare and fruitful to his heart / Than all the bound and printed to his brain' (39). Although he becomes a college teacher, he rejects institutional knowledge for that 'rare' heuristic text produced by his own individualism. Margaret's book as the pivotal centre of Lampman's theme in this poem, a book written in a language Richard does not know, functions as an analogue of the need to translate genre into one's own cultural terms.

The appropriation of formerly developed genres such as the narrative of Lampman's poem marks the degree to which Canadian literature establishes the *tabula* for its inscription. Lampman still remains the product of colonial culture, but his poetic vision is not restricted within or exclusively encoded by imported thematic and generic conventions. The literary kinds colonial poets consider to be appropriate are not necessarily, or always, those they appropriate in practice. It does not suffice that a literary kind is appropriate as a vehicle for cultural expression: the appropriateness of genre ought to be suspect when there are no signs of authentic appropriation. The appropriation process liberates established literary kinds from the aesthetic and linguistic grids that have shaped them as genres within a particular cultural context. It recontextualizes them, and during this process literary kinds reclaim their textual materiality so that they might be assigned, by the writer and her or his culture, a new pragmatic function.[12] Thus the appropriation of literary kinds, and the complexities that entails, takes the Canadian writer a step away from literary anxiety and brings her or him a step closer to the creation of a national literature.

Appropriation of literary kinds is characterized by both repetition and difference. The repetition of established genres recalls the already 'foreign' past within the context of a 'foreign' present. The element of difference that enters this process is accomplished through a double gaze – what we might see in Kierkegaard's terms as a looking backwards and a looking forwards. Malcolm's thoughts in *Malcolm's Katie*, which swing

> ... back and forth between the bleak, stern past
> And the near future; for his life had come
> To that close balance ... a pendulum,

move between the 'then' and 'now' (206) and exemplify the doubleness of the colonial gaze. The gaze backwards is one that fosters the emulation of generic conventions, one that perpetuates the symbolic ties with the mother country by subordinating the present to the past. The second direction of the gaze of recollection will come gradually to articulate the difference between the symbolism (the signified) of the mother country and the semiosis (the signifier, the inscribed) of the new country. It is engendered by looking forwards, by gazing at the gaps in inherited patterns of meaning. The ring Malcolm gives Katie has their initials inscribed in a joined fashion that maintains their distinctiveness despite the absence of a gap between them: 'That "M" is part of "K," and "K" of "M" ... / I like it better than the double hearts' (193). Similarly, the second gaze of recollection functions to give Canadian literature its unity, a unity, however, that does not completely erase the disparate elements within it. The gaze forwards, the recollection of the present and the future, gradually displaces the imported cultural features ingrained in genre without discontinuing the literary tradition.

This displacement delineates the stage where the Canadian long poem of the twentieth century encounters its *other*. An entity without precise origin, a *chora* without clearly demarcated boundaries, the other speaks of origins without origins, of unlimited possibilities and potential, of the long poem's continuous stage of becoming. Openness of form and structure features as its most prominent characteristic. Originally a textual field marked by anxiety about its foreign past, and by the emptiness and namelessness of its present, the Canadian literary landscape gradually becomes a text inscribed by new names and characterized by a more acute sense of which genres better reflect the Canadian literary sensibility.

Frye observes this process, but he also becomes prescriptive about it:

That this development [from Canada as a pioneer country to Canada as a civilized country, part of an international order] is now taking place and will greatly increase in future needs no detailed proof: but it is to be hoped that the poets who do deal with it will maintain an interest in the traditional narrative form. For the lyric, if cultivated too exclusively, tends to become too entangled with the printed page: in an age when new contacts between a poet and his public are opening up through radio, the narrative, as a form peculiarly well adapted for public reading, may play an important role in reawakening a public respect for and response to poetry. There are values in both tradition and experiment, and in both the narrative has important claims as Canadian poetry hesitates on the threshold of a new era. (1971, 154–5)

Frye, obviously, does not merely describe the development of Canadian poetry; he discusses the direction of its evolution, a direction he recognizes in the selection of genre. At this stage, Frye argues, the Canadian poet is no longer plagued by anxiety about the lack of appropriate, or lofty, subject matter or about the uncertain direction of Canadian poetry; her or his concern is now formal in nature. Even so, Frye's statement is informed by his assumption that the poet writes *for* the public, that the public in effect dictates or, if this seems too strong a term, guides the poet's 'experiments.' The same sentiment is echoed in *Anatomy of Criticism* where Frye states that '[t]he basis of generic criticism in any case is rhetorical, in the sense that the genre is determined by the conditions established between the poet and his public' (1957, 247). His reference to radio, although seemingly incidental, is indeed a telling example – think, for instance, of the CBC's literary contests and programs and the extent to which its production rules and strictures determine the kind of writing done for that market.

Margaret Dickie's study *On the Modernist Long Poem* throws some light on the reason why Frye rejects the lyric as inappropriate to the poet's dialogue with the public and focuses instead on the long narrative poem as a more proper vehicle for this exchange. Dickie, like Frye and, as we will see, most other critics writing on the long poem, proceeds to talk about its function by juxtaposing it to the lyric: '[t]he shift,' she writes, 'from the lyric to the long poem was not made swiftly or easily' (6). No matter what these difficulties were, that shift according to Dickie illustrated 'the inadequacy of [the lyric's] private and purified language to shape the *public* themes which they [the modernist poets] aspired to address' (5). The movement is from the short lyric to what Dickie calls the 'long public poem,' the long poem as mirror reflecting the public domain.

But this modern version of epic ethos informing the dialogue between poet (or more precisely poem) and public prescribes to the long poem a strict referential function that translates in effect into a one-way dialogue, a monologic genre. Although Dickie traces the beginnings of the long poem in the 'radical experimentation' of modernism – she has in mind Eliot's *The Waste Land*, Pound's *Cantos*, Crane's *The Bridge*, and Williams's *Paterson* – she finally has to admit that '[m]odernism' *vis-à-vis* the long public poem 'became in the end a conservative or conserving movement, quite different from its revolutionary beginnings' (3, 4). Dickie's argument, like Frye's, implies a definition of the long poem as a genre whose main intent is to represent the public – that is, collective – experience of the society within which it is produced. The poet, in other words, doesn't have to look for inspiration, but is assigned a public muse.

In spite of the various manifestations of genre in Canadian poetry, the long poem has always been there as a specific field,[13] whether 'in the traditional narrative form' that Frye hoped would be maintained or in the form of epic and extended lyric sequences. Genre, when seen as the grammar designating the development of literature, as Tzvetan Todorov sees it, 'is a sociohistorical as well as a formal entity' (1984, 80) providing the reader with an indispensable means by which to establish the parameters of an evolving poetry. Frye's isolation of the narrative form affirms the fact that the long poem has always been one of the most fertile genres in Canadian poetry, but it also displays a somewhat anthropological, almost structuralist, intent that subordinates the long poem as literary text to a 'sociohistorical' referentiality that does not always correspond to the poet's own recognition of reality.

The function of genre, as Todorov says in explicating Mikhail Bakhtin, is to posit the 'relation between the text and the world' so that the reader might study 'the model of the world put forward by the text' (83). Clearly mimetic in its orientation, this is the prevailing function of genre during the first stages of the long poem in Canada. We can understand better its appropriateness if we consider the degree to which certain genre conventions were appropriated.

According to Frye, an important answer with regard to generic appropriation is to be found in the 'mythopoeic imagination in Canadian poetry.' He talks about the martyrdom of the Jesuit missionaries, the Riel Rebellion, the 'forlorn hope at Dieppe' (1971, 148). These and similar themes we encounter, for instance, in Pratt's poetry. Frye remarks that 'there is a certain family resemblance among all these events which makes each one somehow typical of Canadian history. Is there not something in the character of such themes,' he asks, 'that recalls the earliest poetry of our *mother countries*, of the lost battle of Maldon where courage grew greater as the strength ebbed away, or of the reckless heroism at Roncesvalles which laid the cornerstone of French literature?' (1971, 148; my emphasis). Frye's integrative attempt – 'a family resemblance' – reflects the extent to which his concept of mythopoeic imagination in Canadian poetry, besides bearing signs of unity or nationalism, designates primarily a movement inspired by anxiety as well as by nostalgia. The Canadian long poem accomplishes this recollection backwards through the deployment of genres that took ages to develop in the Old World. What we have, in effect, at the beginning of the long poem tradition in Canada, Frye leads us to understand, is a compression of genres. The traces of medieval and Renaissance romances, Chaucer's narratives, and the Anglo-Saxon epics that we can detect in the poetry of that period are all part of the movement backwards that has largely shaped the generic route of poetry in Canada. Whether one intends to interpret Pratt's *The Cachalot* (1926), *The Titanic*, and *Brébeuf and His Brethren* allegorically or otherwise, Pratt certainly echoes a similar deeply felt affinity with the past.

But these diverse choices of long poetic forms, in addition to being appropriate as Frye observes, are also heteroclite. We find in their examples a lack of common generic locus. Generic features that characterize the classical epic, the medieval romance, the narrative poem, and the cycles of lyric poems – genres that developed through a great span of time – are in Canada collapsed within the literature of roughly one century. This simultaneity of diverse forms challenges the grammar of genre as it developed in Europe.[14] It provides further proof that in order to trace the archaeology of the long poem in Canada, and specifically its generic formulation, one has to proceed both synchronically and diachronically.

E.J. Pratt stands at the crossroads of the synchronic and diachronic readings of this archaeological process. His acknowledged reverence for the past, often coupled, as in *The Witches' Brew* and *The Titanic*, with his irreverent parodies of genre and imaginative supplements of history, largely accounts for his choice of what Frye calls traditional narrative. Yet Pratt's narratives, although they may strike the contemporary reader as outdated because of their elaborately rhetorical and prosodic features, are not strictly speaking traditional if we consider his tendency to mix genres and invert their conventions. Pratt was the first 'major' poet successfully to align generic codes with his themes. His long poems might suggest the same desire for epic ethos that we find in earlier poets, but Pratt's deliberate choice of themes of epic proportion justifies his choice of epic and its parodic variants such as romance and mock-epic. Nevertheless, Pratt remains a traditionalist by virtue of his anachronistic ideology and the way it is inscribed in his use of genre. His work, though often compared to that of the Group of Seven, did not have the aesthetic impact theirs had. If 'Pratt's work marks the beginning of a modern Canadian poetry' (3), as Sandra Djwa insists it does, then we ought to talk about a Prattian modernism; nor does he belong to the same 'cosmopolitan-traditionalist stream of A.J.M. Smith, Robert Finch, P.K. Page, James Reaney, Jay Macpherson, and Eli Mandel' (1983, 44), as Frank Davey argues. Pratt has very little, if anything, in common with poets like P.K. Page and Eli Mandel, who are attuned to their contemporary world and poetics. No matter where his greatness lies, Pratt remains aesthetically and ideologically a solitary figure. Even Frye who, like other early Pratt critics, has in the main only praise for his work, observes in his introduction to *The Collected Poems* that Pratt 'has never followed or started any particular "trend" in poetry, never learned or imposed any particular mannerisms of expression' (xiv). As a Canadian literary institution, Pratt stands alone in the tradition of the long poem.

This is so not only because of the idiosyncratic originality with which he approaches his themes – 'great feuds' taking place in a 'dull reptilian silence' (Pratt 1:153), feats of courage presented in elaborate, if not contrived, figures of speech, a great sense of almost baroque detail often bordering on superfluousness or heavy symbolism. Although we see him practising in his narratives the double gaze of early Canadian poets, his is a gaze that insists the world is readable; as Frank Davey puts it, '[t]he only reality which interests him is the knowable one' (1983, 36). I am not referring to his well-known passion for accuracy, which led him to obtain the menu of *The Titanic* and, as Klinck records, even to 'measur[e] the steps up to the bridge [of the *Roosevelt*], to see how far the Captain had to go' (1977, 12) in *The Roosevelt and the Antinoe* (1930). The world's readability in Pratt's long poems is to be found less in the way he unearths historical facts and more in how he views history. History for him is summed up in grand themes that suggest Frye's examples of what 'a poet would naturally be most interested in' (1971, 148). It is no mere coincidence that Frye's examples cited above are stories of war, of defeat and victory, more precisely of the complexities involved in securing a group's or nation's power; if for Frye themes like the martyrdom of the Jesuit missionaries are 'typical of Canadian history' because they reveal a certain historical and sociocultural maturity, then narratives of this kind also typify why and how certain genres are used.

In Pratt's long poems the referentiality of genre is taken for granted; it reveals the literariness of history to the same extent that history is encoded in the writer's choice of theme and form. Pratt's long narratives are long precisely because his themes are meant to be grand; they are informed by the same dialectical consciousness that has shaped Western history. They are delivered in the past tense, the present tense being employed sparingly in digressive sections, such as 'The Multipedes on the Roads' in *Dunkirk* (1941), in dialogue passages, such as the seamen's exchange during the convoy conference in *Behind the Log*, and in speeches, such as the female anthropoid ape's in *The Great Feud* (1926). Although the opening stanza of *Behind the Log* (1947) is written in the present tense, its presentness is meant to intensify the historicity of the events Pratt proceeds to narrate.

There is a language in a naval log
That rams the grammar down a layman's throat,
Where words unreel in paragraphs, and lines
In chapters. Volumes lie in graphs and codes,
Recording with an algebraic care
The idiom of storms, their lairs and paths;
Or, in the self-same bloodless manner, sorting
The mongrel litters of a battle signal

> In victories or defeats or bare survivals,
> Flags at half-mast, salutes and guards of honour,
> Distinguished crosses, burials at sea.   (2:149)

The present tense here functions as an equally rare instance of self-reflexivity in his poetry – Pratt revealing the 'algebraic' logic operating behind the 'graphs and codes' of his own narratives.

Perhaps the most important narrative code Pratt employs in his long poems is that of objective distance, a code that disallows the use of a personalized speaker. Pratt's poems are spoken by disembodied voices; even the 'I' that interrupts the otherwise impersonal narrative of *The Great Feud* is groundless, making no attempt to substantiate the truthfulness of the story it tells:

> Now let the sceptic disbelieve
> The truth I am about to state,
> And urge, with curling lip, I weave
> A legend that is *out of date.*
> Let him disgorge his lie; I claim
> That by a wanton twist of Fate,
> (To which I am by Hera sworn)
> A creature of this sounding name,
> Although three millions years too late,
> Stood on that peak this awful morn.
> It came to pass, one day, before
> Mammals appeared upon the Earth ...   (1:185–6; my emphasis)

As in the opening of *Behind the Log*, the present tense here soon unfolds backwards to enter Pratt's narrative of the past, thus both framing the telling of the legend and deconstructing ('disgorging') the legend's admitted outdatedness. The discourse of the 'I,' far from 'stating' the authenticity of its tale, 'urges' the 'sceptic' reader to 'disbelieve' the validity of the legend. Although these lines problematize the objectivity of the ensuing narrative, the rest of the poem is in agreement with the claim of the 'I.' Even the 'curling lip' that 'weaves' the tale is an ingenious expedient foregrounding truth as artifice, the present already a part of history's pastness; the poem's opening lines, 'Like a quarter moon the shoreline curled / Upon the neck of the ancient world' (1:168), show the extent to which Pratt's present surrenders to the sovereignty of the past, how it curls inside what has already become fact in his imaginary world. In contrast, earlier poets like Howe, McLachlan, and Kirby, by virtue of the stories they tell, record their present with an acuteness that Pratt lacks despite his overwhelming use of documents: whereas their diachronic use of genre documents their colonial condition, his highly controlled narratives reflect his belief in history as design.

Louis Dudek's remark that 'one may place [Pratt's poetry] with the "colonial" poetry of the turn of the century that broke with the culture and faith of the Victorians by discovering a robust and barbarous freedom outside England' (88) is only partly true. For, although Pratt dislodges himself from the colonial thematic and generic imperatives, his discourse does not address the problems of otherness that have concerned the nineteenth-century poets. Whereas those poets empirically acted out the doubleness of their experience, colonialism versus imperialism, this dialectic is produced in Pratt's poetry only by textual inference. From being a condition, an accurate portrayal of reality in the nineteenth-century poem, colonialism becomes an ideological representation in Pratt's narratives. What was verisimilitude has now become artifice. Pratt's is a discourse of war, his rhetoric a rhetoric of conflict. With almost no exceptions, all his long poems revolve around battles. Whether they are of an evolutionary, ecological, or missionary nature, Pratt's wars perpetuate versions of how history was made without questioning the process or its relationship to literary production.

Brébeuf and His Brethren, that 'greatest' and 'most complete Canadian narrative,' is paradoxically the narrative most fraught with the questions raised by Pratt's ideology. This long poem, even though it 'is not epic, or ballad, or romance, or spiritual diary but a hybrid of all these genres,' as Magdalene Redekop observes (52), is monologic in the heroism it presents. From the non-individual, collective heroism depicted in his other narratives, Pratt shifts here to specific historical characters using 'actual document[s] to give,' as Redekop says, 'an objective, dramatized picture *of* a subjective state of mind' (53). As Davey, and before him Dudek, noted, Pratt writes powerfully about power, and *Brébeuf* exemplifies this fascination perhaps better than any of his other long narratives. Brébeuf's spiritual power, his determination to become a martyr – '"I shall be broken first before I break them"' (2:49) – is encouraged by 'The stories of Champlain, Brulé, Viel, / Sagard and Le Caron [that] had reached his town' (2:48). This is only the beginning of the rhetoric of war that marks this poem.

'[C]apturing souls' (2:55) is Brébeuf's desire, and 'For that the first equipment was the speech' (2:53). Language becomes the stage of the war between the missionaries and the Indians. Driven by the 'alphabet of flame' (2:46), his fervent intent to follow the 'winds of God' (2:46), Brébeuf becomes a willing student of the Indians' language.

> Lacking all labials, the open mouth
> Performed a double service with the vowels
> Directed like a battery at the hearers. (2:53)

Similar military metaphors are consistently used in the poem every time the deployment of language is thematized. Although Brébeuf learns 'the rudiments of the Huron tongue' (2:50), he remains unabashedly blind to the Hurons' otherness. His vision of spreading the Word of God is entirely monologic, a monologism supported by Pratt's rhetoric of war.[15]

Brébeuf the linguist operates as a metonymy of colonization. The better his foreign tongue becomes, the more effectively it functions as a bait in 'capturing souls':

> The joy of the Toanché Indians
> As they beheld Brébeuf and heard him speak
> In their own tongue, was happy augury. (2:58)

The overdetermination of Brébeuf's mission allows him to double-talk ('double service'). By speaking their language, he compromises the Indians' otherness. Double-talking as a metaphor of religious conversion is no longer noticed by the native speakers, nor is it perceived by Brébeuf himself as aberrant moral behaviour. Instead, it becomes a trope of cultural resemblance hiding the spiritual appropriation that is the real and acknowledged intent: 'to bring to God / A race so unlike men' (2:57).

In his quest for great heroes, Pratt overlooks the ideological implications of the priests' acts. He becomes an accomplice in their appropriating tactics. Epic conventions are easily put into the service of the missionaries' designs; the epistolary sections, all printed in italics, reveal the priests' physical plight, thus endearing them to the reader; the diary form dramatizes the day-by-day conflict of body and spirit, of the Jesuit missionaries and the Indian fugitives; and brief chronicles put the Fathers' mission into a realistic and political perspective.

(The Founding of Fort Sainte Marie)
1639
The migrant habits of the Indians
With their desertion of the villages
Through pressure of attack or want of food
Called for a central site where undisturbed
The priests with their attendants might pursue
Their culture, gather strength from their devotions,
Map out the territory, plot the routes,
Collate their weekly notes and write their letters.
The roll was growing – priests and colonists,
Lay brothers offering services for life.
For on the ground or on their way to place
Themselves at the command of Lalemant,
Superior, were Claude Pijart, Poncet,
Le Moyne, Charles Raymbault, René Menard
And Joseph Chaumonot: as oblates came
Le Coq, Christophe Reynaut, Charles Boivin,
Couture and Jean Guérin. And so to house
Them all the Residence – Fort Sainte Marie!
Strategic as a base for trade or war
The site received the approval of Quebec,
Was ratified by Richelieu who saw
Commerce and exploration pushing west,
Fulfilling the long vision of Champlain –
'Greater New France beyond those inland seas.' (2:74–5)

This passage reveals the complex forces inciting the missionaries and supporting their work. No reader, as Redekop has shown, can doubt that the Jesuit Fathers act not out of '[s]elf-gain or anything but simple courage' (2:64). But '[t]here is an element of persistent cultural disjunction [in the story of self-sacrifice],' Redekop aptly observes, 'which undermines the affirmation and makes it hard for the reader to surrender to participation in the archetypal story [the crucifixion of Christ]. The martyrdom brings together transcultural stories of dying gods, but the interpretation of the ritual sacrifice reveals cultural bias' (55). The cultural bias forms indeed the poem's centre, the discursive space of a double imperialism: political and spiritual. It is carried out by Pratt's deployment of realistic techniques. Pratt's admiration for the Fathers' love and sacrifice does not suffice as an explanation of the eradication of the Indians' cultural and spiritual difference. Neither does his decision to compose his poem from the perspective of the Fathers as opposed to that of the native people decolonize his text.

Ironically, it is cultural difference that prepares the ground for the fulfilment of the Fathers' desires: their martyrdom.

> The Fathers entered deeper preparation.
> They worked incessantly among the tribes
> In the environs of Quebec, took hold
> Of Huron words and beat them into order.
> Davost and Daniel gathered from the store
> Of speech, manners, and customs that Brébeuf
> Had garnered, all the subtleties to make
> The bargain for the journey. (2:58)

The dissemination of the Word of God is inextricably related to the Indians' purloined speech. Paradoxically, as the Fathers' vows to become martyrs if need be misdirect their actions, so they themselves misread the implications of the need to translate the abstractions of Catholic dogma into the concrete discourse of the Indians.

> But to drive home the ethics taxed the brain
> To the limit of its ingenuity.
> Brébeuf had felt the need to vivify
> His three main themes of God and Paradise
> And Hell. The Indian mind had let the cold
> Abstractions fall: the allegories failed
> To quicken up the logic ...
> ... [Garnier] sent appeals to France for pictures – one
> *Only* of souls in bliss: of *âmes damnées*
> Many and various – the horned Satan,
> His mastiff jaws champing the head of Judas;
> The plummet fall of the unbaptized pursued
> By demons with their fiery forks; the lick
> Of flames upon a naked Saracen; ...
> The negative unapprehended forms
> Of Heaven lost in the dim canvas oils
> Gave way to glows from brazier pitch that lit
> The visual affirmatives of Hell. (2:73)

The self-referentiality produced by the text itself deconstructs the Fathers' self-image. The blind fervour that sends them, holding crosses, in pursuit of the Indians has a disfiguring result. To the natives' frightened eyes and bewildered minds the missionaries must have resembled demons with fiery forks, images of which Garnier sends for. In instances like this, the conflict between the symbolism of the Jesuit Fathers and the text's semiosis exposes the ideological function of Pratt's genre. The priests' realization that they have to translate the metaphysics of their religion into what they hope will be a transcultural visual language bears both a reductive and indeterminate meaning. Their translation of the sacred into the 'popular' dangerously enfeebles Catholicism while graphing iconically the antagonistic and often systematic techniques directed towards devotees and infidels alike by religious institutions. The slippage between the sacred and secular orders of reality formalizes the metaphysical bind Pratt has created for himself; he has reduced the Word of God – that which occasions his long poem – to an anthropomorphic narrative.[16]

The priests soon to be martyred preach what we might call, borrowing a term from Jacques Derrida, 'white mythology':

Metaphysics – the white mythology which reassembles and reflects the culture of the West: the white man takes his own mythology, Indo-European mythology, his own *logos*, that is, the *mythos* of his idiom, for the universal form of that he must still wish to call Reason. Which does not go uncontested ...

White mythology – metaphysics has erased within itself the fabulous scene that has produced it, the scene that nevertheless remains active and stirring, inscribed in white ink, an invisible design covered over in the palimpsest. (1982, 213)

Disseminating the Word of God to the natives is equivalent to spreading over them a veil of invisibility, reading to them words written in white ink. This act, combined with the Fathers' request for images sent to them from France and further amplified by their newly acquired second tongue, brings into question their politics of representation. Pratt's representation both mystifies and demystifies what it sets out to relay; *Brébeuf* narrativizes this palindromic unfolding of intention while, somehow, avoiding the problem: for the Indians, neither system of signification (word or icon) will be understandable because of the lack of intertextual ground. But whereas the Indians declare war acting out of their conscious inability to understand and their desire to preserve their spiritual sovereignty, the holy Fathers operate as linguists condemned to follow the dictates of their misreadings. Despite its various levels of discourse, the poem never exceeds its monologism.[17] Within the layers of the poem's misreadings and unreadability, God appears in advance as an *hors-texte*.[18]

The Indians' final act of war is, thus, textually necessitated; their 'fury of taunt' / 'fury of blow' (2:107) is determined by Pratt's hegemonic discourse. It is only fitting within the textual and ideological constructs of Pratt's poem that 'Speech they [Indians] could stop for they girdled his [Brébeuf's] lips, / But never a moan could they get' (2:107). The linguist missionary has become mute, his muteness being the double sign of his courageous martyrdom and his failure to read the world around him.[19] Brébeuf's silence affirms the invisibility of the Word of God but also testifies to his failure.

Pratt's closing his long poem with a brief section entitled 'THE MARTYRS' SHRINE' and set three hundred years after Brébeuf's 'martyrdom' does not alter the ideological signs I have identified in the poem. The mixed genre Pratt has found here challenges his vision of a readable world. This is the case in his other poetic narratives as well; he writes a new kind of long poem that desires to acknowledge a new place but has a difficult time finding appropriate human characters. Although his use of genre depends on the accretion of disparate forms, Pratt constructs his narratives by excluding rather than including.[20] His ideological, representational, and textual politics show his narrative thrust to be 'out of date.' His choice of non-human or superhuman heroes and his desire to attempt grand themes reflect his world-view. For these reasons it is difficult, if not impossible, to locate Pratt within the archaeology of the Canadian long poem. He articulates, albeit eloquently, the contemporary poets' decision not to endorse what he himself does. Seen from our contemporary vantage point, he has become the point of '*differance*,' standing at the coinciding point of its double meaning of *differing* and *deferring*.[21]

If Pratt created his own thematic and generic ground for the Canadian long poem, Dorothy Livesay opened up that ground in ways that Pratt's rhetoric and world-view could not. Livesay's longer poems, preceded by her first two lyric poetry collections, *Green Pitcher* (1928) and *Signpost* (1932), mark not only her political conversion to left-wing politics, but also an artistic conversion, which she outlined in her prefaces to these poems and in her seminal essay 'The Documentary Poem: A Canadian

Genre.' 'Ontario Story' (1945–7), 'The Outrider' (1933–5), 'West Coast' (1943), 'Day and Night' (1944), 'Call My People Home' (1948–50), and 'Roots' (1966) are all poems in which Livesay suspends the interiority of the lyric mode and moves outwards, towards the public world. This movement has invited many of her critics to look at her poetry in a twofold fashion: Peter Stevens sees 'the essential unity of her work' as being 'emphasized by her publication of *The Documentaries*' and the 'social poems' this book includes (1971, 579); Lee Thompson, talking specifically about 'Call My People Home,' says that this poem is an 'illustration of how genres and media can intersect with a specific historical, topical intent' (49); and Paul Denham sums up 'the most commonly observed dichotomy in Livesay's poetry' as comprising 'that of the "public" and the "private" poems' (87). Dennis Cooley, in a way pertinent to my argument here, locates the import of Livesay's shift:

There is nothing like a crisis in belief to bring a poet to the realization that the word and the world do *not* coincide, that the world we seem to inhabit is misnamed and that we cannot take the pure lyric (or, more accurately: the signifying system we know as lyric) for granted. The lyric cannot *by itself* stand as adequate measure for anyone who finds that inner desire and outer conditions fall far apart. The lyric cannot work when a state, and a poetics, jeopardizes the humanity of its citizens ... Livesay's political conversion can be seen then as a crisis in language and literature as much as a crisis in social formation. (236–7)

Writing while Crane's *Bridge*, Williams's *Paterson*, and Pound's *Cantos* were being written, Livesay saw the long poem as a form organic to the changes occurring in the world at the time.[22] Moving into a different genre for Livesay, as Cooley has shown, was an acknowledgment of the intertextual paths of cultural and aesthetic changes of her time.[23] The poetics of organic relationships characterizing Livesay's work of that period marks the beginning of the long poem as a 'new genre,' a genre that parts company with Frye's 'traditional narrative.' With the appearance of such long poems as James Reaney's *A Suit of Nettles* (1958) and *Twelve Letters to a Small Town* (1962) and Louis Dudek's *Europe* (1954) and *Atlantis* (1967), the modern Canadian long poem began to enter a period of radical change that would open the ground for the long poems of the seventies and eighties.

    Despite the fact that Pratt was instrumental in the publication of *Day and Night*, Livesay writes a long poem substantially different from his. 'Although the poem was written in 1935–36,' Livesay states, 'it was not published until 1940 in *Canadian Poetry Magazine*, which Pratt had launched. Pratt said that he was delighted to find a poem written by a Canadian that was not concerned with the colour of maple leaves, but with the social and industrial scene in cities' (1968, 17). Pratt's support obviously meant a lot to the evolving poet in 1940 and was certainly still cherished when she recorded it in *The Documentaries* in 1968. But in her brief statement, 'The Canadian Documentary: An Overview,' presented at the Long-liners Conference, Livesay argues that Pratt did not succeed in turning history into myth. 'Pratt himself,' she says, 'was too deeply rooted in the nineteenth-century models to be able to use the new media [*sic*] – radio – to full effect' (1985, 128). While revealing her own biases about the public and didactic roles of the poet, Livesay at once credits Pratt for his historical accuracy and remarks that 'Pratt's ideology was Darwinian: "Power comes to the strong." In consequence his long poems do not have political relevance for our times' (1985, 128).[24] Undoubtedly, there are many irreconcilable differences between Pratt's and Livesay's work; but what seems to be the dividing line between their approaches to history *vis-à-vis* the long poem is that Pratt, as I have argued, sees history as design whereas Livesay sees history as process.

The subtitle of 'Ontario Story' '(An Old Woman Remembers),' illustrates that history for Livesay is produced in the present tense. As she lies dying, the old woman enters a realm of time that does not acknowledge the separation from past and present.

> And are there hours, and time
> Omnipotent upon the mantel-piece?
> Ah, May, what time
> What time is it?
> Not four. Not any clockwise time:
> *What time of year?*   (1968, 3)

Memory as a structuring device allows Livesay to represent history as a thing of the present. No longer a master narrative ordering the world, history is reconstructed through the personal memories of one old woman. Yet the old woman herself exceeds the personal to become history personified: the 'golden garden' she and her husband dreamt of in the pioneering days is rendered now as 'this winter sepulchre / These pearly gates of snow' (7) – the 'dark's / Soft pummeling' (3) upon her weathered body. The objectivity and heroic proportions (usually masculine) of traditional history are replaced by quite opposite concepts. History is embodied within the woman's subjective and lyric memories; it is both internalized as what constitutes her self and externalized by a youthful vision that finds its corresponding image in the winter scene surrounding her. Whereas the naïve optimism of youth had encouraged her to aspire to the romantic and universalized conditions of a 'golden garden,' the experience of old age changes the direction of her gaze. From the vertical (metaphoric) function of her gaze, seeking to reveal to her heaven, God, immortality, a universality of specific teleology, we now move to a gaze that is horizontal (metonymic) in direction, revealing, in contrast, an immediately experiential world, a white landscape, that challenges Christian teleology by offering her in effect a double view, that of death (winter) and renewal (the cycle of seasons) in life.

Similarly, the 'prophet' in 'The Outrider' is linked with both the present (the Ontario of the thirties) and the past. Yet the gaze at the past does not cancel out the gaze at the present. Livesay lets the woman contradict herself, perhaps a sign of old age but surely also a sign of the paradoxes inherent in narrativizing one's personal history. The juxtaposition of country imagery – 'chickadees / Find perch on bough' (3), 'apple skins / Curl out initials on the cloakroom floor' (4) – and a rhetoric infused with spirituality – 'Beyond the stream a golden garden lies' (4), 'Omnipotent' time, 'breakfast prayers' (5) to 'Our Father Who / Art not our father there' (6) – allow the old woman both to be situated in ordinary reality and to have access to the otherworldly reality she soon expects to be a part of. The abundance of concrete imagery offers data that document the inner reality of the speaker; it records the subjective world at the same time that it speaks simultaneously of the past and the present. There is a subtle contradiction between the young left-wing poet and her persona's desire to make sense of the present by entering an atemporal (and by implication fulfilling) level of being. But 'The Outrider' has a slightly more elaborate structure than 'Ontario Story,' opening as it does with an apostrophe indebted to Romanticism:

Sing out, you silences! Uncoil, lean hills!

He who was alien has retraced the road
Unleashed, returns to this familiar earth.

The gate falls open at his touch, the house
Receives him without wonder, as an elm
Accepts her brood of birds ...

The old man standing with his hayfork high
Can let it rest, mid-air, and burden fails
And falls within the sun-dipped gloom of barn.   (7)

The imagery and rhetoric echo the old woman's remembrances found
in 'Ontario Story'; in fact, the two poems can be read as a contrapuntal
dialogue in female and male voices. But the apostrophe in 'The Outrider,' delivered in an anonymous voice that can be the poet's or the
poem's own discourse, addresses silence. The paradoxical evocation
– 'Sing out, you silences!' – that begins the apostrophe locates the poem
in an atemporal present that hardly offers the specificity of documentation Livesay has promised us. The outrider of the poem's title
seems to return to this familiar earth from a place reminiscent of Crawford's 'camp of souls.'
   Like an archaeologist, he unearths the labours of that past:

   His coming dreamed of long
In the recesses of thinking, in the hard
Hills climbed, his face a resting-place.
In winter warming hands at roaring stove
His doings smouldering as autumn wood ...
And so it is. Now summer's all swept clean
He comes with eyes more piercing than before
And scrapes his boots – swinging wide the door.   (8)

The shift from the past to the present in this poem is paralleled by
the shift in rhythm and vocabulary in sections II and III, where the
'prophet' speaks of the union activities of labourers.

A thousand men go home
And I a thousandth part
Wedged in a work more sinister
Than hitching horse and cart

Dark because you're beaten
By a boss's mind:
A single move uneven turned
Will set you in the wind   (10)

These shifts suggest what Livesay calls 'the employment of the actual
data itself [*sic*], rearranged for eye and ear' (1971, 267). The data, however, are not foregrounded in a Prattian manner, but are presented
in an alloyed fashion, are absorbed in the tone of the speaker's discourse. We do not read of a few specific labourers and their boss's
resistance to their union activities, but rather of 'a thousand men,' of
'a boss's mind.' The collectivity of the references challenges the specificity (one might even say the assumed objectivity) of documented
data, and functions as a device of persuasion, a sign of how desperate
things are and hence of the need for action. Livesay has her speaker
convey a revolutionary message whose import is tantamount to the
pervasive exploitation of thousands of men. The use of the rhetorical
'you,' at the same time that it stresses the collectivity of the data these
men's lives are based upon, is meant to solicit the reader's understanding and ideological support; we are not spoken to as readers and
outsiders, but are encouraged to unite with the 'thousand men.' This
rhetoric of political seduction reveals the speaker's 'agenda,' and also
points to the extent to which poetry of a certain political persuasion
tends to be monologic in its ideology. Livesay, however, skirts this
problem by her formal experimentation.

When the prophet's 'I' addresses the workers in section II, the poem
unfolds in a faster rhythm, in a combination of oral and written linguistic elements. His voice is both strong in its delivery of political
messages and conspiratorial because of the revolutionary/under-
ground content illustrated by the parentheses framing the section.

(Down in the washroom
    leaflets are passed.
'Say Joe, you sure
    got those out fast.'
    ...

The steadfast lean face
    opposite me

Reads, and alert
  watches to see

Who will respond
  who's first to talk –
Our eyes meet, and greet
  as a key fits a lock.)   (10–11)

This speaker does not communicate politics as monologic discourse. Instead, he wants to subvert the monologic capitalist ideology that usurps the rights of the men he speaks for. The shift from the earlier 'you' to the collective – and therefore politically more effective – 'we' demonstrates the urgent need to change 'historical' conditions. Unlike Pratt, who inserts documents into the narratives he constructs, Livesay affords her readers a view of how history is made and unmade. The data consist of these men's personal lives, their thwarted aspirations and rights, their desire to effect change. This is emphasized by the parentheses that frame these men's voices and activities and create the feeling of an intimate environment embodying the paradox of a will that is at once subjective and collective. In section III and in the 'Epilogue,' in longer lines and in a much more relaxed rhythm, the speaker assumes a different tone, speaks in a diversified language, a language that is still political but that also shows that Livesay's poetics, far from verging on monologism, has a range that exceeds the political.

This range of voice is indeed one of Livesay's accomplishments in the long poems gathered together in *The Documentaries*. Although overtly political in this collection, Livesay does not make propaganda of her long poems. The political and the aesthetic are balanced by her juxtaposition of lyrical and non-lyrical passages, of subjective and objective voices, of narrative and discursive elements. The index to this series of organic relationships is to be found in her definition of what constitutes the long poem as documentary:

the Canadian longer poem is not truly a narrative at all – and certainly not a historical epic. It is, rather, a *documentary* poem, based on topical data but held together by descriptive, lyrical, and didactic elements. Our narratives, in other words, are not told for the tale's sake or for the myth's sake: the story is a frame on which to hang a theme. (1971, 269)

And more specifically:

> the elements of a documentary: topical data, historical and geographic, based on research; no single protagonist; man versus nature which must be dominated if man wants 'progress'; and a view of nature itself as brooding, implacable, but not sinister. (1971, 280)

There is a certain prescriptiveness in her definition, a prescriptiveness that shows her operating with both blindness and insight. Her reading of the long poem as a truly mixed genre that can 'authentically' communicate Canadian experience is indeed the first conscious attempt by a Canadian poet to see the long poem as simultaneously a 'new genre' and an open form. Her preoccupation with theme, however, a theme that is supposed to instruct, reveals her blindness, namely her willingness to subordinate genre to historical necessity, to control the mixed genre of the long poem by means of consistent thematic development. To use Terry Eagleton's words, history enters her work as an ideology that allows her to play with form (72).

Livesay, unlike Pratt, did not attempt the large long poem, primarily, I think, because of her distrust of power systems implied in the monologic discourse of the epic form. For the same ideological and artistic reason, she is interested in anti-heroes; she preempts the monologic and subjective power of the speaking 'I' while, at the same time, restraining the hegemonic implications of objectivity; she gets away with the banality of her rhythms by dramatizing the need for a common, easily recognizable voice. These elements that pervade all her longer poems become even more pronounced when we consider *The Documentaries* to be not simply the result of an editorial decision to publish her longer poems together, but a long poem in itself. *The Documentaries*, complete with the poet's prefaces that accompany each poem, prefigures by way of its structure such long poems as Al Purdy's *In Search of Owen Roblin*, Eli Mandel's *Out of Place*, Robert Kroetsch's *Completed Field Notes*, and Daphne Marlatt's *Steveston*.

The consistencies and inconsistencies that characterize the Canadian long poem from its nineteenth-century beginnings to its modernist versions reveal not a linear history of this genre but the trajectory of a poetry that still, today, seeks a shape. What emerges from the archaeological view of this history is a form that acknowledges the cultural and generic parameters of the tradition along with the very resoluteness with which it often attempts to override them. The patterns of generic appropriation and cultural appropriateness, the recurrent formal and thematic modes and gaps, all these, together with the consistency of length, point to the genealogy of the contemporary poem in Canada. In its Foucauldian implications, this genealogy[25] speaks of the long poem's complicitous relationship with the literary tradition from which it emerges. Because of the major ideological differences between the colonialism of the nineteenth-century long poem and the deconstructive tendencies of its contemporary manifestations, we can establish not a continuous development of the form, but rather an archaeological field, a scattering of formal and thematic origins. It becomes apparent then why, in discussing the contemporary long poem as a 'new' genre, I am in no position to make any claims to knowing its exact origins (though I have traced some of its origins). Nor is the word 'contemporary' meant to delineate a precise historical occasion that might mark the contemporary long poem's radical exit from what is called modern poetry. Instead, it offers a frame of chronological relativity whose margins are not categorically determined and that, as a result, can exceed both in a forwards and backwards movement the ever-tentative line that designates contemporaneity.

'[G]enres,' as Fowler says, 'at all levels are positively resistant to definition' (40). This sobering observation holds all the more for the long poems of the 1970s and 1980s, which I am exploring as a genre whose main trait is precisely this resistance to generic definition. A definition of this kind both affirms and undoes itself. But contradiction in reference to the long poem, as will become evident in the following chapter, is not to be overcome. Quite the contrary. It results in a discourse that invites us to explore it in itself. Although such long poems as bpNichol's *The Martyrology* and George Bowering's *Kerrisdale Elegies* cohere when one reads them, that coherence is assigned to them by the reading act. It enters the poems together with the reader; it is not inherent in the poems. In fact, coherence occurs, is marked, only when the contradictory genre systems of epic, lyric, non-epic narrative poetry and non-literary discourse operating within the long poem posit their various interrelationships. Coherence, then, does not annul contradiction: it brings to light the generic interplay that makes the contemporary long poem a distinct poetic form. The inclusiveness of the long poem does not presuppose a harmonious interrelationship among its mixed literary kinds, nor does it necessitate a complete cancelling out of their idiosyncratic generic elements; instead, it announces a dialogue of genres.

2

A Genre in the Present Tense

[I]f severed they [genres] be good, the conjunction cannot be
hurtful.

Sir Philip Sidney, *An Apology for Poetry*

Lola Lemire Tostevin, *Double Standards* (1985):

for a long time I couldn't decide whether to be story
or poem   one voice or many   the poem always losing its
way as it scribbles towards some equilibrium   while the
story brackets lives   claims them for something it can
recognize   a cast of thousands   costumes   soundtrack

Robin Blaser, *Image-Nations 1–12* (1974):

it is the interchange the form took
like walking in and out of a star
the words are left over   collapsed
into themselves   in the movement

George Bowering, *Allophanes* (1976):

The language
is not spoken,
it speaks ...

history is a thing. A dead language
   in which all words
      describe, & refer,

Frank Davey, *King of Swords* (1972):

The death of Arthur continues.
When I bought her black peignoirs
he was dying, when I wrote her aubades
he was dying, when I took ill at her refusal
his fever rose with mine, his bile
convulsed, upward ...

Dying the death of Arthur, emblazoning ...
& the death of Arthur continues.

Phyllis Webb, *Naked Poems* (1965):

star fish
  fish star

Roy Kiyooka, *The Fontainebleau Dream Machine* (1977):

the Hand of the unseen Poet turning into a
Palimpsest

These quotations grouped together suggest a scene of writing that performs a dance of doubleness, a gesture at once embracing and holding binaries away. Long poems such as Robin Blaser's *Holy Forest*, George Bowering's *Genève, George, Vancouver*, and *Kerrisdale Elegies*, bpNichol's *The Martyrology*, Robert Kroetsch's *Completed Field Notes*, Daphne Marlatt's *Frames, Steveston*, and *What Matters*, Douglas Barbour's *Visions of My Grandfather*, Michael Ondaatje's *The Collected Works of Billy the Kid*, Dennis Cooley's *Bloody Jack*, Christopher Dewdney's *Spring Trances in the Control Emerald Night*, Jon Whyte's two volumes of *The Fells of Brightness*, and Lionel Kearns's *Convergences*, are all examples of how the contemporary long poem, while belonging to the genus of poetry, cannot be fully identified with one of its *eidoi*. By being both outside and inside the established poetic genres, the long poem participates in the category of poetry while defying its limits, the generic laws of its species. This ambivalent positioning marks the deconstructive activity of the long poem. By challenging the monism of the traditional conception of genre, the long poem invites the reader to rethink its laws. One might even go so far as to consider the contemporary long poem as a mutant form bearing only traces of the genres it derives from, a potentially new species or at least a species engendered by generic shifts. The contemporary long poem deliberately departs from the tradition of readily defined generic categories by positing itself as a multi-encoded text that does not adhere to a single set of conventions; its genericity depends less on a given set of generic codes than on the interrelationships of various embedded genres.

EPIC ETHOS

The long poem has always attracted critical attention, primarily, I think, because of its often misunderstood affinity with the epic, one of the most privileged genres. Also, the position in the Western literary canon of individual long poems, such as Homer's and Virgil's epics, Ovid's *Metamorphoses*, *Beowulf*, Dante's *The Divine Comedy*, Chaucer's narratives and the medieval romances, Ariosto's *Orlando Furioso*, Tasso's *Jerusalem Delivered*, Milton's *Paradise Lost* and *Paradise Regained*, Wordsworth's *The Prelude*, Tennyson's *In Memoriam* and *The Princess*, Browning's *The Ring and the Book*, and Whitman's *Leaves of Grass*, to mention only a few, gave to long poetic structures, whether clearly epic or not, an exceptional status. Each a literary landmark in its own right, these poems have either introduced or extended different concepts of the epic (for instance, the heroic, the 'brief,' and the personal epic) or the poetic narrative. Similarly, *The Waste Land*, *The Cantos*, *The Maximus Poems*, and *Paterson* are certainly the quintessential twentieth-century long poems. Despite their formal differences and the distinct ways in which they challenge their literary predecessors, they have become the prototypes of the contemporary long poem by foregrounding length and its generic ramifications.

The generic diversity of all these poems illustrates, as Rosalie Colie argues, that when writers start mixing genres they do so by working primarily with large forms (105, 122). It would be naïve to argue that length in itself could suffice to define the long poem as a distinct genre; by the same token, however, a long poem can only be long. But it wouldn't suffice to resolve such a tautological assertion by specifying

the number of lines or pages that make a poem long. Phyllis Webb's
Naked Poems, a series of brief lyrics and long silences, can be read only
as a single poem, a long poem. And this is not a matter of *reading into*
the white spaces that so luxuriously surround the lyrics; rather, the
reading of this poem takes place processually, as the reader has often
both to backtrack and to continue reading. The issue here is duration
rather than length. Similarly, the slimness of the thirty-seven one-word-
line poems in Lola Lemire Tostevin's *Gyno-Text* (1986) appear hermetic
and resistant to interpretation when read individually –

> synaptic
> reflex
> skips
> a
> syllable
>
> triggers
> flesh
> *flêche*
> to
> the
> target   (np)

– but when read as comprising one long poem they 'scroll' the duration
of birth labour. Length is as much the measure of the long poem as
what endows poems with the ability to unfold at once in more than
one generic direction, to accommodate, while appropriating, seemingly contesting genres. Even in the nineteenth-century long poem,
where length often becomes prolixity, it is length that permits the poets
to waver between the Old World and the New, between description
and idyll, action and nostalgia. But the long poem has not always been
seen as a hybrid, a polyphonic generic structure. More often than not,
critics tend to privilege one of its encoded genres at the expense of
the others.

Edgar Allan Poe was possibly the first writer to draw our attention
to the long poem in a deliberately negative fashion. In his essay 'The
Poetic Principle,' he attacks the long poem as a temporal narrative
because the 'elevating excitement' that lyric poetry occasions 'cannot
be sustained throughout a composition of any great length' (33). Stressing 'that the phrase, "a long poem," is simply a flat contradiction in

terms' (33), he argues further that '[i]f, at any time, any very long poem *were* popular in reality, which I doubt, it is at least clear that no very long poem will ever be popular again' (34). Perhaps one reason that might account for his unwavering position is the way in which, in his essay 'The Philosophy of Composition,' he proceeds to define the long poem as 'merely a succession of brief ones – that is to say, of brief poetical effects' (22). Poe defines the long poem as an aberration of lyric poetry, a failure to sustain lyric intensity, *and* as encompassing lyric poems – the 'long poem' as what it is not. But if indeed Poe was the first to announce the non-existence of the long poem – what Mandel for different reasons called 'the death of the long poem' – why do I bother citing here what so many other critics writing on long poems have cited before me? If there is a contradiction in this seemingly morbid fascination with a definition that undoes what it sets out to define, what is the reader to do with Whitman's indebtedness to Poe? In 'A Backward Glance o'er Travel'd Roads,' Whitman relates the design of *Leaves of Grass* to Poe's assertion:

Toward the last I had among much else look'd over Edgar Poe's poems – of which I was not an admirer, tho' I always saw that beyond their limited range of melody (like perpetual chimes of music bells, ringing from lower *b* flat up to *g*) they were melodious expressions, and perhaps never excell'd ones, of certain pronounc'd phases of human morbidity. (The Poetic area is very spacious – has room for all – has so many mansions!) But I was repaid in Poe's prose by the idea that (at any rate for our occasions, our day) there can be *no such thing as a long poem*. The same thought had been haunting my mind before, but Poe's argument, though short, work'd the sum out and proved it to me. (665; final emphasis mine)

James E. Miller accounts for Whitman's statement by saying that 'in effect, what Poe did for Whitman ... was to enable him to see how to write his long poem without violating "psychal necessity" – that is, by making the long poem out of a sequence of subtly related lyric moments' (1986, 290). He does not take heed of Whitman's conviction that the American poem should not be epic, but this is not the place to discuss Miller's resolution of the astounding discrepancy between *Leaves of Grass* and Poe's resistance to the long poem; a readiness to bypass the issue by calling the poem a sequence of lyrics, as Miller does, is endemic in the most recent criticism on the long poem.

The definition of the long poem by deduction extends beyond Poe.

Critics, who, unlike him, acknowledge the significance of the long poem, also proceed by using deductive if not a priori methods. Michael Bernstein's *The Tale of the Tribe*, an important study of *The Cantos*, *Paterson*, and *The Maximus Poems* as modern epics, contradicts Poe by asserting that the long poem is primarily 'verse epic,' 'a poem including history' (4, 29). Although Bernstein is quick to identify and focus on the radical discontinuity between these poems' projects and that of the epic genre, his intricate argument rests on the premise that epic is the index to these poems. It is worth quoting him at some length so we can see how he tries to accommodate this problem of generic methodology.

'I want to offer,' Bernstein says, 'a series of propositions characterizing epic verse, propositions based upon an admittedly uneasy combination of *a priori* conditions and *a posteriori* conclusions drawn from specific texts.' He then proceeds to define the epic as (a) 'a narrative of its audience's own cultural, historical, or mythic heritage,' (b) that exists without 'the trace of a single sensibility,' (c) whose 'proper audience ... is not the *individual* in his absolute inwardness but the *citizen* as participant in a collective linguistic and social nexus,' and (d) whose main intent is to offer 'its audience lessons presumed necessary to their individual and social survival' (13-4). Bernstein echoes Livesay's as well as Frye's and Dickie's emphasis on the public function of poetry, and specifically of long poetic forms. His 'admittedly uneasy' method of definition simply reiterates the traditional definitions of epic.

Interestingly, however, his anxiety about his method surfaces not so much in the body of his text as in a footnote immediately following his definition of epic.

I have called my four characteristics an uneasy mixture of *a priori* criteria and *a posteriori* features, *inductively* [my emphasis] derived by considering what numerous specific examples of the form have in common. Although such a way of reaching a definition is unorthodox, it is also methodologically necessary, as is the subsumption of my own characteristics under Wittgenstein's notion of 'family likeness.' That is, no single epic need demonstrate *all* of these characteristics; neither does the presence of *one* of these features assure that a given poem is an epic ... Phenomenologically, the epic is a project, an intentional structure to be isolated and distinguished from other intentional structures such as the lyric or the novel. (14-5, note a)

Footnotes, as acts of self-reading, tell us where the slippage between writing and reading figures as a rhetorical turn, revealing the author's uneasiness. In the note quoted above, Bernstein deconstructs his own method: he argues that he has proceeded inductively; yet the text proper of *The Tale of the Tribe* shows that his induced definition is inserted into the long poem *deductively*.

The circularity of his argument points to the limits of his generic approach. In defining '*The Cantos* as an epic ... possess[ing] a recognizable, even if rather elastic, meaning,' Bernstein locates the 'heuristic value' of his 'characterization' in the way 'the responses' to 'previous examples' of the epic will 'guide an initial reaction to the new work.' This recognition is certainly what makes genre an operable literary phenomenon, but Bernstein privileges the recognizable genre at the expense of any other generic elements less immediately identifiable. Although he acknowledges that the poet can 'deliberately manipulate ... can satisfy, thwart, or even seek to "correct" and improve upon the conventions of epic decorum,' he is reluctant to consider what motivates the poet to depart from the epic generic norms the reader can recognize; moreover, he does not seem to be interested in the aesthetic and ideological reasons that inform the poet's refashioning or undoing of epic conventions. On the contrary, he argues that 'the tradition of epic verse has provided a series of pre-texts with which any new poem aligns itself, pre-texts that also directly influence the author's own understanding of how this poem should be structured and what features it must include.' Genre does not function in the programmatic way Bernstein suggests by placing his emphasis on authorial intentionality. He reiterates James E. Miller's own unquestioning acceptance of Whitman's remarks above. But Pound, like Whitman, was not intent on composing a poem exclusively designed around the epic. Although Bernstein is right when he says that '[t]o decide to write an epic situates a certain contract between author and reader ... [that] generates an intentional framework within which the particular exchange, poem / reading, can proceed,' he seems unwilling to account for the importance of generic reformulation or to examine the context within which such changes occur. It does not come as a surprise, then, when he says that the category of '"long poem" tells us nothing beyond the bulk of the volume in question' (15). The rejection of the term 'long poem' because of its presumed lack of specificity reflects the degree to which Bernstein proceeds by means of exclusion; any reference to a poem's 'bulk' is immaterial to him. Yet it is in the very length of poems that the markers of their formal, structural, thematic, and ideological distinctiveness are inscribed and interact with each other.

Bernstein clearly, and perhaps organically given his biases, prefers the historicity of a genre (his appropriation of Wittgenstein's 'family likeness') to the challenge of an emerging form. *The Cantos, Paterson,* and *The Maximus Poems* do rely on history and the epic tradition, but it is reductive to ignore their other major elements and the ways in which they interrelate with various genres. They do not all comply with the generic codes that Bernstein outlines: the many layers of history and their complex interrelationships in *The Cantos* and *The Maximus Poems* cannot possibly be compared to Williams's treatment of history in *Paterson*, which covers only two centuries of local American history; instead of merely representing their audiences' own culture, Pound, Williams, and Olson recontextualize it, often at the risk of estranging their readers from what they are familiar with; there are many instances of the 'inwardness' that Bernstein says is absent in the epic; and, despite the shared didactic tone, it would be misleading to argue that the poets in *Paterson* or *Maximus* speak for the society they supposedly represent – more often than not they criticize it. This is not to discredit Bernstein's reading of the modern epic, but rather to show how overdetermined his application of the concept of epic is. All three poems partake indeed of the epic, but they do so in an 'attempt' to revision the epic as the genre that has traditionally represented a monologic view of history in poetry.[1] Bernstein's method reflects a generic fallacy common among critics: the most easily 'recognizable' features of a text determine that text's genre; it seems to be easier to measure something new against familiar norms than to consider its newness, its generic strangeness. Bernstein's 'attempt' (15) to use history as the 'measure' of the modern epic's definition is problematic, for he does not 'attempt' to examine how history is employed in these poems; an epic rendering of history can often lead to an ideological distortion of the events represented, or, as is more often the case, to an exposition of history's fictionality. There are many long poems dealing with historical material that deliberately parody or avoid the epic genre.

For example, despite Lionel Kearns's reliance on historical facts and oral accounts concerning Captain James Cook, Captain George Vancouver, and the Nootka Indians of the Pacific Coast, *Convergences* (1984) from its opening radically modifies both epic conventions and the reader's assumptions about historical writing.

They arrive. They are visible. They make themselves
present to whatever was here before their coming ...
                              They are in this area
at this precise moment, their spirits merging
with the indigenous ghosts of the place ...
Some of them disappear soon. Some stay on
and for a time become components in a pattern
that grows more stable before it too begins
to change. It is neither good nor bad. It is
flux. It flows in waves and engulfs us all,
a process whose partial record we call history.

A continuous sense of disorder and confusion descends and threatens my life.
My desk is covered with papers that I do
not want to see. What will I do with them?
What will I do with all this information? I
want only to do my work, but how am I to
begin? ... At this moment
I know only that I am here and that
others have been here before and have
left something for me, as I leave something for you. Time is a ritual exchange,
though the gifts move in a single direc-
tion.   (np)[2]

The present tense of the poem alters the reader's relation to history
as the history of the past becomes synchronous with the moment of
the poet's writing. Epic intention here does not suspend the poet's
subjectivity. History, echoing Olson's concept of it,[3] is seen as *istorein*,
the act of storytelling as it occurs, not as conveying a privileged story
closed off by tradition. The poem's double-column format enhances
the duplicitous and double relation to history: on the one hand, it
illustrates how the making of history coincides with the making of
poetry, thereby showing that history is constructed by language; on
the other, it maintains the difference between historical and poetic
discourses, a difference that is further emphasized by the different
fonts in which the two columns are printed.

We cannot afford to ignore the poet's reading and scripting activities
– which *converge* in turn with our own reading act – activities that

contribute to the quasi-epic character of *Convergences*. At the same time, however, it is important to distinguish between the poet's signature in the text and what Bernstein calls authorial intentionality. *Convergences* bears no signs of overriding intentionality, of overdetermination. The incorporation of the writing process into the text manifests the extent to which the text is fashioned during the act of writing, rather than programmatically by the writer's faithful following of the pre-established generic norms and the official versions of the events he describes. Kearns's frequent references to the historical characters' 'genes' and to the 'generations' that followed them foregrounds the extent to which a genre disperses its 'genes' (np), its traces, as the poet reformulates it. Kearns, unlike Bernstein, asserts that historical material alone does not determine the generic signature of the epic.

Atwood's *The Journals of Susanna Moodie* (1970) is another long poem that employs history, this time without epic intention. In fact, whereas in *Roughing It in the Bush* Moodie often resorts to the epic mode, epic is suspect in Atwood's poem because of its ideological workings. As her Susanna says,

> the old countries recede, become
> perfect, thumbnail castles preserved
> like gallstones in a glass bottle, the
> towns dwindle upon the hillsides
> in a light paperweight-clear.   (32)

Atwood subjectivizes history, lets Moodie speak what she left unsaid in her own narrative – the internalized that epic does not embody. What Moodie cannot bring herself to acknowledge in *Roughing It* she declares in *The Journals*: 'Whether the wilderness is / real or not / depends on who lives there' (13). Moodie's condition as a self-consciously split subject in Atwood's poem undoes the highly coded history that Moodie presents in her own hybrid text.

> (you find only
> the shape you already are
> but what
> if you have forgotten that
> or discover you
> have never known)   (25)

It is the position of the subject on the threshold of knowing and not knowing itself that resists the epic ethos in this poem. History is engendered at the moment when the 'I' begins to address itself as 'you.'

Such poems as Eldon Garnet's *Brébeuf: A Martyrdom of Jean De* (1977) encode the epic in order to see it dismantled in the context of other genres and forms – in this case the lyric, the journal, multiple voices, visual devices, and numerous typescripts. The effectiveness of the outlandish episodes in Garnet's *Brébeuf* relies on the reader's immediate recognition that the poem's fictional events ought to be read in the context of the historical events from which they depart. Garnet's desacralization of the religious epic (his Brébeuf is driven as much by lust for 'Mary, Mother of God' [np] as by spirituality) and his deliberate distortion of history become even more pronounced because of his poem's poetic other, Pratt's *Brébeuf*. The focus in Garnet's text as in those by Kearns and Atwood lies on epos, the act of telling.

It is not that the contemporary long poem has no epic traces whatsoever.[4] What I am arguing instead is that, although we often encounter epic elements in the long poem – whether as instances of *mimesis praxeos* or as features intended to subvert the epic genre – it is reductive to conflate one of the most pervasive features of the long poem – the quest – with the epic quest. Quest in this poetry, as was intimated in nineteenth-century Canadian long poems, functions as a metonymy of desire, with the desiring subject not necessarily sharing the epic hero's or citizen's intent. Desire, as Freud, Lacan, Barthes, and Derrida have shown, is born out of lack, out of absence. It intimates the universal human drive to seek a future of pleasure (pleasure not only in its libidinal sense); it also operates as a corrective insofar as it seeks to recuperate the lost past in the form of a desired (desirable) future. As a sign of lack, desire is inherent in the incompleteness of the present, but also negates the present by attempting to exceed or at least to question it. In the long poem, desire manifests itself as the converging point of self and language.

As Lacan argues in 'The Function of Language in Psychoanalysis,'

the function of Language is not to inform but to evoke.

What I seek in the Word is the response of the other. What constitutes me as subject is my question. In order to be recognized by the other, I utter what was only in view of what will be. In order to find him, I call him by a name which he must assume or refuse in order to reply to me.

I identify myself in Language, but only by losing myself in it like an object. What is realized in my history is not the past definite of what was, since it is no more, or even the present perfect of what has been in what I am, but the future anterior of what I shall have been for *what I am in the process of becoming* ... (1968, 63; emphasis mine)

The Word is in fact a gift of Language, and Language is not immaterial. It is a subtle body, but body it is. Words are trapped in all the corporeal images which captivate the subject ... (1968, 64)

The subject's loss in language, discourse as enabling the subject's self-recognition, and desire as the constant element that activates this 'process of becoming' are all behind the quest motif. In this context, the generic imperative that quest and epic ethos operate as a pair is devalued. Desire in the long poem appears in different guises.

Lacan's notion of the materiality of language and the temporality it expresses is of great relevance to an appreciation of the epic traces in the long poem. In discussing Breuer and Freud's 'Preliminary Communication,' especially their treatment of anamnesis (recollection) – a key concept in the epic – Lacan articulates the relation between the singular and plural forms of *epos*: *epos* in the singular means word, speech, tale, song, story, promise, saying, word; it is the plural, *epei*, that stands for epic poetry. Lacan discusses this relation by focusing on the subject's discourse:

He [the subject] has simply recounted the event. But we would say that he has verbalized it ... that he has made it pass into the *verbe* or more precisely into the *epos* by which he brings back into *present time the origins of his own person* [my emphasis]. And he does this in a Language which permits his discourse to be understood by his contemporaries, and which furthermore presupposes their *present discourse* [my emphasis]. Thus it happens that the recitation of the *epos* may include some discourse of olden days in its own archaic or even foreign tongue, or may even pursue its course in *present time* [my emphasis] with all the animation of the actor; but it is like an indirect discourse, isolated inside quotation marks within the thread of the narration, and, if the discourse is played out, it is on a stage implying the presence not only of the chorus, but also of spectators. (1968, 17)

Lacan's focus on the discourse of the other as what produces the discourse of nostos and anamnesis so pervasive in the epic genre discloses how epic ethos is just one of the configurations that desire assumes during the subject's 'process of becoming.' From an epic perspective, it becomes apparent why Kearns's *Convergences* and so many other long poems are written in the present tense. As opposed to the past tense of the epic with its usurping and totalizing effects, the present tense of the long poem validates not so much what is remembered but the act of remembering itself, not the 'true' origins of a bygone past but the subject's 'process of becoming.'

Charles Mair's *Tecumseh* (1886), although dealing with historical material amenable to epic form, is a drama in verse of high rhetoric; as Norman Shrive says, it is 'at times Shakespearean, at others Miltonic, and at others Restoration Heroic, but certainly always lofty' (Mair xix). Don Gutteridge, in writing about Tecumseh a century later, similarly resists the monologic signature of the epic. His *Tecumseh* (1976) is a mixture of documentary prose narratives and lyrics that comprise a structure of many voices, which significantly defer and recontextualize Tecumseh's own voice. The numerous dream sequences – common in classical epics and medieval romances – are used here to introduce the 'imaginary'[5] and to present an intersubjective view of Tecumseh's experiences.

```
a howl was my
first language –
shape of it
shuddering in
I was
        envowelled
in my mother's
arms endlessly
interwound with
sun splashed a
brilliant blood
on us both
we breathe the
earth's green
        air                                           (75)
```

Tecumseh's first word ('a howl'), inextricably interrelated with the mother's own 'howling' as she pushes him out into the world, is by 'nature' double-voiced. Tecumseh, unlike the epic character who has to extricate himself from his mother's bosom and ordinary social functions in order to become a hero, remains within the maternal realm.

> With this hand
> I draw the
> first letter in a
> bitter alphabet:
>
> it is a vowel
> and has no end   (70)

Gutteridge's Tecumseh dispels the epic mythos of the monologic hero. His first word – also 'the / first sentence / [he] uttered ... a / cataract' (79) – has no demarcated beginning, originating as it does from the mother, and 'no end,' for it is both *langage* and *parole*.[6] The alpha, the first letter/vowel, with the omega missing, cogently proposes that language has no telos. Tecumseh's dwelling in the world is marked by *différance*, deferral and differentiation at the same time. His quest is one for language in the present tense, affirming the priority of temporality over the hermeneutic verification of historical events.

> Without language
> there is no
>   catastrophe
> and no poetry
> to make peace
>   with ourselves   (96)

The poem's unfolding in opposition to the warring forces that shape epic structure displays a recalcitrant attitude towards dialectics. Tecumseh's desire to retrieve the beginning of language is not tantamount to a search for a unified origin; although he dreams that 'without symmetry / there is no / vision' (59), his father's at once 'disintegrat[ing]' and 'perfect' face (58, 60) reveals to him a 'shattered symmetry' (60). The epic traces in this poem are there as a sounding board, a measuring device that prevents totalization.

Language as the site where history is made and unmade, where the being of a historical character attenuates the Being of a 'hero,' is also present in Jon Whyte's *Homage, Henry Kelsey* (1981). In his note to the poem Whyte says that '[t]he poem [originally planned as a poem about 'muskoxen'] began to shape itself into epic. My academic work [his MA thesis] on the medieval poem *Pearl* started to inform what I was doing: I would, like the jeweller of that poem, put his poem [Kelsey's account of his journey in Canada in 1690 in rhyming couplets] into a new setting. Hence "homage"' (81). The Al Purdy quotation on the book's cover expresses Purdy's appreciation of the poem by reiterating Whyte's own generic specification: 'Jon Whyte has here used his own writings allied with Kelsey's to change the legend into an epic. ...' Yet *Homage, Henry Kelsey* is not epic except insofar as its tone is frequently lofty, as when Whyte describes, for instance, the end of a pipe-smoking ceremony:

> I stand
> in the middle
> of the long grass
> I turn
> to the north and east
> where the river flows
> I turn
> beneath the sun at noon
> turn
> to the ground
> to the sky
> draw
> the sweet breath of the air
> into my chest
> and
> like a giant heart ebb and flow with wind
> and with seasons   (58)

Epic in this poem does not designate genre but proportion: the expansiveness of the prairie, Kelsey's awe of the New World, physical endurance. Whyte, however, gives an accurate generic description of *Homage* in his preface to *Some Fittes and Starts* (1983), the first volume of the projected five-volume poem *The Fells of Brightness*. Here he says that *Homage* 'incorporates history, myth, landscape, a literary past, and is a foray into "anatomical epic"' (8). The poem's generic inclusiveness makes the poem not an epic but a gathering where the sublime in nature and the rhetorical flowering of Kelsey's soul are placed side by side in moments of silence – '[t]he larynx tightens; the word is drawn back' (48). In the light of Whyte's own definition of anatomy as '"a panoptic treatment of a single subject, or a singular point of view brought to bear on a multiplicity of subjects"' (*Some Fittes* 9), *Homage* is a deconstructed epic, a genre in which monologism is continuously subverted.

The propensity to define a long poem of historical material as epic, then, is not always related to the generic rules that might be found in a text; rather it is produced by the reader's response to the cultural signature of the epic as a privileged genre that tends to 'sing' of historical moments deemed to be important to a culture's development. The epic label in these instances derives from an extra-referential activity – such as Whyte's reading of *Pearl* – that points to models found not in the text proper but in the larger cultural text. It functions as the sanctioning of a writing act that incorporates into historical change enduring codes of utterance. Conversely, the desire to inscribe into cultural history events usually disregarded or minimized by official discourses often leads the poet to appropriate epic elements in order to expose the extent to which their application can produce cultural misreadings. When the epic genre is truly employed for deconstructive purposes, the poet's movement is away from 'idealizing representation ... [and] towards a more complete mimesis' (Altieri 659).

THE LYRIC MODE

In contrast to the epic approach to the long poem, critics like Marjorie Perloff,[7] Joseph N. Riddel, and M.L. Rosenthal and Sally M. Gall trace the long poem as a genre emerging from the lyric. Once again, Northrop Frye has anticipated this argument, this time in his definitions of lyric and epos. Although he makes, as we have seen, a strong case for long poetic 'narratives,' he deals with longer poetic forms other than epic only in scant fashion: '[p]urely narrative poems, being fictions, will, if episodic, correspond to the species of drama; if continuous, to the species of prose fiction' (1957, 293). Frye's theory of genre, whose purpose, as he states, 'is not so much to classify as to clarify such traditions and affinities' (1957, 247), operates according to his 'thematic mode[s]' (1957, 293), thus 'clarifying' the distribution of mythos and ethos rather than designating the formal and structural ways in which mythos and lexis come together. Yet, being aware of the long poem as a distinct poetic form, Frye acknowledges, albeit very briefly, the awkward generic spot in which it finds itself, and to which he consigns it.

We have the three generic terms drama, epic, and lyric, derived from the Greeks, but we use the latter two chiefly as jargon or trade slang for *long* and *short* (or shorter) poems respectively. The middle-sized poem does not even have a jargon term to describe it, and any *long poem* gets to be called an epic, especially if it is divided into a dozen or so parts, like Browning's *Ring and the Book* ... Similarly, we call Shelley's *Ode to the West Wind* a lyric, perhaps because it is a lyric; if we hesitate to call *Epipsychidion* a lyric, and have no idea what it is, we can always call it the product of an *essentially lyrical genius*. It is shorter than the *Iliad*, and there's an end of it. (1957, 246; my emphases)

The instability of definitions and the resistance of certain poems to generic categorization give flexibility to the circular structure of Frye's theory, but also account for the metonymic progression in his discussion of the lyric.

In a short essay on the subject, 'Approaching the Lyric,' Frye insists on the lyric's 'sense of the discontinuous' (1985, 31) and returns to Poe's essay and its influence on the poetics of French symbolism and English modernism: '[t]his essay had, as is well known, a tremendous influence on the French school that runs from Baudelaire to Valéry, and that influence made its way into English poetry in the generation of Eliot and Pound. I imagine that one reason for its influence was the belief that the standard meters of continuous verse had exhausted their possibilities, so that narrative shifted to prose, while long poems, even the poems of that master of the interminable, Victor Hugo, tended to become increasingly fragmented' (1985, 36). Frye's observation is to the point, but it is regrettable that he does not pursue any further the relation between what he calls the lyric's discontinuity and the long poem's fragmentation. Given, however, his thematics of genre, we might guess that discontinuity is related to the treatment of themes, and fragmentation to the presentation of form and structure. In Frye's scheme of things, the long poem thematically maintains its position of subgenre – now seen under drama, now under epic, but usually situated within the lyric domain – whereas structurally it is still in want of 'clarification.'

Perhaps it is because the lyric is such an embracing concept that so many critics of the long poem mistakenly tried to subordinate the long poem's particularities to the lyric's concerns – committing, in other words, a critical fallacy similar to that epic overdetermination. While it is true that the lyric, or rather the lyrical impulse, is inscribed within the long poem, the long poem is definitely not a simple extension or expansion of the lyric. Although the lyrical approach is useful in isolating and studying the lyricism frequently found in the long poem, its value is limited precisely because of its insistence on examining the long poem from the outside. Such an approach locates the genre of the long poem too deliberately within a priori and often honoured generic molds – namely those of the lyric and epic – a strategy that restricts our understanding of its drive and openness. The lyric embedded in the long poem is not a poem that 'does not provide an explanation, judgment or narrative' (Hardy 1), and whose voice 'usually manages to speak only in private relationships or solitude where it relies on more or less than words' (Hardy 2); this is the lyric that reached its apotheosis during the hey-day of the New Criticism. Rather, it is a lyric fracturing its 'wholeness,' parodying its own lyrical impulse; it functions more as a trope than as a genre.

The most extended approach to the lyrical mode of the long poem is *The Modern Poetic Sequence* by M.L. Rosenthal and Sally M. Gall, the first – and so far the only – full-scale attempt at defining the long poem generically. Indeed, the authors' opening statement acknowledges the need to define the long poem as a 'new' genre (3). Ironically, what is immediately noticeable in their study, beginning with its title, is that they soon do away with the 'long poem'; they consider it to be too 'traditional' (26), an uninterrupted narrative lacking the ability to encompass the 'tonalities' (27) of its perhaps 'fragmented structures' (26). Since the existing generic studies of the long poem consider only its specific configurations as epic, narrative, and romance, their dismissal is certainly hasty and not founded on carefully explored grounds. Thus Browning's 'The Englishman in Italy,'certainly a short long poem, and Tennyson's *Maud* 'remain' for Rosenthal and Gall 'long poems in the traditional sense, despite being fragmented in their quite different ways' (26). The problem is not that the points of departure for Rosenthal and Gall's study lie in the nineteenth century – this awareness is obviously important for developing a sense of the tradition of the long poem – but that the authors are reluctant, to say the least, to acknowledge the openness and diversity the long poem can accommodate. Instead, the quality of openness they predictably observe in David Jones's *The Anathémata*, and in *The Cantos, The Waste Land, Paterson*, and *The Maximus Poems*, they attribute to what they call the modern poetic sequence. This is not so much a matter of playing with different generic names as it is an instance of a naming act enervating the genre to be defined.

'[T]he modern sequence,' they argue, 'is the decisive form toward which all the developments of modern poetry have tended. It is the genre which best encompasses the shift in sensibility exemplified by starting a long poetic work "I celebrate myself, and sing myself," rather than "Sing, Goddess, the wrath of Achilles"' (3). The shift in sensibility they observe is fundamental in understanding the genre of the long poem and the way in which it veers from the epic, but their term 'sequence' is deployed in both too limited and too loose a sense to be of any value from a generic perspective. As a result they blur the features of the territory they set out to map. They define the poetic sequence as

a grouping of *mainly lyric* poems and passages, rarely uniform in pattern, which tend to interact as an organic whole. It *usually includes narrative and dramatic* elements, and ratiocinative ones as well, but its structure is *finally lyrical.* Intimate, fragmented, self-analytical, open, emotionally volatile, the sequence meets the needs of modern sensibility even when the poet aspires to *tragic* or *epic* scope. (9; my emphases)

The value-emphasis of their rhetoric exposes the biases of their otherwise insightful study. A sense of nostalgia, the kind Jean-François Lyotard sees as the informing drive behind 'modern aesthetics,' 'the nostalgia for the unattainable' (81),[8] seems to characterize Rosenthal and Gall's emphasis on the lyric.

While Rosenthal and Gall argue that the long poem as 'new genre' encompasses other genres such as the lyric, the epic, and the narrative, their privileging of the lyric at the expense of the other generic elements is fraught with the same problems of reduction we found in the long poem's definition as epic. When they put under one generic umbrella Emily Dickinson's 'Fascicles,' Yeats's 'Words for Music Perhaps,' and Stevens's 'The Auroras of Autumn' along with *The Cantos, Paterson,* and *The Anathémata,* it is obvious that they are engaged less in a generic study than in a study of poetic sensibility that has little to do with any consideration of literary kinds. In this respect, they are very close to Poe. Had they not initially announced that they were going to deal with a 'new' genre, there would perhaps be no problems with their study. No matter how much we want to take advantage of the flexibility inherent in all generic codes, we cannot (as they propose to do) adequately discuss, for instance, Olson's *The Maximus Poems* and Hardy's *Poems of 1912–13* within the same generic framework.

On the one hand, early in their study Rosenthal and Gall talk about the serial lyric as 'the modern sequence pre-eminently' (6), a poem that has transformed its contamination by elements belonging to other genres into a structure that resists frames and determining centres. Momentarily, such a stance promises to be, if not a close definition of the long poem, at least a good one to start from, because it purports to take heterogeneity as its measuring device. Yet their acknowledgment of the sequence as a disparate genre is imbricated in their perception of its fundamentally 'lyrical structure.' In short, their 'new' genre is hardly new. Once more, the desire to privilege one of the long poem's constitutive generic codes at the expense of the others remains paramount. 'Generic hierarchy,' however, what Fowler calls 'relation with respect to "height"' (216), has always been pervasive. Different cultural values allow critics at various times to privilege different genres; if the epic was the literary kind that Bernstein favoured, Rosenthal and Gall vote for the lyric. The implied scale of genres may not be stable, but the inclination to read according to one genre apparently is. Although the long poem is seen as being traversed by multiple forces, it is read as a system whose 'components do not coexist, but struggle for preeminence' (Tynjanov, cited in Fowler 250). Rosenthal and Gall are impelled to resolve its heterogeneity by insisting that its contaminated elements are 'transformed.' Whether there are any traces of contamination left in the long poem as a transformational structure Rosenthal and Gall do not say. Instead, they place the long poem in the very grid of categorization it seeks to evade. They elide what is most distinctive about it: generic contamination.

On the other hand, as their study develops, it becomes clear that what they define as 'lyrical structure' is not the structure of an extended lyric poem.

[I]ts [lyrical structure's] *object is neither to resolve a problem nor to conclude an action but to achieve the keenest, most open realization possible.* This realization is, naturally, rooted in a work's initial pressures but goes beyond them in scope. By initial pressures we mean the human occasion for the poem, its set of awareness, its situation (the felt reality within the poem), its condition of sensuous or emotional apprehension – whatever constitutes an emotional center energizing the poem, which moves towards a state of equilibrium that balances,

resolves, or encompasses these pressures ... The ability to hold in balance conflicting and logically irreconcilable energies, and to identify their presence and intensity, is felt as mastery over contradiction, mastery by poetic conversion into a pattern of unruly but mobilized affects. (11)

Obviously this definition has a lot to do with the lyric poem; however, it also has to do with the 'general' sensibility of literature, more specifically with New Critical tenets about harmony, balance, and reconciliation. It is strange that Rosenthal and Gall should choose 'lyrical structure' as the predominant feature of the 'new' genre when they are aware of its much larger applicability: '[l]yrical structure, incidentally,' they say, 'is by no means restricted to poems. It is a characteristic of all literary genres: plays, novels, short stories, sermons, speeches, even prose exposition. It is, precisely, the concrete aesthetic dimension of any piece of verbal expression' (15). Considering that they profess to be engaged in a generic reading, their wavering between genus and *eidos* is not simply puzzling but indefensible. Their 'lyrical structure' proposes to mould the long poem according to what they present as the universal order of literature.

But although 'lyrical structure' overrides generic distinctions, it still calls, by virtue of its terms, for a close generic rapport with the lyric. Despite the irreconcilable thematic and structural contradictions Rosenthal and Gall observe in the modern poetic sequence, the effect of its lyrical structure, they argue, is that of an 'organic form' (7), a 'lyrical matrix,' which is realized within an 'essential field of emotive reference' (23). It is, ultimately, their emphasis on this emotive locus that subordinates the 'activity' they notice in the sequence to the emotional and psychological motivations of the poetic subject. Thus they do not identify the long poem as one of a *kind*, but as an expression of the poet, turning attention from intertext to poet. Their readings of individual poems reveal that there is hardly any difference between the actual poet and the lyric subject. This not only contradicts their own critical argument, namely that the lyrical structure of the sequence predominates over its particularities – which are what contaminates it – but also implies that the thematic and structural activity Rosenthal and Gall focus on becomes virtually lost, neutralized by the 'equilibrium' they are eager to locate beneath the 'surface variations' (307) of the sequence. Their privileging of a deep structure – the level on which the 'organic whole' of the poem (again reminiscent of New Criticism) is realized – is virtually imposed on the poem by the readers. Rosenthal and Gall fail to take into consideration that the fragmented form of some of the sequences they examine does not represent 'wholeness' but helps to foreground the shattering of the illusory idea of wholeness as an essence that artistic works presumably aspire to.

Their reading of Jones's *The Anathémata*, although sympathetic and sensitive, betrays their discomfort with long poems that resist easy resolution, or dissolution for that matter, within that vague field of 'emotive reference' (295–9, 306–7). It appears that Rosenthal and Gall wistfully, if not wilfully, ignore the various 'signs' of Jones's writing, signs that he shares with his readers in the preface to *The Anathémata* (9–43). They disregard the poem's subtitle, 'fragments of an attempted writing,' which illustrates that Jones is not interested in reconciling the contradictions of his poem or in drawing its discontinuities within a single 'continuum,' as they claim (307).

> There's conspiracy here:
> Here is birthday and anniversary, if there's continuity
> here, there's a new beginning.   (Jones 51)

Continuity or a moment of realization for Jones does not mark a moment of 'equilibrium' but rather the paradoxical progressive and regressive unfolding of his long poem from one 'deposit' of history to another. Furthermore, Rosenthal and Gall's regret that Jones's poem lacks the 'confessional dimension' (299) of the sequence is nothing other than disregard for what the poet himself seeks to accomplish; he says in his preface that 'one is trying to make a shape out of the very things of which one is one-self made' (10). The simultaneous internalization and distancing implied here, in keeping with the poem's refusal to comply with the demands of any specific genre, let alone chronology, is entirely ignored by Rosenthal and Gall, who also disregard the poem's layout – its intricate structure – as well as its various levels of discourse. Bewildered, they search for a lyrical self as opposed to a self that defies any centralization of its 'emotive' and 'psychological tonalities.'

Their methodology would not help their readers make head or tail of similarly intricate long poems, such as Fred Wah's *Breathin' My Name with a Sigh* (1981), *Waiting for Saskatchewan* (1985), and *Music at the Heart of Thinking* (1987), which, although informed by the lyrical mode, dwell in the intervals of lyricism and narrative. Indeed, it wouldn't be entirely inappropriate to argue that, like Kroetsch's *Completed Field Notes*, these three books comprise one single long poem whose design is to be inferred from Wah's compositional 'practice of negative capability and estrangement' (*Music*, Preface, np). Wah challenges the intelligibility of genre while inscribing his poems in the rift that occurs among various generic codes.

> Sentence the true morphology or shape of the
> mind including a complete thought forever
> little ridges little rhythms scoping out the total
> picture as a kind of automatic designing device
> or checklist anyone I've found in true thought
> goes for all solution to the end concatenates
> every component within the lines within the
> picture as a cry to represent going to it with the
> definite fascination of a game where the number
> of possibilities increases progressively with
> each additional bump Plato thought   (*Music* 6)

The slippage between subject and object, referentiality and self-reflexivity, makes the poem a host to difference. It goes so far as to sublimate the contesting generic forces at the 'heart' of the whole 'sequence.' It evades interpretation by making interpretation its theme. Plato's bumps become the analogue of the reader's hermeneutic process. As mimesis can only be approximation –

> the air
>
> as it comes out ahead of me
> wah[h], wah[h]
> ...
>   wuh[h]
> ...
> to cool the soul
> no, to cool the heart
> he says (Aristotle)
> on breathing
> animal   (*Breathin'* np)

– so the long poem can only approximate the lyric; not a lyricist, the poet breathes out his dispersed self. The phonemic association between Wah's name and breathing reaches towards essentialism, but it is an essentialism reminiscent of Olson's proprioception, pointing out in turn that whenever meaning is born there is also a hint at non-meaning: the inarticulateness of an animal's wuh-wuh, the poet's breathing, the orality of his discourse recorded on the page, breath as air and therefore always already outside the poet – all inhabit a differential space that defines naming while establishing contiguity. Historicized and contextualized, the long poem's subject is at once apart and a part of, responsive and resistant to the world.

Rosenthal and Gall's attempt at discovering a 'lyrical structure' in all sequences is a wilful misreading of the long poem's desire to make differentiation its primary trope. Douglas Barbour's *He & She &* (1974), a love poem, is an example of how the lyricism embedded in the long poem hesitates to reach its full potential: 'Lady, lady, what / the hell can i say?' (3) is a lyric apostrophe to the beloved, but also an ironic reminder that the long poem's attempt to achieve an 'organic whole' is encumbered by referents that are at odds with the aesthetic and societal values encoded in the tradition of such love sequences as Sidney's *Astrophel and Stella* and *He & She &*. Barbour's poem begins with a direct challenge to the unity promised by the title:

Someday im going to write a poem
about our fights:

it will be full of
casual errors like

they are.   the blunt
edge of
rapier remarks.   bruises
from pulld punches   (1)

The poem is at once about love and discord; the result is an often humorous and deliberate collage of lyric occasions focusing on inflated trivialities:

'Sorry i broke
your fingernail   i
was only trying to help.

```
Open a door
thought   pave your
way:   only
trying to help.'

The broken nail
does it well:
demonstration/
man & women act
together ...                                                    (20)
```

What we might consider to be mutually exclusive cultural and aesthetic codes come together within the generic gaps of the long poem. As Barbour says elsewhere in the poem:

```
Maps are subtly out of date
you must re-survey /
                        tentative
he wonders   where? / how?
to begin this reconnaissance

                        a new
lover   lost
in these somehow unwarranted
spaces / changes unlookt for                                    (4)
```

Dislocation, a theme consistently used in the long poem, declares a yearning that exceeds the lyric's potentiality to locate the self. It is not that dislocation produces impediments not conducive to the prolongation of lyric intensity or that narrative can better accommodate what the lyric's brevity leaves untold; rather, the absence of epic nostos becomes a nostalgia for the lyric. But as Paul de Man says, '[n]o lyric can be read lyrically nor can the object of a lyrical reading be itself a lyric – which implies least of all that it is epical or dramatic' (1984, 254). The long poem keeps the lyric in abeyance while bespeaking it.

Joseph Riddel argues that 'the theory of the lyric, rather than being antithetical to any notion of the long poem, indeed is the only theory of the long poem' (466). Riddel does not look for the organic whole that unifies the fragmented nature of the long poem; he focuses instead on the lyric's constant questioning of its own form and structure. He does not simply insist on the workings of lyric in the long poem; he is interested in the aporia it generates, that plays through all language, and inevitably produces doubled readings (the undecidable) or defines literature as that kind of text which can never be reduced to a closed spatial reading, either as a dialectical or a self-mirroring play ... The lyric, then, undoes its own frame, or repeats the 'force' of framing with its own metaphorical violence – a play of displacements which the modern 'long poem' only makes explicit. The lyric is irreducibly temporal, a text never present to itself. It represents the flaw of myths of origin.

Perhaps, then, the 'long poem' has become our model of 'reading' (or better, re-reading) as decentering. (466–7)

Riddel's wish to see the long poem as 'our model of "reading" (or better, re-reading) as decentering,' like Frye's argument, extends the lyric beyond strict generic specifications, but it does so in a way that gives us a different understanding of how the lyric and the long poem converge, however contradictory this convergence might seem. In Riddel's formulation the lyric is no longer considered to be a pre-established genre: it engenders its own tropes, generates its own reading. Such a notion, while working against the essence of genre, moves towards the formulation of a textuality reminiscent of Barthes's *écriture*;[9] *écriture* threatens to become a non-genre *par excellence*, a textuality that purports to be produced and to perform independently from any literary orders. By calling this kind of textuality lyric, however, Riddel suggests what Evelyn Cobley, in her discussion of Bakhtin's genre theory, calls a 'genre [that is] both constant and infinitely variable' (328).

The epic is one of the generic variables Riddel locates in the long poem: the long poem, he says, 'represents the undoing of the dream of the epic to produce a myth of origins, to return upon itself' (477). But Riddel's privileging of the lyric, together with the epic traces, does not make the long poem what Gary Saul Morson calls a 'boundary work,' a work that is 'uncertain which of two mutually exclusive sets of conventions governs' (48). Neither the lyric nor the epic can be seen to dominate the other, for the long poem derives its energy from the interaction of these, among other, generic elements. Riddel's argument that the energy of the long poem derives predominantly from the lacunae he identifies in the lyric suggests that the long poem transgresses the limits of genre; yet its transgression should not be confused with the flexibility of the codes of *a* given genre, in this case those of the lyric.

Riddel is not alone in positing the lyric as a non-genre *vis-à-vis* the long poem. Extending Frye's theory of genres, Andrew Welsh also argues in *Roots of Lyric* that '[l]yric is ... less a particular genre of poetry than a distinctive way of organizing language'; 'we can see,' he says, in 'Williams' *Paterson* and Pound's *Cantos* that there are basic conflicts between the traditional demands of a long poem and the very different organization of a lyric-centered language' (21). Welsh does not tell us what the 'traditional' demands of the long poem are, but he moves beyond Frye when he relates the lyric to certain linguistic structures that can be found in the long poem. Lyric as a non-genre is not, in contrast to its positioning in Frye's generic theory, constituted by the contract the poet and the public accept about the conventions of writing and reading. Rather, for Welsh, it comes forward as an aspect of the poem's linguistic phenomenality.

In this respect, both Riddel and Welsh seem to move towards Paul de Man, who states that '[t]he lyric is not a genre, but one name among several to designate the defensive motion of understanding, the possibility of a future hermeneutics' (1984, 261). The motion de Man talks about is the troping of language, the rhetorical turns the reader has to follow in order to become part of the poem's intelligibility. According to de Man, the lyric moves away from 'description' towards the 'materiality of an inscription.' 'Description, it appears,' de Man says, 'was a device to conceal inscription' (1985, 65), a device that revealed only the phenomenality of the lyric subject's experience. The lyric, then, signifies a certain inscription, which is part of its intelligibility, and a certain reading.

This reading, since it breaks through the lyric's 'description,' is not an act of mimesis; instead, it is what de Man calls an allegory of reading. In the de Manian lexicon, '[a]llegory names the rhetorical process by which the literary text moves from a phenomenal, world-oriented to a grammatical, language-oriented direction' (1985, 69).[10] The trajectory of such a reading illustrates a different functioning of the lyric poem's self-referentiality, one that changes the direction of but does not thwart interpretation, one that discloses its own contradictions. It is this kind of lyric that the long poem encompasses: not that literary kind which is relatively short, articulated by a single speaker's apostrophe, framed by a specific occasion, and focusing on the speaker's emotive locus, but the self-referentiality that binds the subject's writing and reading acts as they are materialized through language. The pure short lyric, a 'monological form' (Rajan 196), does not allow the subject's otherness to speak through. And when it is present in the long poem, it occurs not as the intrusion of what William Rogers calls an 'anomalous voice' (81), a voice defying its conventional generic codes, but as a deliberate undoing of those codes, an anti-lyric, the kind of anti-lyric the reader finds in Lola Lemire Tostevin's 'sophie (1988).

Tostevin's lines 'espaces vers vers où? / vers quoi?' (53) evocatively articulate the tentative generic topos that the lyric inhabits in her long poem, certainly not a topos of a claustrophobic monologism. The pun on 'vers,' reinforced by the rhyming repetition and the question marks, discloses what the lyric cannot, by traditional definitions, contain. In 'sophie, Tostevin inscribes in her 'anti-lyrics' the otherness the lyric tends to subsume:

> listening to Lady Day you forget about lyrics   hear
> the mystery of voice trace in time a space between
> the lines   one note above   one note below   the melody
> flowers beyond measure   too marvelous for words   give
> me more and more and then some   (9)

While Tostevin speaks through the most recognizable lyric trope – apostrophe – the double meaning of 'lyrics' elucidates the deceptive neatness of the lyric mode and exposes the rupture between what carries the lyric, 'voice,' and what it fails to 'measure' – 'give me more and more and then some.'

Orality, privileged by the traditional lyric, gives way to writing:

> I write because I can't sing   I am the book exiled
> from my voice in search of a melody but like the woman
> who is blind because her eyes are filled with seeing
> and like the woman who is deaf because her ears are
> filled with hearing I am mute because my voice is filled
> with words and unlike music I can only be understood
> and not heard   (10)

Tostevin totally subverts the very conditions of the lyric: voice, hearing, music. She reveals the blind spot in the lyric mode, its inability to hear its own sound. Muteness becomes an enabling condition that requires readers to shift their reading strategies; we can no longer 'speak' of this poem's 'speaker,' as we cannot, with any degree of certainty, 'speak' of the poem's lines or prose. Tostevin's employment of the lyric is informed by her desire to undo both gender and genre categories. Although the dialectic between speech and writing reminds us of Derrida's deconstruction of the metaphysical tradition – the same *philo*sophical tradition that 'sophie apostrophizes – Tostevin, in her book's middle section, entitled 'by the smallest possible margin,' turns her Derridean strategies against Derrida; and she does the same with the lyric trope, thus showing that 'harmony doesn't exist before the lyre' (11). The lyre – like philosophy, like genre theory – is merely the instrument that facilitates the performance. Unity as an artificial idealized state discloses the ideology of the lyric.

'Lyrical structure,' then, results in a closed world, a strait-jacket enfolding the self as loving subject and as loved object, its voice not 'natural' but coming out as it does from 'vacant mouths gaping on the shelf   sallow skull / of the eastern moon minus its black tongue' (35). Tostevin demonstrates that the lyric, far from functioning as an idiolect, operates as an ideologeme that mutates the subject from the world. 'Black tongue' double-speaks Tostevin's intent: it suggests print, writing, but it also speaks of her suspension of the lyric until the very end of her long poem where 'the muse has learned to write'

a poem   the gold red rind of a rhyme   *a rimmon*   a garnet
the bony pulp of a pomegranate   the acid taste of crimson   the
sensuous pleasure of seeds that speak to the tip of the tongue
the curving stem of knotted rootstock   the nodding flowers of
Solomon's seal   it is all here in song   in this weed and rain
filled garden (where voice is the site) its body distinct ...   (74)

Writing here bears all the moisture of the rain-filled garden, becomes a song, a song, however, that does not reinstitute the lyric in its ge-net(r)ic form, because the instrument now is not the lyre but the pen, its ink restoring the liquidness of the genre with a difference. Image of nature and artifice open up the dialectical structure implied in the lyric's ideology.

Tostevin accomplishes this lyrical paradox with 'the measure of an extended hand' (74) covering, but not necessarily bridging, the distance between a sealed mouth (11) and Solomon's seal. As a long poem, *'sophie* thematizes the interrelatedness of long form and lyric line, testifying to what Charles Altieri calls the 'betweenness' of the long poem, that 'historical, stylistic, and epistemological condition' according to which there 'can no longer be a clear transition from corrupt surfaces to revivifying pattern' (655). The lyric might remain as one of the strongest generic signatures in *'sophie*, but it is not ratified as such. The double figure of the distance and proximity defining the lovers' condition in the poem also defines the interval between lyric and anti-lyric:

vingt-cinq ans

longue distance parcourue par un couple en mouvement
tous les deux s'emparant de l'espace et du temps
tous les deux à s'inscrire quoique tu demeures pour
moi absent

intervalle

petite dépression qui se façonne comme par un glacier
le nous du passé se dissout et pourtant la question
reste fondamentale   qui a désavoué mon corps? qui
la [*sic*] métaphorisé?

le toi pensant au moi pensé?   (55)

Tostevin undoes the monologism of the lyric by showing its method of 'unknowing,' by departing from its generic conventions, which, exhausted, function only as metaphors. Yet she also lets 'sophie speak *and* write, and does so in both French and English.

The lyric as the presumed locus of the self, a crypt hiding its historicity, often assumes this anti-lyric condition in the long poem.[11] There is, in other words, a gap between the poems we read and what we are told makes them lyric. Ralph Cohen's comment in his essay 'On the Interrelations of Eighteenth-Century Literary Forms' throws some light on the behaviour of the lyric, as well as on the critical approaches that rank high the lyric elements in the long poem: critics, he says,

are mistaken in assuming that the distinctiveness of kinds was agreed upon; they are mistaken in assuming that the rules specified the kinds; they are mistaken in assuming that each kind was bound to a clearly defined specific effect. Rather, the poetic kinds [are] identified in terms of a hierarchy that may not have been all-inclusive (since not all possible forms [are] specified) but [are] all interrelated. And this hierarchy can be seen in terms of the inclusion of lower forms into higher. (35)

The perplexity that arises from generic studies of the long poem is informed by such assumptions. Whereas many of the altered forms of the epic and the lyric in the long poem result from the attempts to deal with their exhausted conventions, their recontextualization also signals an equally important attempt at questioning the ideologies embedded in these kinds. Many critics cannot tolerate the generic incompatibility they encounter in the long poem; although they redefine the literary kinds that purportedly govern its structure, they ignore the semantic and ideological shifts produced by the combinations of various generic features.

What Rajan says about genre sums up the tension between the epic and lyric readings of the long poem.

A semiotics of genre, to complement the structural study of genre begun by Aristotle and the thematics of genre completed by Frye, would see the pure lyric as using its proximity to song in order to mute the gaps between signifier and signified by conferring on the words the illusory unity of a single voice. By contrast, narrative, which dramatizes the gaps between what is told and the telling of it, is always already within a world of textuality, of interpretation rather than origination. A more complex case is that of drama, which at first sight seems to share the lyric proximity to the order of voice. In fact drama deconstructs that order, and reveals the textuality even of voice. (196)

As Rajan's remarks implicitly confirm, the long poem, although not necessarily narrative in form, has the ability to absorb into its large structure lyric, dramatic, and other disparate elements, thus creating a textual process of 'betweenness.' This betweenness is not a matter of simple deviation from previously established generic conventions; rather, it is a matter of multiple encodings and decodings, of shifting value systems, of infraction.

A GENRE IN THE PRESENT TENSE

The most consistent attempts to define the long poem in Canada have been made, interestingly enough, by poets themselves, beginning as we have seen with Dorothy Livesay's 'The Documentary Poem: A Canadian Genre.' But even before Livesay, another writer, George Bowering, in 1964 began to edit *Imago*, a magazine exclusively dedicated to the publication of long poems. In his opening editorial, Bowering stated his purpose clearly: 'This *Imago*, the magazine ... is intended ... for the long poem, the series or set, the sequence, swathes from giant work in progress, long life pains eased into print: Blake's "Marriage of Heaven & Hell" welcome ... So as to submissions: send thick mss, the cumbersome thing the ragbag mag wont have room for' (*Imago* 1, 2). As was his plan, from wherever he happened to be living (Calgary, London, Montreal, Vancouver), Bowering edited twenty issues of *Imago* (1964–74), which presented an array of long poems in their entirety or in excerpts, most of them Canadian. The importance Bowering – and other writers, such as Kearns, Davey, Fawcett, Marlatt, and Wah (all published in *Imago*) – assigned to the long poem was reinforced in 1970 by *The Long Poem Anthology*, edited by Michael Ondaatje, complete with a preface in which he unequivocally stated that 'the most interesting writing being done by poets today can be found within the structure of the long poem' (1979, 11). More recently, the debate was reopened by Robert Kroetsch's essay 'For Play and Entrance: The Contemporary Canadian Long Poem' (1980), and Frank Davey's 'The Language of the Contemporary Canadian Long Poem' (1981); it culminated with the publication of the proceedings of the 1985 Long-liners Conference.[12] These activities provide us with evidence that we are dealing with the development of a conscious genre,[13] as is particularly attested by the poets' own statements on their long poems in Ondaatje's anthology. There is no consensus among these poets as to why they write long poems or how they write them; their common fascination with the form, however, suggests an acute awareness of a certain poetic practice.

   The most notable debate on this matter is to be found in the essays of Kroetsch and Davey. Written in twenty-four parts and thereby parodically evoking the epic, Kroetsch's essay reflects his usual critical style – that is, it is at once incisive and elliptical. 'For Play and Entrance' successfully outlines the major concerns of the long poem, but it is riddled with problems. Kroetsch argues that

The problem for the writer of the contemporary long poem is to honour our disbelief in belief – that is, to recognize and explore our distrust of system, of grid, of monisms, of cosmologies perhaps, certainly of inherited story – and at the same time write a long work that has some kind of (under erasure) unity.

And yet the long poem, by its very length, allows the exploration of the failure of system and grid. The poem of that failure is a long poem. (1989, 118)

Kroetsch, accurately I think, delineates the ideological intent behind the writing practice of the long poem, but his poetics of failure introduces a deceptive process. Indeed, he defines failure by ironically adopting the values of the cultural system he deconstructs; he also seems to define it, as Davey points out, from a male point of view. The overriding metaphor in his essay is that of desire held back, desire not quite sublimating itself. 'In love-making, in writing the long poem – delay is both – delay is both technique and content' (117). The poet not so much as lover but as a subject resisting his falling into love, onto the body of otherness; the long poem not as love-making but rather as a machine of desire, an object in perpetual ecstasy – a condition few long poems, not even Kroetsch's own, reflect.

Davey says in his interpretation of this argument that Kroetsch

reads the energy of the long poem as sexual energy, and delay as postponement of a terminating orgasm. This theory, in my subjective view, has unhappy implications for the life-long poem (not to mention the life itself should it bear any close relationship to the poem), and contains at least a hint of exclusively male perspective; not surprisingly, it is linked by Kroetsch to a view of the Canadian long poem as a narrative of disappointment and failure. (1983, 185)

Davey is right in his critique, but his objections remain too literal, and he reaches towards an essentializing female desire. Kroetsch's rhetoric of desire does not speak of gender or of anatomical difference; rather it speaks of the ideologically phallocratic configurations assigned to gender roles. For example, the following statement, in the context of Kroetsch's reading of Webb's *Naked Poems*, betrays not gender bias but the blind spot in what is taken to be normative behaviour by the very ideology he questions: 'the poet, the lover, compelled towards an ending (conclusion, death, orgasm: coming) that must, out of love, be (difference) deferred' (118); both subject and object of love in *Naked Poems* are female, but Kroetsch doesn't differentiate between Webb's 'hesitation ... to write the long poem' and her 'insisting on ... a way out of the ending of the lyric' (118). His measure of the long poem does not intend to be phallic; it is so by default.

Instead, the long poem emerges from Kroetsch's essay as a desire machine (re)producing – *ad infinitum* (we are led to speculate) – its 'pressure toward madness,' its 'protests' against closure, against 'accuracy and source' (119). The deferral of orgasm that Kroetsch finds inscribed in the length of poems is nothing other than the long poem's seduction by process, its unwillingness to submit to any pre-formalized versions of closure. Desire, as we have seen, informs the quest in the long poem, but this is not the kind of desire Kroetsch discusses: '[a] perpetual delay as we recognize the primacy of the forthcoming and as yet unmade discovery' (119). The biomechanics of desire, for Kroetsch, in its continuous deferral and prolonged delays, is sexualized, but fetishizes to the same degree both female and male bodies. This kind of desire renders itself, paradoxically, undesirable; it debilitates the poet, as it is configured, for instance, by Kroetsch's 'The Sad Phoenician,' originally entitled 'The Sad Phoenician of Love.' The Phoenician, a self-acknowledged failure in love, can find sublimation only in his desire for language, in his 'trading' in the alphabet, his repeated reversals of signs. Yet the applicability of Kroetsch's theory of delay deconstructs itself by means of his own warning signals: 'DANGER: deferral (delay delayed) of the encounter. With god. With the muse. With the lover' (124). The danger lurks less in the encounter than in the delay itself; it is his notion of sexual deferral that desublimates and de-individualizes the long poem's process. The long poem (sometimes writing as love-making, sometimes the poem as the body of thwarted love) surfaces as a body without organs, self-engendering – '[d]elay is the mother of beauty' (132) – with no need for mediation, no room for the other. (This theory, ironically, is hardly supported by Kroetsch's own long poems.)

This is certainly not a case of Don Juanian erotics, for the poet as lover cannot possibly prolong pleasure without leaving the desired body. The Kroetschian poet/lover, however, is trapped in his own body: '[y]ou, poet, giving birth to yourself. The contemporary Canadian long poem as birth and trauma' (123). The solipsism implied here is not inscribed in the contemporary long poem as I see it; it is implied, though, in Kroetsch's imaging the poet as both a writing machine and as the force (desire) that feeds that machine. Despite Kroetsch's polemical stance against humanism, the poet in the process of giving birth to himself remains a monologic subject who doesn't accede to the ideological signature of the long poem. Kroetsch's focus on failure does little to disengage the poet from the very binary structures that he rightly says the long poem seeks to disperse. Birth and trauma, delay and orgasm, unity and disunity – Kroetsch's gestures of erasure simply redraw the same figures but in different configurations. The long poem as feminine text – a site of birth and trauma – discloses the hiatus in his argument; behind his 'ferocious' attack on closure, there lies his real fear, fear of beginnings: '[p]oets, like lovers, were driven back to the moment of creation; the question, then: not how to end, but how to begin. Not the quest for ending, but the dwelling at and in the beginning itself' (118).

How to begin indeed. Kroetsch, obviously, situates his theory of delay between the discursive and the figural; the poet as creator is a subject marked by the maternal signs of birth and trauma and is the same poet who, pressed by the 'endless need to begin' (123), must abnegate his very creation, himself as desiring subject desired by language. Beginning anew, an important recurring trope in the long poem, does not always have to be instigated by a 'war within'; Kroetsch's casual references in his poems to such texts as 'the eggplant poems,' (presumably) begun but abandoned, are jokes, but jokes with a Freudian twist. They declare as much fear of beginnings as fear of closure. 'The erotic and erratic erotic' (126) in the long poem intimates the possibility of failure, but not Kroetsch's seemingly romantic version of it. Failure is annulled by the potential to begin again, and again.

Yet, despite the precarious condition of desire in his essay, Kroetsch is the first (poet) critic to attempt a formalization of the primary concerns of the contemporary long poem in Canada. He speaks of its undoing of 'narrative grammars,' its interlacing of epic and lyric intents, its 'archaeology that challenges the authenticity of history' (119), its fragmentation, its obsession with self and place, its continuous falling into language. Not surprisingly, the summation of his argument is to be found in yet another contradiction in his essay:

entrance / en-trance!

We write poems, in Canada, not of the world, but to gain entrance
to the world. That is our weakness and our strength.

Dare to enter.
Dare to be carried away, transported.

Is not the long poem, whatever its inward turn, finally the poem of
outward? As we come to the end of self, in our century, we come again
(consider the critical writings and poetry of Frank Davey) to the long

poem. We become, again, persons in the world, against the preposterous
notion of self. We are each our own crossroads.   (132)

If in his scenario discussed above desire and delay impede communication by keeping the other in abeyance, here, he suggests, the effects
of deferral are assuaged by entering the world. At this point – already
dashing off – Kroetsch does not quite tell us how this entrance is to
be achieved. We can infer, however, that it is mitigated by the shift
from coming to becoming – '[w]e become, again, persons in the world.'
The movement from the poet as solipsistic lover residing within a
product of self-made *jouissance* to the poet as person, a denizen of the
world, is an important moment in Kroetsch's antithetic text. It points
to the performative function of the long poem: the long poem not
envisaged as a static system, but as 'play,' as performance. This performative function renders all its generic boundaries problematic.

In outlining the major features of the contemporary long poem,
Frank Davey stresses 'the impulse not to delay but to prolong, to have
the poem not be about time but in it, not to be about the life but
within it' (1983, 188). The shift in emphasis from delay to prolongation,
though significant, is one that cannot be easily resolved, because it is
not a question of either/or. The length of the long poem, a matter
also of 'depth or breadth' as Davey remarks (183), is inextricably related
to its temporality; 'length,' Davey argues, 'also speaks about time –
that the writer will take his time, engage time, encompass its passage'
(183). The temporal movement of the long poem measures the distance
that separates it from the centre of experience. Yet Davey's emphasis
on anticipation – the long poem 'anticipates more rather than post-
pones' (185) – is operational only if understood in the context of having
no conditions or knowable object attached to it.

Bowering's *Allophanes*, an example Davey himself cites, creates various kinds of anticipation, but its continuity does not depend on the
delivery of what the reader might anticipate; instead, it depends on
a series of swerves that shuttle the reader off to surprising destinations.
A highly intertextual poem, it engages the reader in conflict with its
self-consciousness and cryptic allusions. As its title indicates, *Allophanes*
keeps resituating the reader from alchemy to modernism, from baseball diamonds to 'Hera's clitoris,' all the while locating its temporality
in the poet's ear – 'I cock my ear. What I want to hear is the voice
that enters my secluded study' (1979, 329). Anticipation is part of the

long poem's process, but it is infected by temporality, thereby dispersing its desired object.

Similarly, the success of Davey's own *The Abbotsford Guide to India* (1986) relies less on the fulfilment of the reader's anticipation, carefully set up by the poet, than on a continuous unfurling of surprises that disclose the extent to which the poem revolves around an absent centre. Anticipation is constructed by the particularities of the poem's conscious interplay with generic modes such as the guidebook, the travelogue, the documentary, the prose poem, and *le récit*; they bring to the fore the unconscious operation of universal codes embodied in a tourist's perception – the tourist metaphorically pointing to the reader. If the poem's opening line, 'Abbotsford is the centre of Canada & India is the centre of the world' (3), offers a signal as to what the reader might anticipate – a subversion of codes and ideologies – the poem itself coyly delays the fulfilment of this anticipation by creating more and more anticipatory occasions.

Documents

...

You are advised to obtain a Tourist Introduction Card & Liquor Permit, although you are unlikely to need it. Parsees prefer to have their bodies disassembled by vultures. Your international health card should list immunizations for typhoid, diphtheria, smallpox, polio and cholera. A passport stamp is a contextualized signifier. The Parsee mortuary platforms are called the Towers of Silence. File a currency declaration on arrival; keep certificates of all currency conversions. An autographed poster of your minister of external affairs is not necessary. Indian clerks will be helpful whenever you enter the wrong line. You must present your passport in order to register at a hotel. Cows have the right-of-way. Carry the phone number of your hotel. The bodies of Hindu children & harijans are disposed of in rivers. The Delhi luggage carousel may soil your bags with grease. Indian merchants & professors delight in the exchange of business cards.   (10)

This passage, like most of the other prose pieces in the book, is written in a matter-of-fact tone that reinforces the surface value of the text. The abrupt shift from one statement to another displays a discontent with the grammar of tourism's anticipatory narrative, and does so by bombarding the reader (and the prospective tourist in India) with an overflow of warnings that might produce the opposite of the desired effect. Georges Van den Abbeele observes that 'a tourist attraction has three components: a sight, a marker, and a tourist ... The most important and interesting component of the tourist attraction is the marker, without which the tourist would not only be unable to recognize the sight but the sight itself could not exist as such' (4). Davey's reader, as a tourist-to-be led through an incongruous chain of seemingly unrelated markers, becomes a tourist in the text suffering from textual and cultural shock. The heterology of *The Abbotsford Guide to India* resists the self-incorporation and assimilation that the fulfilment of anticipation requires.

Davey's juxtaposition of various discourses ranging from the lyric expression of a peacock's cry to pseudo-scientific pronouncements alerts the reader to the partiality, the unpredictability, and the inherent falsehoods of any simple attempt at providing a guide to India as cultural text.

> & there's still this singing beggarwoman back in Srinagar. Who never wanted to be a story. Who didn't want to be a signifier. & in the possible gravel field there's a bunch of women & children in ragged shawls & jackets examining some coins & small bills piled in the centre of a dirty cloth. The woman from the river is there, & a couple of ragged men. Our possible text is there too but it can't hear the dialogue. It would gladly stage a rock concert but it can't 'solve the problem' of characterization.
>
> (63)

If characterization is resolved at all in this poem, it is by Davey's escaping from the lyric trap of the 'I' by shifting the discursive space from which the 'I' speaks; the subject/object dyad in this poem never achieves any significant stability. This not only testifies to the performative function of the long poem, but also indicates the extent to which anticipation is part of the long poem's 'play.' As Davey's text examines its own ideological motives, so the reader's aborted anticipation prevents India as text from being subsumed by the touristic fallacy that otherness can be appropriated.

Later in his essay on the long poem Davey unwittingly deconstructs his initial premise about anticipation: '[t]o see more than can be anticipated. To be surprised' (1983, 190). The structure of surprises in *The Abbotsford Guide to India* affirms the temporality of the long poem. The more self-conscious the reader the more complicitous she or he is forced to feel with the tourist; the greater the surprise – 'Maybe

"maybe" is a story' (1986, 62), 'Each day the Indian elephant re-invents himself' (1986, 79) – the more rigorous the sensation that communication becomes ex-communication. Surprise by definition is meant to deconstruct anticipation. In this respect, Kroetsch's delay (as decoded above) and Davey's prolongation, which encompasses an 'announcement of futurity' (1983, 183) and surprise (1983, 190), are equally important as they mark the long poem's trajectory.

Delay: its meditative turns, its hesitancy to begin, its pauses, detours, and double-takes; prolongation: the rupture of what both Kroetsch and Davey call discreet occasion (119 and 183, respectively), a remission of time, making a thing process. Both delay and prolongation show the poet to dwell in language and hinge on the inscription of excess in the long poem. Whereas delay and anticipation operate against a preconceived ending, prolongation functions according to momentariness, situating the long poem both within and outside a time continuum; it liquefies the unmasterable margins of time – past, present, and future. Delay and prolongation extend the aporetic structure of the long poem – its apostasizing from truth, its long measure versus its simultaneous disdain for and coyness about saturation. Although prolongation comes as a riposte to delay, both of them function as engendering and not as organizing principles – what Davey suggests especially with regard to prolongation.

Davey's concept of prolongation by surprise is interrelated with two other important aspects of his argument: the long poem's resistance to sequential narrative, and its autobiographical impulse. In this, his argument does not differ much from Kroetsch's. More specifically, he states that the long poem operates '[i]n distrust' of '[s]equential narrative [as] an organizational system, a language, a structure of signs that speaks of certain assumptions about reality: that it is linear, directed by cause and effect, excluding in its constructions and focusses' (1983, 184). Although Davey does not see delay as one of the engendering principles of the long poem, it is precisely the combination of delay and prolongation that results in its non-linear narrative structure. The irreducible temporality of the long poem counters the unifying force of sequential narrative. The impossibility of satisfaction that Kroetsch detects in delay is coupled with the unceasing deferral of endings that both he and Davey observe in the long poem.

If 'sightseeing,' as Van den Abbeele argues, 'constitutes a kind of basic narrative sequence' (4), cohesion in *The Abbotsford Guide to India* is promised by anticipation but delivered by the consistent erring that surprises incur. The traveller's movement and his camera's shifting angles, which, through a certain kind of pictorial delay, register visually those sections of reality that go beyond the tourist's self-consciousness, show that '[t]ourism can never be more than rhetoric & device' (Davey 1986, 90). From this obsession with India as place whose *genius loci* the traveller tries to understand, he emerges as a poet/tourist, a wanderer forever remaining in exile within the very narrative he wishes to inhabit: this kind of tourist/poet cannot abide the text he creates, perhaps the penultimate surprise in the contemporary long poem.

Amber
(A Visitor Thinks Long Poems, Thinks Amber)
...

What someone did here, what I did, was go on building ... Building toward the missing beds in the harem. 'Keeps your mind off your troubles,' my grandmother said, as she crocheted the unneeded doilies. Then Aurengzebe gets angry. The Americans raise the interest rates ...

& so I'd been thinking these were my ruins. Thinking big, thinking
long poems.   (Davey 1986, 50–1)

Surprise effects the widening of the circle Davey intends to break out of. Building towards a structure within which the poet's grandmother is kept company by Aurengzebe (from Dryden's long poem) results in a negative unity. The poem's subject knows that his epistemological endeavours will be deferred, a deferral that prolongs the act of knowing – 'Thinking big, thinking long poems.' In this, time in the long poem is not an erosive power, a reified concept; yet engendered as it is by language, it directs the poem and its reader towards a subjectivity that becomes knowable only when the subject, by an act of self-consciousness, becomes the object of its discourse.

The long poem's heterology, acknowledged by both Kroetsch and Davey, does not lack the kind of irony that Davey argues it does. 'The contemporary poem,' Davey tells us, 'tends to use a subtext of low cultural standing, to do no borrowing of structure from it, and rarely to use it to subject the main text to ironic commentary' (1983, 186). Yet not all the examples of subtexts of low cultural value cited by Davey support his argument. Pratt's *The Titanic*, 'used' by Davey himself in *The Clallam*, the holy grail romances 'used' by him in *King of Swords*, and Moodie's *Roughing It in the Bush* 'used' by Atwood in *The Journals of Susanna Moodie* could hardly be called subtexts of low cultural standing and thus compared to Kroetsch's 'use' of a seed catalogue and a family ledger. For instance, the subtexts in Tostevin's *'sophie*, ranging from Pythagoras, Plato, and Derrida to the Bible, are anything but low.

The problem in Davey's argument lies in his concept of 'usage' as well as in an implicit hierarchy that orders cultural texts and their codes. Even if we accept a distinction between the intertexts as low and the long poem as high, such a reading won't account for the extent to which the long poem is commensurate to the elements it embodies. They are not subtexts but sources become an integral part of the long poem, because they are not just used for background purposes; they are appropriated. Their participation in the textuality of contemporary long poems thematizes (by questioning) their low or high cultural status, thus effecting not a simple reversal but a revisioning of the rules of representation and ideology.

The lacunae in Davey's argument are resolved by his subtly altered position in a later essay, 'Countertextuality in the Long Poem' (1985), subsequently republished in a slightly revised form as 'Recontextualization in the Long Poem' (1988). In the original version, Davey said that it is 'useful to note that works like those of Pratt or Kearns or Sid Stephens' [*sic*] *Beothuck Poems* have many notable precursors in this attempt to make past speak to present or to make the present reader recreate past texts' (1985, 38). Bracketing the problems in seeing Pratt's use of historical sources in the same terms as Kearns's or Stephen's, we find a significant 'revision' in the revised essay; referring to the same writers, Davey now tells us that they 'have many notable precursors in this attempt to mark past events with present ideologies, or to make the present reader rewrite past texts' (1988, 131).

Far from being a simple change in diction, this rewriting substantially alters the argument Davey presents in his first essay on the long poem. As he states in both versions of his second essay, the 'impulse of these [works] texts is not really to document; it is to appropriate, co-opt, [re-envision] re-cast for one's own needs and times' (1985, 39; 1988, 132; brackets refer to the first version). This position is echoed by Stephen Scobie who observes that the historical 'events which make up this [long poem's] narrative are documented, historical happenings, although the poet will frequently modify or shuffle these events, or add to them purely fictional incidents' ('Amelia' 269). The irony informing the appropriation suggested by both Davey and Scobie is two-fold, aimed at both the source employed and the long poem employing it; it doesn't speak, however, at least not directly so, to the ideological function of the treatment of documents in the long poem.

Davey's fortuitous change of 'countertextuality' (implying a dialectic relationship) to 'recontextualization' speaks to that, but Scobie insists on seeing this irony in Livesay's terms: 'this irony [of the relationship of poet to persona] is the major form assumed by the "dialectic between the objective facts and the subjective feelings of the poet," which continues to be, as Livesay perceived, the central characteristic of the genre' ('Amelia' 269). This dialectic is operative only when the poet is willing to take for granted the stability of documents constructed by official historical discourse. When Scobie, like Davey, 'feel[s] the need to subvert [his] own definition, or, in the current terminology, to "deconstruct" it' (1986, 245), he notices 'the distance that the continuing poem has come from that "documentary" form of the long poem with which [he] began' (1986, 251). He declares that 'in the continuing poem, everything becomes fictional, even the most seemingly personal of autobiographical details' (1986, 249). The shift of terms broadens Scobie's first definition and makes it more inclusive, thus emphasizing the long poem's self-questioning as well as its questioning of the self, but it threatens to do away with the concept of the document altogether. It is one thing to question the fictionality of a document's presumed objectivity and another to suggest that a document ceases to have a referential function in the long poem. The recontextualization of historical material in the long poem effects a negative dialectics[14] by documenting the fictionality that often informs binary structures privileged by history; the result is the deconcealment and reordering of the referential hierarchical values in traditional historiography. The ideological power of the long poem as a genre lies in its ability to redirect the referentiality of its components, to alter the position of its referents, whether they are the genres or documents it borrows from. While remaining referential and ironically employing dialectics, the long poem derives meaning otherwise.

Doug Jones's 'Kate, These Flowers ... (The Lampman Poems)' (1977), far from reflecting a dialectical relationship with the past, positions itself on the threshold of both its precursors and its antecedents.

Kisses are knowledge, Kate
aphasia confounds us with a new
tongue
     too Pentecostal, too
Eleusinian, perhaps, for us
moderate Anglicans   (76)

These lines double-speak, compelling Jones's reader to see them as
timebound yet as escaping the determinism of time frames. They are
consigned to the residues of the past but they are the product of the
present. The poem's speaker cannot redeem the past because the past
is precisely what engenders the poem's writing:

     this country where
desire becomes restraint
refractory, silence
our orator
     and thus apparent
paradox
     until the petalled flesh
speak as to the deaf and blind   (79)

If there is any master-narrative here it is one that ensues from 'paradox' – 'silence / our orator' – the very paradox of discovering one's
presentness in the difference of the past. Jones's Lampman sublates
his own identity and historical specificity, his otherness being an ironic
comment on Jones's own writing strategies.

Similarly, Don Gutteridge's *God's Geography* (1982) confiscates the
past in order to reinvest it with the poet's own desire. Following two
pages of documentary material, the poem opens by showing that the
past becomes its own antecedent.

me: here
and that two-
edged jaw
biting
     milk
       flesh
         air

and

me:

      there   (11)

We read the 'here' and 'there' as the now and then, but the poet's autobiographical gesture that recounts the 'I' as 'me' renders the subject as object. This linguistic distancing and historical gesture has a twofold function: synchronically, it shows that identity partakes of the past and present; diachronically, it prevents a complete conjunction of the two, thus revealing that the otherness of identity is incommensurable with a complete totalization of past sources.

The long poem's treatment of historical sources does not necessarily perpetuate the hierarchical values embedded in them. Instead, they are dissolved and reconstituted with a difference. Whether these sources are about the detritus of past lives, personal histories, or major historical events, their putative ideologies are not domesticated but problematized; the effect is a retracing of present habituality, this as a result of the temporality of the contemporary long poem. Even when the long poem is contaminated by what it sets out to question, its manifold structure assures us of its otherness. The ambivalence of its relationship with its many intertexts is irreducible. This is not to suggest that the long poem shies away from taking a stance, or that its generic heterogeneity always results in hermeneutic perplexity. On the contrary, it makes its task to show, in Davey's words, 'truth's variability' (1985, 33; 1988, 124). This variability, however, is misinterpreted by critics who readily define the long poem as epic because of its tendency to incorporate documentary material. Its treatment of documents does not necessarily lend itself to the epic genre as such, although the desire to record poetically a historical situation or retrieve an individual from historical misinterpretation or anonymity often derives from the poet's recognition that the ethos of the material is or has the potential to be epic. We could detect, for example, in Michael Ondaatje's *The Collected Works of Billy the Kid* (1970), George Bowering's *George, Vancouver* (1970), Florence McNeil's *Emily* (1975), Gwendolyn MacEwen's *The T.E. Lawrence Poems* (1982), Ed Dyck's *The Mossbank Canon* (1982), Dennis Cooley's *Bloody Jack* (1984), Stephen Scobie's *The Ballad of Isabel Gunn* (1987), and Paulette Jiles's *The Jesse James Poems* (1988), an epic ethos in the way they present their protagonists' histories. In poems like these, which focus on documents dealing with a central figure, the poets' intention is not to reify in epic terms the figures taken from history but rather to subvert both the given 'truths' about these characters and the value systems that have informed them. These poems posit themselves as supplements to the documents they employ because they both appropriate and add to what they find in history.

Thus Scobie's *The Ballad of Isabel Gunn* recasts the recorded adventures of Isabel in epic light and fills in the gaps of her silence with a poignancy that deconstructs the presumed authenticity of archival material. Nevertheless, *McAlmon's Chinese Opera* (1980), although more closely interrelated with documents, lacks the epic ethos of *Isabel Gunn*. The tragic pathos with which McAlmon is described as a hobo – 'Nights I spent camped out with nothing / except the night itself to talk to, / debating the serious question of whether / it might have been better not to be born' (14) – is far from suggesting any epic qualities for this modernist anti-hero. Yet he emerges in these poems as a strong character, for his wilful failures if nothing else. It is McAlmon's voice, at once plaintive and full of rage and contempt for his contemporaries, that gives *McAlmon's Chinese Opera*, described with telling uneasiness by Scobie as a series of 'poems,' the structure of a long poem. Scobie's biographical outline in the 'Afterword' (certainly intended to be read as preface, given the well-known documentary background) is deconstructed by McAlmon's speaking 'I,' which immediately transforms biography into autobiography. This undoing of genre is in keeping with the sources Scobie has available, namely the numerous autobiographical and biographical works, including McAlmon's own, that talk of Paris in the twenties. A self-conscious writer, Scobie tells his readers that they should 'accep[t] the McAlmon of these poems as a character in a historical fiction' (93), a character 'best described by Dorothy Livesay ... when she talks of a "conscious attempt to create a dialectic between the objective facts and the subjective feelings of the poet"' (93). But if there is a dialectical relationship implied between the autobiographical and the biographical material, it is subverted, even exceeded, by McAlmon's 'I.'

'What I never wanted / was pity,' he states at the very beginning of the book; what he wanted instead was precision:

I wanted them to draw me as I was:
the line straight and hard,
the muscles firm, not tired at all
nine hours a day

at a dollar an hour
in 1921.   (7)

Caught in the middle of his unrequited desire for respect and accuracy,
and residing in the precarious position of speaking in a voice that is
spoken by another writer (Scobie), McAlmon manages to exceed the
singularity of the first-person point of view of these poems. For what
allows him to speak at all is, ironically, the intertextuality of his voice,
the extent to which it speaks from within a tradition that he dismissed
as much as it dismissed him. The tension in *McAlmon's Chinese Opera*
is to be located between poet and character, but also between character
and history. It is this kind of negative dialectics that informs McAlmon's
opera: its inarticulate libretto is both a parody of modernist epistemology and an expression of McAlmon's personal anguish. Defying
his own dialectical position at this point, Scobie records McAlmon recording his opera in the third person:

The only thing that stopped them dead
at any party, any bar, was always
McAlmon's Chinese Opera, a long
high wordless toneless wail
that filled the empty sky inside my head
and got me thrown out on the street
to seek the perfect audience of dawn.   (48)

Both author and reader of this opus, McAlmon tempts the reader with
an objectivity that the documents about him cannot claim. His opera
attains significance because its momentariness evades documentation
and thus, paradoxically, invites both paraphrase and distortion. Documents, in this book, are rendered by Scobie (contrary to his earlier
position), as lies – 'There was the lie I told to Glassco, / that I'd joined
the Canadian Army' (68). The document as lie, as an ineluctable fiction,
transforms McAlmon's Chinese Opera into a text:

The hand that reaches out
to turn the radio off
is parchment skin and hollow bone.
The mind has already shut itself off,
but somewhere in the darkness between stations
a voice is screaming down

the airwaves of the long dead years
McAlmon's Chinese Opera.   (73)

A shriek that haunts the tradition he almost embraced and that wilfully
ignores any borders, this text extends beyond its own voice (its speaking 'I') by challenging its very materiality. Dissonant and cacophonous,
McAlmon's Chinese Opera as a work of art speaks of the dissolving
power of the anti-aesthetic in aesthetics. Its 'Chinese discourse,' besides
estranging the artist himself from his work of art, invites an act of
translation that has no source, no origin or precise point of reference,
only an object translated imaginatively – McAlmon's Chinese Opera – at
once its double and entirely different.

The document as lie also informs The Ballad of Isabel Gunn. Although
Isabel, too, speaks in the first person (a signal of Scobie's ideological
inversion of documents), the specification 'ballad' is somehow at odds
with her own singing 'I.' A ballad implies a diachronic relationship
between singer and character or event, even when the character is
allowed to speak in the first person; Isabel's ballad instead is in synchronic relation with her own 'I.' Despite the many ballad elements
in the poem itself, it is Scobie's own act of entitling the poem The
Ballad of Isabel Gunn that accomplishes the same ideological distancing
we find in McAlmon's Chinese Opera. The ballad signifies not only Scobie's
narrativization of incomplete documents but also the extent to which
a story like Isabel's can be told only after the acknowledgment that
it has been co-opted. An attempt at a cohesive narrative is bound to
contribute further distortion to the already distorted documents.

Isabel's speaking 'I,' although it succeeds in retrieving her from the
silence and invisibility to which her nineteenth-century patriarchal society relegated her, does not convey a sense of solid identity. On the
contrary, it is conditioned by the story she tells, namely of her donning
a male disguise in order to follow her lover, John Scarth, to Canada,
and of her assuming a new name, John Fubbister. Her ballad not only
sets the 'facts' straight, but also reintroduces into the story the very
desire that inspired her journey towards Labrador, a land that 'refuses
the human gaze' (19):

And later, when all the stories were told
over and over, they always assumed
it was his idea: the words they used
were 'seduced,' 'debauched': he took me with him

to be his plaything, to keep him warm
(as if I was one of those Hudson's Bay blankets!)
and I, poor girl, weak-minded like all
my deluded sex, let him lead me along
like a goat on a hank of old rope,

...

The stories never tell how long and hard
I pleaded with him, I cut my hair
and dressed in corduroy, he laughed to see
and then grew still.   (12)

More than her 'becom[ing] a man' (21), it is desire for the other that makes her an exile both in Canada and, later, in the domain of love. By becoming a man, she also becomes her own other, her otherness doubled by taking on her lover's first name, John. Again, a negative dialectics informs this documentary character's sense of othered identity: the poem's last line, 'I am not unnamable. I am Isabel Gunn' (58), far from asserting her recovery of her truly documented identity, testifies both to the fictional and referential function of documents. Her naming act constitutes both unnaming (she is no longer John Fubbister) and renaming (she resists her 'real' name, Isabel Fubbister).

The unreliability of documents is further emphasized by the uncertain paternity of Isabel's child, an uncertainty Scobie inserts into the story by having Isabel, after being abandoned by Scarth, mate with David Spence Junior, a historical character but not one involved historically in Isabel's life. Scobie's deliberate fictionalization of documents reinforces Isabel's deconstructive act of naming. The self-referential line, 'I have found a man who will write this for me' (28), with which Isabel begins her dictation of a letter to her lover through a James Brown, illustrates in its matter-of-fact tone how her identity is caught in the tension between her speech and the poet's (and Brown's) writing, and points to the multi-authority of documents. Although this letter is invented by Scobie, its documentary form does not suggest intentionality; instead, it addresses the question of how documents can usurp identity and reality, an activity that, as Isabel Gunn herself knows, is fraught with ideological implications. A document that is or becomes a lie questions objectivity at the same time that it creates an alternate referential system in which the artist's cognitive power is subjected to the ideology of the genre she or he uses.

The deception intrinsic to documents can also be detected in long poems of a different documentary nature, namely those that choose to record the *genius loci* of a particular geography. In Douglas Barbour's *A Poem as Long as the Highway* (1971), John Marshall's *The West Coast Trail Poems* (1977), Daphne Marlatt's *Steveston* (1974), David Arnason's *Marsh Burning* (1980), Monty Reid's *The Alternate Guide* (1985), Birk Sproxton's *Headframe:* (1985), and Frank Davey's *The Abbotsford Guide to India*, the poets find their documents as they go along, or invent them in a manner organic to their process of writing, or even identify as document what is considered to be superfluous in other recording processes. Thus the title of Reid's book aptly demonstrates that his poem 'grew out of [the] extraneous material' that the field guide to the natural history of Alberta he edited could not contain (7). Many long poems of this kind 'document' places that lie outside the delegated centres of power. The outlaw figure, the failed artist, the silent/invisible woman of the documentaries dealing with single historical figures are replaced here by Sproxton's Flin Flon, Arnason's Gimli, Marshall's Pacific rim, Marlatt's Steveston, Suknaski's Wood Mountain, Whyte's Rockies, and Davey's Abbotsford – places traditionally viewed as lacking a locus of energy, as being culturally irrelevant. The documents in these poems are informed by the desire to redraw cultural geography, to shift the designated centre off centre.

For example, the opening line of Barbour's poem, 'a poem as long as the highway' (np), unequivocally declares how the long poem is engendered by and itself generates the documents that comprise it. As he says,

> construction is
> slow as
> growing is,   where
> growing is knowledge

The long poem discloses to the reader that which remains unknown in the known, and suggests that there will always be something unknowable in both its own structure and the structure it incorporates. While acknowledging this, Barbour also declares:

> Yet the road
> like the poem progresses,
> through particular landscapes
> to a certain truth

This truth, however, as we have already seen, has variable content, a content whose signification depends on the observing subject and on the temporality of the long poem as a genre in a state of becoming. When the subject is not given priority, the intentionality pervading inherited documents is rendered obsolete; in this light, documents speak of the past as well as of the present. Their depth and surface are no longer in dialectical conflict because the traces of their making are clearly inscribed in, and often produced or altered by, the writing process.

> All this
> weather and landscape as history:
>
> and my mind records that thought,
> and knowing, I curse the lack
> of paper, pen;   I'll have to try
> to hold it there
> until we return to camp
> and I can write it down.
>
> Not quite the way
> it appeared.

Although Barbour cannot prevent immediate perception from becoming document – from being recorded 'Not quite the way it appeared' – his willingness to acknowledge loss, to locate himself in the intervals that inevitably occur between subject and object, takes his poem away from the positivism normally assigned to historical sources.

> geologist, surveyor, artist:
> crowsfeet on a map, the heavy
> colours cut and carved, numbers
> and weight, percentages, all
> methods to paraphrase
> certain immensity.

The irony of 'certain immensity' accentuates the irrelevance of methodology in an enterprise that will only result in paraphrase. Paraphrase, besides offering inadequate description, presents the documented reality as a passive object, finished and done for. But *A Poem as Long as the Highway* affirms, in its processual making, the constitutive energy of subjectivity in constructing a world 'documented' by a negative dialectics. The poet 'on the highway' is not a single (singular) subject gazing at the mountains that 'rest in distance'; the mountains 'assume pupils' / widening,' 'wait to be described.' As object/subject, the mountains activate the critical difference the long poem introduces in the treatment of documents; attributing to them an awareness of passivity brings into question the dialectical relationship between subject and object. Besides co-opting the mountains, the act of paraphrasing indicates the limits of the geologist/surveyor/artist's presumed sovereignty.

If, despite its questioning of documentary authenticity, the long poem has a tenacious relationship to documents, it is because its genre is constituted, to borrow Philippe Hamon's term, by 'a semiotics of *knowing*' (96);[15] this semiotics challenges the status of its sources as well as the various rhetorical strategies involved in the long poem's (re)shaping of sources and of itself. This semiotics of knowing also informs the writing of serial poems as it has been practised by Jack Spicer and Robert Duncan, and by their close associate in Canada, Robin Blaser. The serial poem moves towards an entirely new definition of the document through its emphasis on dictation, an emphasis that shifts the poet's attention from questions regarding the authenticity of sources to issues relating to poetics. The gradual growth of Blaser's *The Holy Forest* superbly exemplifies the compositional implications of dictation. As Blaser says about his own work,

I'm interested in a particular kind of narrative – what Jack Spicer and I agreed to call in our own work the serial poem – this is a narrative which refuses to adopt an imposed story line, and completes itself only in the sequence of poems, if, in fact, a reader insists upon a definition of completion which is separate from the activity of the poems themselves. The poems tend to act as a sequence of energies which run out when so much of the tale is told. (1970, 17)

The serial narrative of this kind of long poem depends on dictation, 'the unknown, or the outside [that] enters the work' (1975, 273). Dictation opens up the poem's field of reference to include what one's own personal and emotive world would normally be blind or oblivious to, namely 'messages' Spicer called Martians. These 'messages' 'always come from elsewhere, from outside, from an Other, and in this they are distinguished from significations, which can arise from the [poet's] personalist interior' (Rasula 57). What is dictated is absorbed in the serial poem, but it is not entirely erased as a message from the outside. The opening lines of Bowering's *Allophanes*, 'The snowball appears in Hell / every morning at seven,' were dictated to him, as he tells us, in Spicer's voice. Blaser's *Image-Nations 1–12* (1974) and *Image-Nations 13 and 14* (1975), *Cups* (1968), *Syntax* (1983), and *Pell Mell* (1988), through different typography, italics, and quotation marks clearly designate what comes from the outside; yet it is these sources that, while maintaining their otherness, engender the poems themselves. The result is a disjointed narrative that presents the poet as a reader situated within a world of coding and encoding, a double and ongoing process that is at the heart of the serial poem's making.[16]

We encounter a similarly intense and generative relationship with outside sources in long poems that we might call conceptive.[17] Conceptive poems like Wah's *Music at the Heart of Thinking*, Kroetsch's *Mile Zero, The Sad Phoenician*, and *Excerpts from the Real World*, Tostevin's *'sophie*, and Betsy Warland's *open is broken* (1984) and *Serpent (W)rite* (1987) are primarily poems of ideas that offer themselves as responses to or extensions of ideas by other writers. The intertextuality that plays a major role in the construction of most long poems is here foregrounded not as footnotes or background material, but as direct source to become an integral part of the poem. Thus Wah's *Music at the Heart of Thinking* conceptualizes in its writing practice the function of language and story by way of responding to Olson (Wah's teacher and a great poetic influence on him), bpNichol, Victor Shklovksy, Julia Kristeva, Nicole Brossard, and others; Warland, in both her long poems, deconstructs the way women's signature has been inscribed in the world and in texts; Kroetsch's sad Phoenician meditates on the letters of the alphabet; and bpNichol in his *Martyrology*, through his lifelong meditation on language, meditates on the long poem itself. The narrative emerging in these poems is a narrative that resists summation because the ideas conceptualized cannot possibly be fully contained by these poems or by any other single text. In the conceptive poem there is no seam separating the long poem as text from the textuality that engenders it; the source becomes part of the poem itself, speaking its own otherness, showing how the long poem is itself another practice of intertextuality.

The cumulative effect of outside material in the long poem, be it generic, historical, or conceptual, shows the poet of long poems to be a reader. As Kroetsch says in his statement on *Seed Catalogue*, '[t]he writing the writing the writing. Fundamentally, I mean. The having written excludes the reader. We are left with our selves as critics. We want to be readers. The continuing poem makes us readers' (1979, 312). If we were accustomed to thinking of reading as genre, the long poem would offer a reading *par excellence*. 'Writing,' as Culler says, 'can itself be viewed as an act of critical reading, in which the author takes up a literary past and directs it toward a future' (1980, 50). The long poem, then, is a rereading of writings, a rewriting of readings. But if we are invited to consider the poet of long poems as a reader, there is no specific or legitimate reason to assume that the long poem's decentring is the 'explicit,' as Riddel argues, manifestation of the lyric's own undecidability.

George Bowering's account of his process of writing *Allophanes* explains why the long poem derives its energy from more than one generic source.

What I want to hear is the voice that enters my secluded study. I don't care, really, to enquire of it where it is coming from. If it is loud enough it is all round one ... I am aware of myself as audience ... As I get older, I come more to realize that my activity as a poet composing is an extension of my desirous childhood Christianity ... I mean it. If I hear the gods instead, I am acknowledging, like it or not, my adulthood. (1979, 329)

Bowering as poet/listener cannot determine what he hears, nor can he determine in what genre voices or rereadings mark the long poem's field. The nostalgia that we detect in Bowering's statement is similar to the nostos that informs the protean movements of other long poems such as Spicer's *A Fake Novel about the Life of Arthur Rimbaud*, *Billy the Kid*, and *Holy Grail*, and Al Purdy's *In Search of Owen Roblin* (1974), Barbour's *Visions of My Grandfather* (1977), Andrew Suknaski's *Montage for an Interstellar Cry* (1982), and Ron Smith's *A Buddha Named Baudelaire* (1988). This nostalgia cannot be expressed through the lyric alone, no matter how much the lyric generates its own aporias.

Behind this *longing*, behind this writing of rereadings, there are also traces of the epic and the non-epic narrative traditions, traces that are often translated into the compulsion simply to tell a story, a telling that engenders its own mode. This is how Roy Kiyooka, for instance, points towards the non-lyrical decentring of these other poetic traditions: 'the slowly turning propeller of our adamant History proposes that the yet-to-be-written Canadian Epic will be a wind-borne series of discreet images, 4000 lines long, with an ocean at either end for ballast. everytime I re-read the F.D.M. [his long poem *The Fontainebleau Dream Machine*] ... I re-invent myself. "it" is a musical score for a small ensemble. a window, sky-light an open door' (1979, 332). The diverse compositional nature of the long poem illustrates that generic limits are indeed elastic: they can stretch, extend, or fold within and without. Nonetheless, the long poem transgresses not the limits of a single genre but the limits, the frames, of various genres, such as those of the lyric, the epic, the narrative, the drama, the documentary, and the prose poem.[18] Only if we remain constantly attentive to the dynamics of its various generic components will we do justice to its protean form.

In this context, the title of Eli Mandel's essay 'The Death of the Long Poem' announces that it is not a genre that has ceased to exist but one that

takes its definition in a period that ... resists definitions, as it resists system, grid, cosmology, belief. Perhaps for that reason it presents itself in a series of paradoxes and remains, in one sense, an unsatisfactory notion. From its beginning, wherever that might be, it is an affront to the denials it apparently intends to affirm. In other words (and the long poem always insists on the other words) it exists as a poetics that denies its existence. (1985, 19)

These acts of resistance and denial allow the long poem to be at once an insidious form and a circumscribed genre. Contrary to Mandel's conclusion that 'the long poem cannot be a form – its endless process resists the very definition of structure, centre, foundation we want to put upon it' (1985, 21) – it can be a form; in fact, it is a form defined by its ideological proclivity to turn away from coalescent assumptions and towards the dazzling discontinuity accompanying excess. To appropriate Hayden White's words, it is the form of the long poem that 'constitutes its ideology,' a form that encompasses questions pertaining both to writing and to cultural problematics (10).

The long poem enters the margins of genres by appropriating the concept of genre. The proliferation of its form, while questioning the conventional notion of unified genres, depends on their very conventions. It exposes what Derrida calls 'the law of genre.' 'As soon as the word "genre" is sounded,' Derrida remarks, more radically than any other critic on genre, 'as soon as it is heard, as soon as one attempts to conceive it, a limit is drawn' (1980, 56). It is these limits and their proven flexibility that constitute the long poem's readiness, its desire, to bend and tease the very 'laws' of genres it borrows from. Through its ability to accommodate in its form and structure radically disparate elements, it displays the extent to which its textuality continues (conserves) and parodies (reverses) their traditional functions.[19] Making no claims whatsoever on generic purity, it solicits other literary kinds, going as far as to break the hymen of its own genre. Its particularity as genre is tantamount to its resistance to generic definition.

This is why, I would like to stress again, a generic reading of the long poem should not valorize one of its novelized genres at the expense of another. The long poem not only works against any attempt to retrieve the matrix of the specific genres that engender it, but also parodies the nostalgia for the retrieval of generic origins while incorporating this search within its own textual body. The implicit denial of an overriding structure of generic authority posits the long poem as an instance of *mise en abyme* – a genre without a genre, one might even say. It is no longer an *eidos* but the act of *eidenai* itself, not a fixed object but a mobile event, the act of *knowing* its limits, its demarcated margins, its integrated literary kinds. The long poem ceases to be a kind of a kind by becoming the kind of its other. Hence its ungrammaticality as a 'new' genre.

The contemporary long poem accomplishes its inscription of otherness through its temporality,[20] specifically the present tense. The present tense calls for the deconstruction of the lyric, epic, narrative, and other elements found in the long poem. It is employed to explore new complexities of the lyric utterance in relation to the subject that enunciates it. Although many lyrics, as George T. Wright observes, are also written in the present tense, the present tense of the long poem operates differently. It is not a matter of using what he calls 'mental verbs – *I think, I see, I consider*' (564), which declare the function of the simple present tense, but rather a direct result of its performative act.

Sharon Cameron's discussion of the present tense in the lyric helps us to understand its different usage in the long poem.

[the lyric's present] seems to contain a multiplicity of temporal features that we ordinarily think of as mutually exclusive. It is past-like as well as indicative of future. It locates action temporally, but not in time as we know it. Although timeless, this present tense implies duration ... A present that houses the past as well as the future and that, moreover, evades spatial location and fixture is very close to the creation of a temporal myth built between past and future, real and imagined time, this world and some other. (132)

The present tense of the lyric, even when it is not meant to re-present the occurrence of the subject matter's occasion, is fixed on the occasion of the present moment of writing; yet, the present tense of the lyric remains silent about itself; it does not enunciate its presentness. As Cameron suggests, in spite of the spatial and temporal dislocations incurred by it, the present tense of the lyric, forgetting as it does its verbal materiality, expresses not so much the present as the permanence of myth. 'Given the desire,' Cameron remarks, 'to frame the present in the stasis of perception, it is easy to see why the lyric confuses present tense with the *presence* that ... will bring them [temporal fusions] to a halt' (207; my emphasis). In contrast, the present tense of the long poem does not seek to fuse other temporal dimensions; nor is it its objective, as we have seen, to evoke metaphysical or mythical presence. The presence it speaks of is that of the materiality of language, namely how the writing act progresses in time. By foregrounding the materiality of language the long poem demonstrates that its meaning derives from language as act (not as representation); it also shows that its present tense functions as the vehicle of its signification process, a process equally derived from the acts of writing and reading.

The poet, engaged in an ongoing process (a fact that partly accounts for the length of the long poem), composes in the present tense through a dialogized, in contrast to the lyric's and epic's monologic, 'I.' The traditional dichotomy between spectator and actor, signifier and signified, is erased. The two functions become interchangeable, the distance between them breaks down, the writer finds herself or himself at times lost in a fluid world where everything is possible. This is an experience we too share as readers. When we enter into the present-tense world of the long poem, we cannot tell with certainty to what extent our reading graphs our recognition of the poem's own inscription or becomes an 'allegory' of its own interpretation, its self-referentiality.

A further consequence of the long poem's unfolding in the present is the decentring of the self, the questioning of the Cartesian ego. The present tense, because it remains by definition inconclusive and constantly in motion, designates the tentativeness of the self; it manifests itself as the enunciating subject of its performative act.

The dialogic enunciation of the self and the aporias it gives rise to lead to the loss of epic distance in the long poem, even where we can detect strong epic elements. The epic as a genre is marked by the transferral of a represented world into the past. The long poem, by contrast, attempts to deal with the inconclusive present; it recalls the past not so much as a presence entirely lost, but as a presence that, unavoidably, is what in its different configurations the long poem inscribes. It is, in part, through this attempt to retrieve the past that the long poem practises a critique of the culture that produces it, for it seeks to explore not the tradition of the past but its genealogy. From the monologic world-view represented in the epic, from the intense 'cry of the heart' in the lyric, we move to a world-view that continually affirms, and is constituted by, the present.

The grounding of the self in the present tense contributes to the discursive form of the long poem. That discursiveness results partly from the long poem's preoccupation with locality, and partly from its mode of enunciation. Although locality is a concern pervading Canadian literature in general, its treatment in the long poem recasts it as a distinct theme that shapes its form. Together with the documentary material that often goes along with it, locality may designate the place that generates narrative; but, more than that, it causes its own temporalization and the liberation of documents from fixed interpretation. At the same time, locality also becomes the field of writing, namely the space where the long poem's inscription and process are thematized.

In a similar manner, the long poem's discursiveness marks the loss of authorial distance. The main consequence of this loss is that the single-minded narrative of the traditional epic, together with its implicit overview, is erased as well. As a result, narrative is replaced by discourse – enunciation itself. The linearity of narrative now takes the form of a dialogue between different levels of discourse and genres that tend to privilege an awareness of the writing act, while speech still maintains its significance through the voice's textuality.

All these generic and thematic modulations allow the long poem to sustain its performative action. The performative utterance, as Emile Benveniste says, 'does not have the value of description or prescription but ... of performance. This is why,' he continues, 'it is often accompanied by indications of date, of place, of names of people, witnesses, etc.; in short, it is an event because it creates an event.' In conflict with its resistance to an all-descriptive generic definition, the long poem's specificity with regard to its components presents its disjunctiveness as the site of the performance. Benveniste's recognition that there is 'in the performative a peculiar quality, that of being *self-referential*, of referring to a reality that it itself constitutes by the fact that it is actually uttered in conditions that make it an act' (236) reflects the degree to which it is the poem's writing process that materializes its performative function. Its reflexivity is in keeping with its readiness to act upon the infelicities it might recognize in the literary and cultural systems encoded in it. This is the promise it offers.

3

Locality in the Long Poem

ORIGINS WITHOUT BEGINNINGS: ROBERT KROETSCH

What has come to interest me right now is what I suppose you can call the dream of origins. Obviously on the prairies, the small town and the farm are not merely places, they are remembered places. When they were the actuality of our lives, we had realistic fiction, and we had almost no poetry at all. Now in this dream condition, as dream-time fuses into the kind of narrative we call myth, we change the nature of the novel. And we start, with a new and terrible energy, to write the poems of the imagined real place. (Kroetsch, in Ondaatje, ed. 1979, 311)

Robert Kroetsch's 'dream of origins' speaks of the desire to locate an origin, a desire ingrained, as we have seen, in the archaeology of the Canadian long poem. When this desire, often in effect a memory of colonialism, privileges absence, it locates origins in a place that has not been directly or recently experienced – Europe, the Old World. In Kroetsch's poems, however, the desire for origins does not privilege the place *from* which his ancestors came, but rather the place *to* which they came – the small prairie town, the New World.

Although his early long poems, *The Ledger* and *Seed Catalogue*, deal with the place he was born in, the tension that generates the desire for place occurs when the poet no longer inhabits his place of origins. Locality in his poems derives from a profound sense of dislocation. Thus Heisler (his home town) becomes Bruce County (the place where some of his ancestors first settled), 'the green poem' (*Completed Field Notes* [*CFN*] 12), which becomes Heisler again, which becomes in turn upstate New York, the prairie, and Nanaimo; which becomes Winnipeg, then Banff, Greece, China, Germany, and so on. Locality in Kroetsch's work is informed and shaped by 'arrivals ... departures ... arrivals' (*CFN* 17). Whereas individual locations maintain their geographical and cultural singularity, the poet's revisiting only affirms his dislocation, a condition that not only prevents the fulfilment of his 'dream' of re-entering the place of origins but also belies the notion that there is such a place.

'The acceptance of origin in Kroetsch's text,' as E.D. Blodgett argues, 'is manifested primarily in the integrative arrangement of texts on the page: the page, by becoming a picture-space, immediately makes of history, memoir, and the play of origin a static activity in the temporal sense' (201). Yet, whereas the reality of the poet's origins is re-enacted by what Blodgett calls the 'picture-space,' the awareness Blodgett describes is not necessarily static. Kroetsch's 'dream of origins' is fundamentally a dream of motion, a dream of dream-as-desire defined by dislocation. The dream is occasioned by the writing process that recasts origins in the field of language.

Despite his rhetoric of nostos, Kroetsch does not undertake a journey of nostalgia. His arrivals and departures mark instead the movement of the nomad as poet. 'We write mandalas,' Kroetsch says, 'towards a cosmology that cannot be located. Towards a cosmology that, possibly, we do not wish to locate. Like Wordsworth, we spend years on the prelude. Like Stevens, we make notes towards a supreme fiction' (1989, 77). Memory and dreaming become the substitutes for the homeward journey. As the title of one of Webb's poems reminds us, 'The Place Is Where You Find It' (1982, 134). Entirely at home with language, Kroetsch distrusts the absolute certainty that any single place might offer him. In this respect, although Kroetsch has repeatedly acknowledged Williams's influence on him, *Seed Catalogue* is not as close to *Paterson* as the reader might expect. *Paterson*, while proclaiming the significance of locality and, at the same time, shifting from setting to setting, remains located on the same ground. The city of Paterson, the library, the waterfalls, the park, the doctor's office are all firmly mapped within the territory that fills Williams with 'local pride.' In contrast, Kroetsch's treatment of locality, like that of his contemporaries, is characterized by the continuous juxtaposition of place beside place, and by the cultural and ideological intertextuality emerging out of such 'picture-spaces.' Far from being a negative condition, Kroetsch's dislocation exposes the risks inherent in centralization. 'The placing of place,' he says, 'but not as in the American poem of (Paterson, Gloucester) place.' The placing of place inscribes what the eye sees – '(place: the eye / consumes itself: time)' (1989, 121) – and also what the poet's gaze fails to see, namely the absence that has been inscribed in the Canadian cultural landscape. Absence in and of place informs the configuration of locality in his long poems. The paradoxical inscription of this absence is in keeping with the long poem's generic contradictions and its ideological and cultural traits. The poet can fully inscribe absence only in the present tense.

In this context, the stone in 'Stone Hammer Poem' becomes the measure of presence and absence, of origin and place.

1.

...

the stone is
shaped like the skull
of a child.

2.

This paperweight on my desk

where I begin
this poem   was

found in a wheatfield
lost (this hammer,
this poem).

...

7.

The poem
is the stone

chipped and hammered
until it is shaped
. like the stone
hammer, the maul.   (*CFN* 1–4)

The stone – by means of image, simile, assertion, metaphor, metonymy, and repetition – is object and poem and place and dream, all
at the same time. 'This won't / surprise you,' says Kroetsch: 'My grandfather / lost the stone maul'; 'he [Kroetsch's father] found the stone
maul / on a rockpile'; 'I keep it / on my desk / (the stone)' (*CFN* 5,
6, 7). The stone as a found, lost, and retrieved object triggers the poet's
imagination and becomes transfigured into its namesake, a 'found'
poem. It functions as a heuristic device that sets up spatial limits while
breaking down the finiteness of geography; it helps the poet locate
himself within a familial territory that, significantly enough, lacks a
centre. The grandfather and the father represent the values of the
Old World, so the poet enunciates their presence in the past tense:
they are the figures that delimit the beginning of this tradition as well
as the place of loss. The past, and what it represents, is framed by the
poet's present, the present tense of his location and writing process
alike.

The loss of centre-as-place and of place-as-centre, the absence of
demarcated boundaries, posits Kroetsch's 'dream of origins' as the only
substitute for real, geographical place. Russell Brown observes that
'that loss is a precondition of the eventual finding' (165). It is indeed
a precondition of finding a place, but the eventuality Brown is looking
for is simply not there; or, it is but at the same time it is not. Kroetsch's
obsession with beginnings defies any eventual finding of place because
he resists telos. His long poems, although they stand by themselves,
form 'a continuing poem,'[1] the present participle an adjective marking
the mazing path he follows in his attempt to find a place. The 'doubleness,' according to Brown, that loss and finding seem to suggest,
is also reiterated by Robert Lecker:

in [Kroetsch's] long poems, as in the best verse in *Stone Hammer Poems*, we
note several points of tangency and ongoing concern: an involvement with
establishing through poetic language a particularly Canadian and western sense
of place, a desire to represent a peculiarly *double* sense of Canadian experience,
and a need to find a sense of personal and public origins that may be dreamed

by the poet whose task it is to write his world into existence. (1986, 125–6; my emphasis)

In discussing Kroetsch's individual long poems, Lecker ignores the cumulative effect of *Field Notes*, the 'continuing poem' that, by gathering the individual poems together, transcontextualizes them. Similarly, Brown states about 'Stone Hammer Poem' that it 'consoles us [about its sense of loss] in rather traditional fashion by suggesting that there are recompenses – the most notable of which is the creation of *this* poem' (173). But Kroetsch writes, '[s]ometimes I write / my poems for that / stone hammer' (*CFN* 7). If the plural of 'poems' suggests anything it is not a doubleness but a plurality. The poems can be read individually as long as they remain independently published. But the design of *Field Notes*, together with the subsequent publication of all the volumes into *Completed Field Notes*, reveals the poem's process of differentiation that is incurred when its parts are transtextualized. When read together, their internal echoes, their contradictions and reversals, all manifest the plurality of Kroetsch's sense of place.

The poet finds the lost place he dreams about only to lose it again – '[t]he poem itself, surfacing. The poem of the place, the place lost. Things fall into place in the poem,' he states in his epigrammatic way (1989, 122). This delay is evidence of the generic function of locality. Locality in the long poem, although a central concern, is decentralized. And for Kroetsch specifically, locality lies outside the logocentric tradition: '[t]he problem of the writer of the contemporary long poem is to honour our disbelief in belief – that is, to recognize and explore our distrust of system, of grid, of monisms, of cosmologies perhaps, certainly of inherited story – and at the same time write a long work that has some kind of (under erasure) unity' (1989, 118). Kroetsch refuses to be seduced by the soothing promises of the logocentric tradition that say origins can be found. The very act of finding a fixed place of belonging is put, as he says, under erasure.

'Mile Zero,' as it appears in its rewritten and augmented form in *Advice to My Friends*, the second volume of his 'continuing' (but now, he claims, 'completed') poem, visualizes formally and structurally this erasure. The incomplete lines that attempt to frame the pages by forming parallelograms, the diagonal lines that point to the dialogue of the facing texts graph that erasure: erasure not only because they resemble the Heideggerian and Derridean 'X' crossing out a word in order to release its coerced meaning, but because they suspend (visually and verbally) and therefore subvert and recontextualize the original version of the text. Blodgett's 'picture-space' again comes to mind. But here erasure erases itself and becomes its own supplement, for Kroetsch not only maintains what is deleted within the text, he also comments on his erasure tactics.

---

*I have removed from this stanza the single line

(her breasts were paradigms)

(originally in parenthesis, as indicated) because I am somewhat offended by the offhand reference to paradigm ... The concern with *nostos* is related to a long family history of losses: *e.g.*, the paternal side of the family landing in New York in June, 1841, aboard the *Pauline*, and the mother of the large Kroetsch family, settled in Waterloo County, Ontario, a few years thereafter widowed, the early death of the poet's mother in Alberta, a century after that first un-homing. Both quest and goal become paradigmatic (RK).   (*CFN* 132)

Origins can be dreamt, but they are unoriginal; they exist only as traces that contain the lost, deleted place without formalizing it. '[I]f all begins with the trace,' Derrida reminds us, 'there is above all no originary trace' (1974, 61). Kroetsch engages himself in a continuous search for an origin, but his search is informed less by nostalgia for a lost place and more by a desire for difference. 'Un-homing' is the name he gives to locality. Hence the metonymic route he follows.

It is significant that *Advice to My Friends* ends with a poem about the poet's mother (who died when he was thirteen), its last line being 'Mother, where are you?' (*CFN* 218). After a series of long poems searching for origins both in, and in places other than, Canada, Kroetsch has located the trace of matrilinear origins. It is not a coincidence that it has taken him a decade since his first long poem (1975) to write about his mother in 'Sounding the Name' and 'The Poet's Mother' (1985). He comments on this himself in 1981 when he says in 'Mile Zero': 'is not the mother figure the figure at once most present in and most absent from this poet's work?' (*CFN* 132). Kroetsch's questions paradoxically affirm that place can be lost, misplaced, displaced, or even hidden by his own patriarchal tradition. This loss, however, is supplemented by his writing, the performative act of his long poems – the poet become his own mother. The simultaneity of presence and absence in his poetry forms a teasing figure, the shape prolongation takes. This is why the place he reaches by tracing his mother's presence, a presence also put under erasure, is only the space a question mark takes.

Appropriately, the question 'Mother, where are you?' is answered by the questioning of this question, the very last poem of *Advice to My Friends*:

Envoi (To Begin With)

There is no real
world, my friends.
Why not, then,
let the stars
shine in our bones?   (*CFN* 219)

The last, at least so far, sign of Kroetsch's continuing poem is, again, and almost predictably so, given his poetics, a question mark, a suspended closure. Place cannot become self-identical with what marks the nostalgic desire that drives the poet towards a place. Kroetsch dreams about place not as topos but as tropos. It is only as real as the forever receding and appearing figure of *mise en abyme*. His condition of dislocation enables him to locate the equivocal desire that sets the poet after new beginnings. It is important that the 'non-originary' origin of the dreamed place Kroetsch reaches, ever so tentatively, at the 'end' of *Advice to My Friends* is the same as that in the beginning of *Field Notes*: bones. Bone neither as weapon (what Brown argues for), nor as the 'privileged signifier' of the phallus (as Lacan would have it). Bone as both and as more ...

It is evident that the 'dialectical tensions' Lecker observes as 'central' to Kroetsch's work are deceptive (1986, 126). 'There is only one release,' Lecker argues: 'find the home place, reinstate the stone ... [H]owever, the stone's true home cannot be guessed at.' In spite of his occasional deconstructive vocabulary, the dialectical pattern on which Lecker insists does not reveal Kroetsch's vision of place in its entirety. Trying to emulate what he calls Kroetsch's 'wedding oppositions,' but equating opposition with contradiction, Lecker adopts an approach (128, 129) that bypasses the parodic reversals that are so ubiquitous in Kroetsch's long poems. Oppositions may balance, but contradictions do not; Kroetsch's concern with place is dialogical not dialectical.[2] Because of

Kroetsch's troping with contradictions, the referentiality of locality in his long poem is constantly suspended by the metonymic nature of his writing and by his nomadic movement from place to place. Kroetsch is interested in the semiosis of place, not its semantics. Hence the semiotic intentionality behind his dislocation, an intentionality that both eschews complete identification with place that might lead to closure and therefore blindness, and intensifies and prolongs (and delays) the dreaming, writing process. The 'long' search for one's place allows locality in the long poem to blend the real place inhabited in the past or the fictive place inhabited now by the poet with the textual place she or he creates. Yet this blending is immediately resisted by the absence (cultural and other) present in the Canadian landscape, an absence that permeates the long poem as well. The inclusiveness of the long poem makes it possible for place and absence (the locus of desire) to be inscribed in its textuality.

This is why Kroetsch's obsession with place reaches, more often than not, beyond the dreamed memory of real place. 'His dream of origins' is frequently rendered as a rewriting of the dream of Eden – another imagined (and desired) place – a rewriting that evokes yet another dimension of the colonial mentality. Kroetsch's long poem decodes the absolutism and dialecticism of the dream and human drama of the Garden of Eden. Although there is in his poetry an abundance of gardens, he does not deal with this archetypal place in traditional dialectical manner. The prelapsarian innocence and guilt consequent to the Fall are continuously reordered. Here is what he says early in *Seed Catalogue*:

Winter was ending.
This is what happened:
we were harrowing the garden.
You've got to understand this:
I was sitting on the horse.
The horse was standing still.
I fell off.   (*CFN* 32)

The parodic reversal and its ironic humour in these lines work against the consoling promise entailed by the dialectical structure of the myth of Eden; the fall is presented as a non-event.

In talking about the garden in Kroetsch's poetry, Lecker observes that '[a]ll of the senses are opened to the garden that must be saved.

This can be done by reinterpreting the myth of Eden not as a fall from innocence but as the birth of possibility. Better still, the birth of possibility depends upon the fall, for only when these opposing forces are synthesized does true creation begin. We are back to Kroetsch's dialectical concept of vision as a collection of meetings between mind and matter, time and space, voice and silence' (132). Whereas Lecker is right in arguing that the garden in Kroetsch's long poem marks the birth of possibility, he implicitly supports the tradition Kroetsch works against when he suggests that possibilities emerge out of synthesis. Insisting on seeing Kroetsch as a structuralist, Lecker does not pay due attention to the heterogeneous movements that mark the long poem in general, and Kroetsch's poem in particular. The variable formal and thematic elements in Kroetsch's poetry recontextualize Eden in a way that frees consciousness from the humanistic versions of the myths of place, self, and language, ultimately from the closure of harmony and synthesis. The effect of the differentiation process incurred by the multiple shifts from place to place is not synthetic but synergetic.

Kroetsch's questions at the end of *Seed Catalogue* disperse Eden by dissolving its impossible dream of unity: '*How | do you grow a garden?*' (CFN 49), '*How do you a garden grow? | How do you grow a garden?*' (CFN 50). The garden is used as a principle for organizing the unstructured space of the prairies. Kroetsch's repetition with difference exemplifies *how* he appropriates place by overcoding locality: the tonal and syntactic transformations of the same question, the ungrammaticality of his grammar, are an attempt to decode the memory of the original origin, namely that of nature.[3] The grammar of Kroetsch's narrative is one of dislocation, a dislocation enunciating what has become of nature as the 'original' origin. By deconstructing the notions of originality and origin, Kroetsch alludes to the underlying ideology that has constructed these very myths. Even nature as memory[4] – a shared memory of human origins – does not maintain its status as the symbolic *chora*. Kroetsch's garden is both trace and residue. He is left with language alone, and his search for origins affirms his desire to represent what is lost. He does so largely in a non-mimetic fashion: nature survives as trace, but its representation is deferred through continuous dislocation.

In his later poems Kroetsch moves gradually away from the garden – the trace of nature as myth/symbol – and towards other versions of locality. In *The Criminal Intensities of Love as Paradise* the paradise remains in the title, unattainable and unrealized in its humanistic interpretation – a horizon retreating. The poem takes place 'in elk meadow / or forest' (*CFN* 90); the lovers are '*Standing near a waterfall*' (91), reminiscent of the Fall as well as of Williams's falls in *Paterson*; or go '*Into Town*' (95), Jasper, a parody of a tourists' paradise; or find themselves in '*Campsite, Home, Away From*' (98). Movement serves as dislocation and/or detour from origins. 'Un-homing' marks the grammar of these lovers' movements.

Is desire itself, then, the origin of desire? In *Letters to Salonika* Kroetsch says: 'to desire an end to desire / is to desire' (*CFN* 159). There is no precise originary point in the motion desire produces. This movement without beginning and without end becomes more poignant in Kroetsch's *Advice to My Friends* where cities and archaeological sites assume greater importance. The change of setting here marks a shift that can be viewed within the larger context of Canadian literature, a shift that George Bowering points out in an interview with Daphne Marlatt: '[s]o the whole thing about a New Eden was just a crock. They were just making a New Babylon when they came over here' (1979, 75). As the garden is seen to be the prototype of nature before the Fall, so Babylon is seen as the prototype of the city after the Fall. The garden as Eden can be understood only in dialectical opposition to the city: as the space of innocence (both in the sense of locality and concept), the garden precedes the city, by definition a profane habitat, and determines the degree of the city's expansion – not to exceed the boundaries demarcated by the garden. The city as Babylon, in contrast, works against this spatial dialectic: it is a city not situated outside the periphery of the garden but containing the garden within it. Kroetsch indeed creates a Babylon in *Excerpts from the Real World*, where his visit to the real Babylon ends this long poem. Whereas in *Field Notes* and *Advice to My Friends* the origin as garden leads him to his dead mother, in *Excerpts from the Real World* the origin as city leads him to Ishtar. It is certainly more than a coincidence that in the endings of these long poems the elusiveness of locality and dislocation is inscribed in the feminine.[5] Given, however, the polyphony that characterizes the generic plurality of Kroetsch's long poems, displacement is just one of the ways in which locality is treated in this 'new' genre.

THE POET AS PEDESTRIAN: DAPHNE MARLATT

William Carlos Williams's treatment of locality has largely influenced the focus on the concept of place in the long poem, a concept that does not necessarily derive from dislocation or from dreaming, as is the case with Kroetsch's long poems. Williams's notion of 'local pride' that prefaces *Paterson* reverses the direction of the 'dream of origins' of the early immigrants in North America. This parodic inversion accomplishes in the long poem the two impulses that Linda Hutcheon identifies as the primary functions of parody: '[p]arody is fundamentally double and divided; its ambivalence stems from the dual drives of conservative and revolutionary forces that are inherent in its nature as authorized transgression' (26). The conservatism that Hutcheon talks about does not refer to the maintenance of a conservative political tradition but to the conservation of a constantly reviewed and revised literary milieu. Thus the 'local pride' behind the 'dream of origins' in the long poem legitimizes locality in ways that invite the reader to rethink the very notion of origin. But the treatment of locality in the long poem does not always go as far as its origins, whatever they might be. Quite often, locality is taken to be what it literally is: local place.

Bowering talks about this pressure on the local in an interview with Caroline Bayard and Jack David:

The word that we [West Coast poets, mainly those of the *Tish* group] used all the time was 'locus,' which we liked partly because it came out of Olson, partly because it didn't say setting, it didn't say place, it didn't say landscape, it didn't say all those things that are literary devices. Every time you use one of those terms you posit a person who is saying, OK, now how can I organize all this into a literary work. But if you said locus, it implies trying to find out where you are. It implies, I'm trying to locate myself. We didn't know much about our own skills and we didn't know hardly anything about the place that we lived in so those two things were built simultaneously. (Bayard 79–80)

Bowering's 'locus,' as his reference to Olson implies, relies heavily on Herodotus' notion of writing about locality and history, a notion that has little to do with displacement and a lot to do with locating oneself within a specific place, a conscious and ideological position. Kroetsch's strategies – the distrust of the eye, the deferral of the poet as beholder – find in this poetics a different rhetorical configuration.

If Thucydides was the father of traditional historiographic discourse, Herodotus was the father of history as an art form. Thucydides was the historian of logos, the historian who distinguished historiography from mythology by carefully scanning available information and tracing facts to their causes. Herodotus, on the other hand, practised a history that privileged the eye, as in personal observation, and took as much interest in the description of people and events as in the act of story-telling, the narrative rendering of facts – the division of his *Histories* into nine books, each named after one of the muses, is a reflection of this. 'To satisfy my wish to get the best information I possibly could on this subject,' Herodotus says in the second book of his history, 'I made a voyage to Tyre in Phoenicia' (120). The visible, what the eye holds in its gaze, determines the mode as well as the matter of history. Herodotus' history, tested on his own pulse, shows how place may remain 'in place' until the eye becomes a locus of knowledge. Or, as Olson remarks, '*istorin* in him [Herodotus] appears to mean "finding out for oneself," instead of depending on hearsay' (1970, 20). The historical act for Herodotus is identical with the etymology of history: to look for oneself, to learn by inquiry, to tell a story. Such inquiry leads to self-knowledge, a knowledge constructed largely through the way in which it is conveyed to someone else. Whereas for Thucydides logos refers primarily to reason, for Herodotus it refers to the act of telling: logos becomes *legein*. The emphasis of the Herodotean mode of history on the gaze locates the writer's self in a field that is at once that of writing and of place.

The immediacy of the poet's gaze renders history in the present tense. As Katharine R. Stimpson says, '[t]he past presses the historian as the present does the poet' (159). Olson's poetics of localism has had a great influence on many Canadian poets, especially those on the West Coast such as Fred Wah and Daphne Marlatt.[6] His 'kinetics,' the ability to perceive place in time, is largely actualized through the immediacy of perception accomplished by the poet's gaze. As Roland Barthes says,

the gaze is not a sign, yet it signifies. What is this mystery? It is that the gaze belongs to that realm of signification whose unit is not the sign (discontinuity) but *signifying* [*signifiance*], whose theory Benveniste has proposed. In opposition to language, an order of signs, the arts in general derive from *signifying* ... [L]iterally, gaze cannot be *neutral*, except to signify neutrality ...

Science interprets the gaze in three (combinable) ways: in terms of information (the gaze informs), in terms of relation (gazes are exchanged), in terms of possession (by the gaze, I touch, I attain, I seize, I am seized): three functions: optical, linguistic, haptic. But always the gaze *seeks*: something, someone. It is an *anxious* sign: singular dynamics for a sign: its power overflows it. (1985, 237–8)

The enabling power that allows, in fact invites, the gaze to enter locality resides in its threefold function (optical, linguistic, haptic), which seems to be equivalent to the expression of desire. 'History as place,' according to Olson, 'verifies the desire' (1970, 26). Since Olson does not specify what *the* desire is, the definite article might be taken to suggest that desire is the first locus, the mobile field, the poet inhabits; it is what *moves* poetic language. Desire endows the subject of the gaze with dynamism, what Olson calls 'kinetics,' the ability to perceive place in time, in process.

Located in the ongoing present – not the timeless present of the lyric, but the present of the writing process – the gaze has access to the past while looking ahead, towards the future. It locates itself at the crossroads of past and future: the pen traces the gaze, the eye follows the hand; from seeing (reading) to writing as reading. The anxiety, the desire of the gaze as sign, suggests that the gaze is always on the go. Yet the anxiety inherent in the gaze as sign doesn't simply signify desire. 'Voir est un acte dangereux,' Jean Starobinski says, reminding us of Orpheus, Narcissus, Oedipus, Psyche, and Medusa (1961, 14). The danger and desire evoked by the gaze are in keeping with the long poem's consistent attempt to question the ideologies informing not only what it records but also the strategies through which it attempts to read the world. In the long poem the gaze is where skin (the inner/outer) and place (outer) meet.

Daphne Marlatt's *Steveston* reflects the processual view of locality that the long poem takes. In Douglas Barbour's words, *Steveston* is a 'complex perception which engages the place as process in time' (1978, 182). Marlatt herself has repeatedly acknowledged the importance of Olson to her form and to her obsession with locality. Perhaps this is why most readings of *Steveston* discuss its 'rootedness' by privileging the concept of place in motion: place in *Steveston*, a number of critics have argued, is engendered by the confluence of the Fraser River and the poem's processual form. Marlatt, too, makes the same point more than once. In 'Text and Tissue,' for example, she said to interviewer Ellea Wright that '*Steveston* was a book I wrote in which I was trying to *imitate* the flow of the river in long, long extended sentences' (4; my emphasis).[7] Locality, she suggests, ceases to connote stability and becomes place as flux: the river holds the eye as the poet's gaze follows the motion of fluid place, a paradox that capitulates some of the contradictions inherent in the long poem.

But the river in *Steveston*, despite Marlatt's insistence on it as a primary force, is just one dimension of locality. The Fraser River is seen by Marlatt, but her gaze can hold only its Heraclitean elusiveness, its constant flow and renewal.

Pour, pour

> from its bank) this river is rivering urgency, roar
> (goku, goku) thru any hole ...
>
> 'This river is
> *alive*,' he says ...
>
> ... some seed as
> imprint or, continuance, continuing to pour/down as light, or time,
> this town down stream its own downpour ...   (17–18)[8]

The river, so powerful as physical presence and socioproductive force alike, is ubiquitous. Its ubiquity is one that relies on presence as well as absence, often exceeding its physical reality to give way to social reality, 'this town down stream.' By 'imitating' its flow, one might say, Marlatt renders it as an organic metaphor that accounts for her proprioceptive engagement with locality and her writing process. At the same time an image and a floating signifier, the river is subjected to representation. As the livelihood of the Japanese Canadians residing in Steveston, it is represented as both space and mode of production. Marlatt's mimesis of its flow is not mimesis strictly speaking; it is a complex decoding process, for she translates the river's representation, not its fleeting reality; she presents the social and economic impact of the river on the Japanese community of Steveston. '*Steveston*,' she says in an interview with Gilbert Bouchard, is 'about a Japanese-Canadian fishing community on the Fraser River – what I did was to try and develop a syntactical movement that would parallel the ongoing movement of the river on to the sea' (7). Her focus on the river, in other words, enables her to produce the signification of her long poem: locality is presented as an open site to be graphed by sight.

The fact that the primary locality in the poem is not the river has been intimated by some of Marlatt's statements about the genesis of the poem. As she says, '[w]ith *Steveston*, my interest was occasioned by taking a Sunday drive there in the spring of '71 or '72 and finding Star camp, the last extant cannery camp, little houses, shacks still standing – it was about to be torn down, the people had moved out. You could sense a whole life there in what they had left behind. Again I wanted to find out more about it, about what that life had been like.'[9] Marlatt becomes a special sort of historian when she encounters this landscape. But the landscape that immediately fascinates her is, obviously, not the river. It is the human habitat, its ecology, the story it tells of itself. Davey is the first critic so far who has not exaggerated the river 'localism' most critics find in *Steveston*. In his essay 'The Explorer in Western Canadian Literature,' he points out that in *Steveston* 'it is not just place but time and place, or place in time, which are to be explored and mapped' (145).[10] The primary locus in the poem is the town itself, the social, fabricated space that defines the texture of *Steveston*.

The town, like the river, is presented in all its multiplicity:

Steveston as you find it:

> multiplicity simply there: the physical matter of
> the place (what matters) meaning, don't get theoretical now, the cannery.
>
> (23)

The poet resists the temptation to theorize because of the fear that theory, when unmediated, might abstract and distance. But Marlatt's Olsonian poetics – recorded in a journal she 'kept during the Summer of '63 Conference, Vancouver' – includes the theoretical in writing as well as the universal:

Olson: 'the DETAILS interest' – why? because 'truth' i.e. concrete reality – exists only in THEM & the whole is an abstract assumption made by the MIND – yet the excitement breaks forth in the mind's jump from details (clicking into place) to form the whole. (1975, 76)

The abundance of details in the poem is an attempt to create a visceral image of Steveston, to people the page with what peoples the town. At the same time, the layers of details decode the structural levels of life as seen by the poet:

> That I persist, also, in seeing *them*, these men,
> who are cut down to one day a week: their technology too great for
> the crop to bear, $600 worth in one day off one boat. The persistence
> that has always in the industry characterized them. He *knows* he's an
> expert fisherman, tho deprecates, 'Oh one day a week's easier for an
> old man like me.' But idle, how strange that idleness sits on one
> given to work – A glass of water, a glass of sevenup, in town, at a
> cafe counter. So familiar it's boring. But for the dream that surfaces
> when the young woman from *out there* walks in, with whom, momentarily,
> over a hamburger & a glass of water, he connects.   (52–3)

The poet's seeing, economical and social conditions, pride, erotics: all these informing details, while recording what the gaze contains, countervail the totalizing effect that the eye might have on what it touches.

Even when the poet's eye sees the past of the town imaginatively, the details of the recording process render imagination as real as reality itself. The opening of the poem is, as Lecker puts it, a 'step into Steveston's past' (1978, 65) and a step into its 'continuous present':

> Imagine a town running
>
>   (smoothly?
> a town running before a fire
> canneries burning
>
>   (do you see the shadow of charred stilts
> on cool water? do you see enigmatic chance standing
> just under the beam?   (13)

Roy Miki is convincing when he points out that '[t]he town Steveston ... is approached simultaneously as a literal place with finite history and a figural place where the imagination dwells' (1985, 77). The poet's gaze transgresses the temporal boundaries of the past and the future. The site produced by the imagination and the gaze alike is, as Marlatt says, the '[c]ity as the image of a social paradise' (Bowering 1979, 75). There is a shift here from Kroetsch's memory of paradise to Marlatt's present-tense experience of paradise as a social environment. Steveston is polis as the space of the imaginary, polis as community. As Marlatt herself says, appropriating Olson: '& "polis is eyes": we use our eyes to see/be aware of all that is around us – leads to individuals & their unique awareness (I am complete *in my own body* & thus "polis" is also my/your body: each cell as individual/complete one aware of others, working with others but in itself at same time → cosmos' (1975, 79).

But this correspondence between gaze and locality does not imply that the poet, as an outsider to the community of Steveston, engages in some version of voyeurism. Voyeurism, 'le désir de posséder par le moyen de l'oeil,' as Starobinski defines it (1961, 19), is not what constitutes Marlatt's act of writing. Voyeurism is defined by the distance between the subject viewing and the object viewed. Marlatt's gaze, instead of freezing in its hold the motion of the town and keeping the town at a distance, introduces a different erotics: desire that brings together the body (the poet's / the locals'), the town, and language.

Marlatt's scopic drive recreates the town as a writerly text. The textuality of the poet's gaze, as it translates itself into discourse, goes beyond creating an optical artifact of the town.

> The place? These kids, who live by the sea & know
> nothing of boats. But orders, orders of power, of hoarded wealth.
> Insistent, hey you guys, to break in on what the others are earnestly
> engaged in: Somebody's pants! Got any money? Look, batteries,
> gasoline a licence – I could be driver of a boat. Hey, cool!
> this is a masterkey you know, it'll open up that door.   (34–5)

'The place' reverberates with voices. The poet works with the eye but with the ear as well. The voices of the locals are inserted in direct speech, the result being a hybrid of voices. Marlatt's own voice is dialogically related to the voices of the locals. She articulates this dialogism in the present tense because it affirms her presentness, the proprioception of her writing act.

Through the eye, the ear, and the performative act of her discourse, locality ceases to be place only. It becomes a living archive. The archive, Foucault tells us, 'does not have the weight of tradition ... cannot be described in its totality; and in its presence it is unavoidable. It emerges in fragments, regions, and levels ... It establishes that we are difference' (130–1). The town as a living archive does not function as the border of past, present, and future; it revokes, instead, the notion of origin. In her attempt to 'find out' about the town, Marlatt posits herself as an archaeologist operating in the present tense. Archaeology does not seek the beginnings of things; it establishes discontinuities, finds meaning in the gaps, the fragments and shards, it discovers. In

Steveston Marlatt allows discontinuities to exist in the 'continuous present' of the poem.

Place, then, is located on the ground where the poet walks. Marlatt's history begins at ground level; each one of her footsteps links one site to another. If Kroetsch is to be seen as nomad, Marlatt is the poet as pedestrian. Walking, moving within a locus that exists outside the body but that is also created by it, is synonymous with Marlatt's archaeological process.

> She runs in the
> throat of time, voicing the very swifts & shallows of that river,
> urging, in the dash of it, enough to keep up, to live on.   (65)

> What do the charts say? Return, return. Return of what doesn't
> die. Violence in mute form. Walking a fine line.   (76)

> To live in a place. Immanent. In
> place. Yet to feel at sea. To come from elsewhere & then to discover
> love, has a house & name. Has land. Is landed, under the swaying
> trees which bend, so much in this wind like underwater weeds we think
> self rises from.   (79)

> (fishy as quick slime, saying, it's here, & here, & here,
> this self

> whose wealth consists of what?
> A house?   (80)

Marlatt as walker, as archaeologist of streets and canneries and people, always translates the signs of spatiality she sees around her into something else. Accretion – 'the accretion of all our / actions' (70) – parataxis, the deferrals of main verbs, are the poetic devices that prolong her archaeological discourse, that extend the poem 'out to sea' (86) – its last words. In the landscape the sound and movement of language and body offer a stunning choreography of infinite possibilities. Locality in Marlatt's poem is not merely a theme, a setting that might be replaced by other themes or settings. As an element shaping her long poem, locality is always there yet it is never static, a fixed place awaiting description.

The scriptive act, almost always recorded in the long poem, foregrounds the letter of geography, writes the alphabet of place in more ways than one. The poet of long poems seems to be more concerned with the fixity repeated by the act of writing, a concern that speaks yet another generative principle of the long poem. Even when we move from Marlatt's treatment of locality in *Steveston* to Eli Mandel's own radical reading of place in *Out of Place*, locality remains a prominent issue. Marlatt locates herself in a strange place; Mandel revisits a familial and, therefore, familiar location. The sites are different, movement follows a different trajectory, but locality and the anxiety (desire) it entails remain equally central.[11]

THE SYNTAX OF PLACE: ELI MANDEL

In the entry that introduces the journals of *Life Sentence* Eli Mandel poses the question: 'When do language and place become identical?' (1981, 55). Although he does not provide an answer, within the grammar of his question there is already an implicit assertion: language and place can become identical. The convergence of these two orders of reality is a matter of time: '*When* do language and place become identical?' Mandel also asks. Mandel's journey in *Out of Place* has as its point of departure the question asked in *Life Sentence*. The delay of the convergence of language and place is articulated when he locates the focus of his question in the *process* of 'becoming identical' as opposed to an achieved still point of being identical.

This question functions as the main intertext behind the generic structure of many Canadian long poems: the search for language in place; the search for place in language. Recording geography, a scriptive but polyvalent act, is a primary component of the long poem. *Out of Place* exemplifies this persistent concern through its formal and thematic elements. Here begins the wandering of the written word in a place that, although structured by the poet, cannot quite contain the poet himself. When the poet's journey reaches an ending, after *Out of Place* reaches the hands of its publisher, Mandel asks, again in *Life Sentence*, another question: 'Will it be evident that *Out of Place* tries to be a book existing in the gaps between its poems, its absences?' (1981, 62). He locates the substance of the poem in an absence that we can trace if we observe the poem's warring forces: past and present; written records and writing; man and woman; the self and its other. These gaps between the poems, these absences, suggest the erasure of the binary complexity that threatens to lock the poet between the landscape he visits and the mindscape of his language. Mandel's poem is situated on the edge of a mimesis that soothes by offerings of illusory fixity and of a fiction that opens up vistas nominally blocked off by the mimetic act.

Language and place in *Out of Place* become identical through the poet's displacement, a displacement that exposes the illusions of factuality that have shaped our notions of self and place, a displacement that reveals fiction as the way to discovery. *Out of Place* is a long poem that disseminates its own making and writing. Mandel divests himself of the longing to return home; his longing instead is to break out of space as a particular locality that locks the self within it.

Before the poem as poem begins, the reader confronts Ann Mandel's 'Preface.' The 'Preface' is the first example in the book of the desire to break out of space. Because of its location and its function as preface, it marks the ground the reader has to traverse. Yet it also foregrounds its own expulsion from Eli Mandel's text and its inclusion as one of the poem's main intertexts. While it introduces the poem, it also presents itself as the sum total of the signifying forces at work there. It is the seam that connects the empirical historicity of *Out of Place* with its materiality as text. This junction, as will gradually become clear, reveals, too, the presences that Eli Mandel erased in the poem, without, however, denying their centrality.

Derrida observes that '[t]he signifying *pre-cipitation*, which pushes the preface to the front, makes it seem like an empty form still deprived of what it wants to say; but since it is ahead of itself, it finds itself predetermined, in its text, by a semantic *after-effect*' (*Dissemination* 20). Ann Mandel's 'Preface' fights against its generic marginality, its empty form, by its central location on the page (7–8).[12] And although it is written retrospectively as the semantic after-effect of the poem, it is important that it does not announce in the future tense, as many prefaces do, 'you will read ...' It is written in the past tense: '[k]nowing we could not take those papers from the vault, yet curious to know their contents, we moved into it and settled down for whatever stay seemed necessary' (7). The past tense of the 'Preface' intimates the reader's experience of *Out of Place*. It contains both the past of the poem – the history of its making – and its presence as text.

The past tense of the 'Preface' also becomes the reader's future. Although the 'Preface' does not prescribe a particular interpretation of the poem's text, it does delineate the semantic horizon of *Out of Place*. Yet after reading both 'Preface' and poem, the reader notices that the 'Preface' as an empty form and the fullness of the poem's meaning cancel out each other's intention. The 'Preface' re-verses the poet's attempt to excise from his poem all but one reference to the vault, which I take to be the originary topos of *Out of Place*. This single reference in Eli Mandel's text appears in the poem 'the hoffer colony,' which, like the 'Preface,' is situated within the vault. The 'Preface' is the after-effect of the poem's meaning as well as the pro-gram of its making – its departure point. Ann Mandel, the poet's journey companion, is the first I/eye through which the reader enters the poem. Her 'Preface' outlines the itinerary of *Out of Place*.

As Ann Mandel's 'Preface' stands outside the poem, so the poet is 'out of place' in her 'Preface.' Eli Mandel is not foregrounded as a poet, as the person who initiated the journey. He is placed within the language of the 'Preface,' within the space occupied by the pronoun 'we,' which carries the main thrust of Ann Mandel's brief but eloquent narrative. Benveniste states that,

If there cannot be several 'I's conceived of/by an actual 'I' who is speaking, it is because 'we' is not a multiplication of identical objects but a *junction* between 'I' and the 'non-I,' no matter what the content of this 'non-I' may be. This junction forms a new totality which is of a very special type whose components are not equivalent: in 'we' it is always 'I' which predominates since there cannot be 'we' except by starting with 'I,' and this 'I' dominates the 'non-I' element by means of its transcendent quality. The presence of 'I' is constitutive of 'we.' (202)

Ann Mandel's 'I' dominates in the 'Preface' not only as one of the elements of the plural subject of 'we' but also as a separate 'I.'

At first *we* could make no sense of things, and I spent long hours staring from the black interior to the blazing doorway. When my eyes burned past that white rectangle, I could see long beige and yellow prairie grasses ... I knew the grain elevator was to the right but refused to lean forward to see, leaving the framed picture intact. (7; my emphasis)

The departure of the 'I' from the pronoun 'we' emphasizes the absence of specific reference to Eli Mandel, who remains anonymous and not clearly enunciated as a 'he'; only the love-making references in the opening paragraph of the 'Preface' indicate who the companion of the 'I' is. The poet in the 'Preface' is a mute presence, a silent reader of the records they find in the vault.

It is the evocative style of Ann Mandel's 'Preface' that initially engages the reader. Her 'Preface' is a poetic overture that transcends the marginality of the ordinary preface by positing itself as a 'primary text' (Hartman 5).[13] In a book such as *Out of Place* where the poet's self and its locality are the informing concerns, the reader cannot consciously ignore the enunciative silence of the 'Preface' that posits the presence of the poet as a shadowy figure in the dark interior of the vault. The effacement of the poet discloses the 'Preface' as the double of what goes on beyond it. The 'Preface' is by definition the residue of writing of *Out of Place*, yet it is, too, the breath that releases what prompted Eli Mandel to open the gaps between his poems. It is what draws the reader closer to the core of the poem; better still it is what defers (prolongs) the direct confrontation with the poem.

Although the 'Preface' precedes the poem, it does not stand outside it. The 'Preface' contains both the silent poet and the seeds of the poem he is going to write. Moreover, it originates the motion that links in *Out of Place* difference and identity, the self and its other, absence and presence. The silence and the absence that the 'Preface' inscribes through its own writing render it as the *supplement* to the poem. As Derrida observes,

The supplement adds itself, it is a surplus, a plenitude enriching another plenitude, the *fullest measure* of presence. It cumulates and accumulates presence ...

But the supplement supplements. It adds only to replace. It intervenes or insinuates itself *in-the-place-of*; if it fills, it is as if one fills a void. If it represents and makes an image, it is by the anterior default of a presence ... [T]he supplement is an adjunct, a subaltern instance which *takes-(the)-place [tient-lieu]*. As substitute, it is not simply added to the positivity of a presence, it produces no relief, its place is assigned in the structure by the mark of an emptiness. (1974, 144–5)

The 'Preface' as a piece of writing of a marginal nature frames the poem; as a supplement it is the threshold to and a part of the interiority of *Out of Place*. It reveals the central idea of the poem, that of writing.

Writing, the subject and matter of *Out of Place*, finds its first configuration in the image of the vault – the vault as it is described in Ann Mandel's 'Preface.' The vault confronts the reader through a series of familiar symbolic recognitions. It is the womb one exits from and whose security (Freud tells us) one longs for; it is a place of death, of old records, of the past one retreats to, but it is also a place of life once Eli and Ann Mandel move into it; it is Jung's unconscious, the hidden self. Each of these interpretations operates in the poem. But the symbolic configuration of the vault that most clearly points to the absences on which *Out of Place* rests is that of Plato's cave.

The doorless vault, like Plato's cave, has an 'entrance open to the light' that invites the Mandels to enter its dark interior. In the light that surrounds the Mandels everything else appears obscure; everything else, that is, inside the vault. Papers of accounts and invoices, pages from magazines and from a 'diary or fiction of a kind' (8) litter the floor of the vault. These scattered documents are the shadows of the past. They are memories of lives put to sleep on paper. Their writing is sown on the floor of the vault by *ghost* writers, writers of another reality.

A look at Plato's allegory illuminates the happenings in the vault. After the prisoner released from Plato's cave

come[s] out into the light, [he] finds his eyes so full of its radiance that he [can] not see a single one of the things that he [is] now told [are] real ... He [needs] to grow accustomed before he [can] see things in that upper world ... Now imagine what would happen if he went down again to take his former seat in the cave. Coming suddenly out of the sunlight, his eyes would be filled with darkness. He might be required once more to deliver his opinion on those shadows, in competition with the prisoners who had never been released, while his eyesight was still dim and unsteady; and it might take some time to become used to the darkness. (230–1)

Ann Mandel's experience, after her 'eyes burned past' the 'blazing doorway,' evokes the experience of Plato's figure. 'Bringing my sight back into the room required another period of blindness before the layered white paper emerged from the dark. Then colour, a greyness reappeared, and the corners of the cement vault' (7). This experience stands, as Plato would put it, for the 'upward journey of the soul into the region of the intelligible' (231). But whereas Plato values the world of the shadows as a paradigm that reveals unreality, the Mandels view the shadows as being animated, realized by writing.

When the Mandels enter the vault, they step into 'the double world' that Eli Mandel describes in *Out of Place*.

the double world:

> it is variously believed that this world is the
> double of another, as in Plato, Swedenborg, Malebranche,
> some of Immanuel Kant, Arthur C. Clarke, Isaac Asimov,
> Stanley Kubrick
>   Two clocks set at the same time in
> identical universes should stop at the same time.
> This clock is a shadow of that real clock. When I
> look at my clock I have no way of knowing whether I am in
> the first or second universe ...
> Nothing on either prairie changes though the winds blow
> across immensities your heart would shrivel to imagine
> knowing they pass between the worlds and can be heard to do
> so on the road to Wood Mountain. That is what was written
> in the rocks.
>
>   (53)

It is writing again that discloses the presence of the 'double world' whose boundaries merge with those of 'this world.'[14] The 'double world' is the supplement to this reality. The vault, situated as it is on the edge of these two worlds, consists of a duplicitous reality. It is a place where opposites meet in order to lose their polarity: the 'we' contains the 'I'; the poet inhabits silence in order to enter the realm of writing; the poet's companion moves from critical discourse to poetic language; the past rises to meet the present. It becomes evident that the confounding of these opposites in the space of the vault, instead of reestablishing their dialectics, accentuates the doubleness of their presence. The dynamics of the vault infuses this polarity with a desire for totality, a desire for an absolute intelligibility the truth of which is not revealed but written. Writing, what is 'written in the rocks' – the written records of the vault – becomes the spatial surrogate of the place that Eli Mandel seeks to inhabit. Language and place become identical in the greyness of the vault. As Mandel said once, '[b]ooks are always writing us' (Arnason 89). The written records incite him to embrace the impossible dream of plenitude.

Eli and Ann Mandel, once inside the vault, are both haunted and hunting. They are haunted by the insignia of the ghost writers, the records of Eli Mandel's ancestors. The vault, like Plato's cave, is a prison. It is a prison of language, for the Mandels become the preys of the writing they feel compelled to read. Hence the 'gloom' and the 'uneasiness' that Eli Mandel confesses to in 'the hoffer colony':

and in a concrete vault its floor
littered with prairie I find
scripture a farmer's exodus Israel
                 ... I begin
to feel gloomy about possibilities

...

I look uneasily at grain inventories   (38)

But whereas the Mandels' psyches are threatened by their imprison-
ment, by the drawing force the records exercise upon them – 'our
work proceeded over days,' says Ann Mandel (7) – their own presence
threatens in return the internal purity of the vault.

The Mandels breach the silence that surrounds the place. Within
the encompassing walls of the vault, space and writing succumb to the
bodily functions of the visitors, to the scrutiny of their reading.

What pages we were not reading and sorting served for mattresses, sheets,
and head rests. When we decided a page was insignificant for our purposes
or saw it was blank we placed it in a pile to use for wiping ourselves or for
after love. Others became serviettes, sunshades, etc. (7)

Content or the absence of content determines the function of writing.
'[W]riting,' Edward Said says, 'is a ceaselessly changing triangle of en-
cipherment, decipherment, and dissemination' (20–1). The Mandels'
presence introduces an element of profanity in the vault, which stores
within its concave space traces of people long dead. The body of writing in the vault is purloined from an existence that has remained un-
stained by exterior presences. Pages now become conjugal sheets. The
Mandels break the hymen that has protected the interiority of this
writing from any outside interferences. Their presence consummates
a relationship between the past held in the vault and the present that
now flows into its hollow. The neutrality of the written records is
erased by the intimacy created when the Mandels employ writing in
a merely physical way. The vault is after all a prison that does not
remain inviolate to the Mandels' desire to unmask its complicity.

The interior purity of the vault is violated by the Mandels' desire
to impose an intelligible order on the scattered records. As Ann Man-

del says, '[u]sing sentence structure from bottom and top lines, we put the sheets together in what we conceived was the right order, then began to read' (8). But the vault belongs to no one, and so its scattered records signify the Jewish diaspora. The reading order Ann and Eli Mandel try to establish is, then, an attempt towards an anti-diaspora, an attempt to put an end to displacement, to reverse the direction of unwanted dispersal, to return to the promised land. The power by means of which both parties – ghost writers and present visitors – threaten to overwhelm each other is solely that of language. Through the grammar of language the poet and his companion transform the litter of the vault into the order of letter. 'A peculiar tale emerged, the pilgrimage west of a man and wife from the east to the place of his birth, home of his ancestors, a search for a lost home. Evidently the place they came to was this farm' (8). What is this tale but the double of *Out of Place*, the double of the journey west the Mandels take?[15] And in the light of Mandel's Jewish heritage, the journey west evokes (marginally) that of Joseph and Mary, returning to their home town, there to (re-)create the Word. Writing, found within the space of the vault, sustains that old journey, whereas Ann Mandel's 'Preface' and Eli Mandel's poem are a repetition moving both backwards and forwards, a duplicitous translation of a past and a present that encounter each other in the stained sheets of the vault. The deferred lives of the ancestors are now released as the Mandels discover a narrative grammar behind the ungrammaticality of the records, a grammar that finds its Platonic paradigm in the vault. The ghost writers and the poet and his companion become figures in an intertextual dance that is held on the floor of the vault, the space of writing.

It is evidently the Mandels' reading act that initiates this dance. But although they are under the rule of the shadows in the vault, inspired (breathed into) by the old voices, their reading activity detracts from the harmony of their dance. The Mandels' reading process violates the meaning of the old texts. To quote Kroetsch, '[t]he grammar of narrative remembered, even if it can only occasion in mistelling' (1989, 128). On the level of writing, Ann and Eli Mandel are identified with the 'man and wife from the east,' Joseph and Mary; on the level of reading they are displaced by the writing they read. The reading 'I's are not identical to the 'I's of that couple. The Mandels' reading act, invited by the silent ciphers, emancipates them from the vault as the last stronghold of the past and proves these old records to be writerly texts. The reading the records initiate is the first step towards the process of writing *Out of Place* that will articulate the reality of place as a reality that can be grasped through words.

'The last pages were missing,' says Ann Mandel at the end of her 'Preface,' 'but we could see the end. We put down the story and turned back toward the vault.' The missing end of the narrative is imagined before the narrative of *Out of Place* begins. The writer of the 'Preface' delivers the poet to his poem, which will be an inscription of deviations. *Out of Place*, in turn, is only the preface to a poem that Mandel seeks to write. When he goes west he begins a quest that is too processual to have a definite end. In his interview with David Arnason, Dennis Cooley, and Robert Enright he says:

We're travelling through the Prairies, we've encountered the gods; the gods are in storm; they hold us up; and we look at them; we've awestruck; and then we move to another set of gods, and then to another time. So the answer is: yes, I think I'm so fascinated by process that I spend a lot of time trying to work it out in [*Out of Place*], always, and to learn the ways of drama in poetry – the speaking voice, your structure being anything but a form put on. It is an event, an inevitable event of ordering. (71)

The quest can be ordered only through the structural repetition of encounter with gods of one time and then with gods of another time and so forth. But the epic ethos of Mandel's quest does not offer him the consolation of a foreseeable ending. Hence the Mandels' turning back towards the vault. The vault they turn to now is the vault of 'another time.' It is a vault of the present world, the resource the poet must revisit in order to confront its dark interior through the light of his own language. The vault becomes a metonym of *Out of Place* pronouncing the absences that bind Eli Mandel to his self and to the place of his origins.

While in search of his beginnings in the vault, Eli Mandel is pursued by the ghosts' voices beckoning him to enter onto the road of exodus. He says at the end of 'the hoffer colony':

before we take our easy leave
how should we understand
prophecies and miracles? (38)

The gloom and uneasiness that Mandel felt inside the vault, while engulfed by the old ciphers, are gone once he sets out to translate his reading act into writing, wandering within the space of his own language. It is a wandering that promises no return to a place of pure origins. The ghost writers, Mandel's ancestors, are the original demiurges of *Out of Place*. Eli Mandel, the double of these ghosts, slips into the difference that separates him from his origins; he slips, that is, into his own writing. As Andrew Suknaski puts it in his characteristic way, 'Wowk, in *Out of Place* you returned to find your WORD in some magical cipher' (20). Mandel delivers himself to the omnipotent fictionality of language where his true origins lie.

Like a contemporary Odysseus, Mandel has passed through the region of the dead, the vault, without dying. His passage, like that of Odysseus, has been inspired by nostos, the desire to return home. The concept of nostos in *Out of Place* is actually what predicates (prefaces) the two distinctive journeys that underlie the structure of the poem. These are the journey home – that is, the journey back to Estevan, Saskatchewan – and the return from darkness – that is, the exodus from the greyness of the vault. The first journey frames the second, not so much out of geographical necessity as out of the need to repeat the mythic structure of nostos. The root of nostos, *nes-*, in its 'earliest reconstructible context' means 'a return from death and darkness,' and is also the root of *noos*, which means mind, intelligence (Frame ix, 23). The descent into the underworld, no matter what mythic configuration it takes, is perhaps the most important ritualistic step the homecomer has to take before his wish to return home is fulfilled. (Given the presence of Ann Mandel, the poet's passage is also comparable to Orpheus' journey.) It becomes clear now that the Saskatchewan Mandel revisits is not his destination. The actual journey towards home is the route he follows after he emerges from the vault. Thus locality in *Out of Place* is not a place to return to but a place to exit from.

The Platonic configuration of the vault in Ann Mandel's 'Preface' accentuates this double journey. After Plato's prisoner emerges from the cave he says that he would rather 'be on earth as a hired servant in the house of a landless man' than return to the cave (230). These words, however, that Socrates puts in the prisoner's mouth, are a direct quotation from Achilles' statement to Odysseus when they encounter each other in Hades; but Achilles' statement in *The Odyssey* concludes that he would rather 'be on earth as a hired servant in the house of a landless man than be a king over all the perished dead' (180). The ascent from the cave to the light of the sun in Plato's allegory is, of course, a metaphor for the intellectual ascent from a *topos doxastos* to a *topos noetos*. Through Plato's dual scheme of illusory opinions and intelligence that directly echoes Odysseus' homecoming, Mandel's own nostos is revealed in all its ramifications. His memory, what maps out the movement of his nostos, has to be purged of the extraneous material that misleadingly presents Estevan as the destination of his journey. Mandel's purgation involves the emptying out of notions of home as a locality that welcomes the wayfarer by offering him comfort of teleological import. For this reason his purgation had to take place within the space of the vault.

Mandel's desire to return home is a desire to valorize the past and an affirmation of his displacement. This valorization, however, is not practised by a warrior/hero as the epic tradition demands, but by a man of language whose fate was set in the past 'by fowl.'

> On Fridays in Regina the difficulties become acute, how to
> smuggle two live chickens in a burlap sack down the street
> of Ukrainian neighbours, past two alien churches, one Russian
> Orthodox, its onion domes looming over me (alien afraid as
> Klein would say) like a Chagall version of shtetl-life, the
> other Greek, its angular priestly spire aloofly critical
> of the gross yiddishkeit of chickens. Their obstinacy, their
> cunning. How do they manage to wiggle their obscene squawking
> heads through burlap? Why should my fate be set by fowl?
> The murderous notions in my head on Friday, Sabbath eve:
> 'chicken you'll die before the ritual blessing, that's for sure',
> detestable the squalid hut to which I move, its bloody
> rows of funnels, feathers stuck to crusted blood of slaughtered
> birds.
>
> I think of god, his commandments regulating the sanctity
> of chicken soup, appeal the case to high authority. 'It isn't
> fair' I say. 'To whom' my grandfather's omnipotent
> reply, 'you or the chickens?'   (67)

The young boy's journey here is again a homeward journey, but this time, accompanied by the signs of his ethnic origins, Mandel's experience is not that of nostalgia but that of embarrassment if not shame. The young boy is 'beside' himself because the chicken by squawking voices the difference of his identity. The parody of the Jewish ritual is also a parody of his self-characterization. The ritual, for Mandel, is a passage of literal transition: his walk through the various neighbourhoods obliges him to recontextualize his ethnic identity within a setting of multiple ethnic elements. His appeal to authority (the grandfather) for the affirmation of his ethno-ego position is parodied as well by the authority figure who displaces the young boy even within the context of his own statement.

The fact that the answer to young Mandel's question is another question – 'you or the chickens?' – upsets the codes of epic heroism while illustrating the alternate positions that can incur from recontextualization ('you *or* the chickens?'). This parody destabilizes the function of the hero as well as the concept of identity: the transference to the chickens as the figure of otherness misplaces the young boy within his own system of justice, propriety, and selfhood. The chickens as an indicator of the parodying act deflate the importance of the homeward journey by exposing the notions that faith in the ideals of home is quite often a blind faith and that identity is no less than a heterogeneous concept. This same parodic marker also points out that displacement is a misdirected form of referentiality – '*you* or the *chickens?*' – which often relies on binary opposition – 'you *or* the chickens?' – and which only deceptively leads towards self-definition.

Referentiality as displacement is accomplished here by means of the present tense. The 'Epilogue,' unlike the 'Preface,' is written in the present tense, which has a double function. On the one hand, the simple present tense can be used to express an act that displays the frequency and repetition ('On Fridays in Regina ...') of the recounted event.[16] In this respect, the present tense functions as the historical present, which achieves simultaneity for the sake of narrative vividness. Yet the past thing evoked is temporally nullified where Mandel creates a sense of universalized continuity by extending locality towards a national geography: 'Meanwhile the chickens continue to squawk, past Eleventh Avenue, down the mean streets, St John, Halifax, Montreal, Toronto, Ottawa, to where the gleaming razor waits' (68). The present tense here does not designate time; it has a generalizing function.

Yet the continuity incurred by the use of present tense is tied in with the ritual Mandel describes, a further erasure of the distinction between past and present. The present tense of the repetitious event Mandel narrates coincides with the occasion of the recounting, which is also linked to his act of enunciation.[17] What is interesting is that the present tense of enunciation – which operates purely on a linguistic level – displaces the past the writer wants to retrieve and relocates it within the present. The effect of this linguistic instantaneousness is a certain ambiguity, for it is not clear (linguistically) whether what happens 'on Fridays in Regina' is lived, relived, or still continues to happen in Regina. As Christine Brooke-Rose says, '[t]ense is either used to blur order ... or it becomes wholly a category of voice' (314). The blurring of narrative time in *Out of Place* relocates the past within the poet's present, thus further frustrating his attempt to return to that place and time. Moreover, the present tense works against mimesis by foregrounding the notion that what exists does so only on the level of the poet's writing act. The past is not represented but re-presented by Mandel's enunciation. This emphasis on the performative act contributes to the critical and ideological difference the long poem introduces in its treatment of the past.

The employment of the present tense throughout *Out of Place* encounters a moment of paradox in the 'Epilogue.' The structural posteriority of the 'Epilogue' as a genre is paradoxically cancelled by the fact that a part of it, 'Pictures in an Institution,' was previously published in Mandel's earlier book, *An Idiot Joy*. But the epilogue's posteriority is also inverted by its present tense, whereas the textual anteriority of the 'Preface' is inverted by its past tense. It is this inversion that allows Mandel to inhabit the textual place he creates. If he privileges the past at all, he does so by determining it not 'by fowl' but allegorically, namely by reading and writing otherwise. The opening poem of *Out of Place* asserts this.

the return:

in the estevan poem, for example,
how everyone can be seen eating
or is it reading
            but not everyone
there is myself in the souris valley
forty years later
            Ann
looking at wild flowers
cactus   their thick colours

>I remember how I dreamt
>
>her   (13)

The first place of return after the exodus from the vault is 'Estevan, Saskatchewan,' not Mandel's hometown, but a poem of his that first appeared in the *Minotaur Poems*. Writing is the place towards which his nostos has led him. As Peter Stevens says, '[l]andscape and page have become one' (58). It is Mandel's writing act that modulates his present, liquefies the past, stirs the stillness of the abandoned vault, and reopens the 'doors of Perception' (15).

The return to the geographical Estevan can be completed only by metonymic substitution: from geography to genre. The name of place loses its stability; it becomes signature, the name bearing the mark of its occasion. The materializing imprints of Mandel's words on the page are the supplement to the gaps in his memory, the double of the sheets he finds in the vault. His writing act transforms his displacement into the discovery of his self within the space his words occupy.

The 'Preface' as text discloses Ann Mandel's own place in the poet's homecoming. Instead of the warrior/hero coming home to a Penelope, we have the writer, his destiny 'set by fowl,' going with his female other to the lost place. In the 'Acknowledgments' Eli Mandel says that the 'companion and guide is of course a familiar figure in tales of journeys' (75). As a companion Ann Mandel both triggers and witnesses the shedding of the poet's old self; as a guide she is the presence (anima) that mediates between the poet and the underworld, redoubling thus his encounter with his *doppelgänger*; as the writer of the 'Preface' and the eye and maker behind the photographs that accompany the text of *Out of Place*, she enters the space of writing and becomes one of the voices that participate in the making of the poem.

The intertextuality, then, that informs the generic plurality and structural complexity of the long poem is first actualized in *Out of Place* by Ann Mandel's presence. More specifically, the interplay of voices and texts emphasizes that the monologic authority of the poet is 'out of place' in a poem that explores the absence of place as a fixed ground. The female voice of the 'Preface' not only accompanies the male voice of the poet when he sets out to create the space of writing both of them are going to inhabit but also suggests the importance of the period of gestation spent in the vault. One might want to push this even further and suggest that the female voice of the 'Preface' begets the poet's voice – that the poet echoes her.

Beyond this, however, the 'Preface' is the first marker in the poem pointing out the flexibility of generic boundaries. Despite the suggestiveness of its title, *Out of Place* turns out not to be marginal. Even though Mandel's journey has been presented according to the epic conventions as dramatized by their parodic inversion, his quest consists not of a continuous epic narrative but, quite the contrary, of lyric discourse, prose poems, letters, and photographs taken by Ann Mandel. This generic plurality illustrates the poetics of indeterminacy that characterizes the long poem in general while, at the same time, delimiting the flexibility of *Out of Place*.

The lyrics that comprise 'The Return,' the first section of *Out of Place*, localize the quest within the poet's experience. His personal quest assumes its epic character only because he foregrounds himself as a quester who is a poet. Thus Estevan, a geographical site, is replaced by 'estevan, 1934,' a linguistic site – the ground actually sought by a poet. This transference is further accentuated by the reflexivity of the lyric discourse, accomplished through repetition and recollection in Kierkegaard's sense of these terms. 'Repetition and recollection are the same movement,' Kierkegaard says, 'only in opposite directions: for what is recollected has been, is repeated backwards, whereas repetition, properly so called, is recollected forwards' (33). This double movement, together with its many detours, exemplifies the generic structure of *Out of Place* as well as its tension between the past and the present.

It is precisely this pendulous movement that points out how referentiality operates in the long poem. 'The return,' for instance, manifests this double movement simultaneously: the 'estevan poem' mentioned in the first line of 'the return' is a recollection of the 'estevan poem' written years earlier, becoming thus a reference outside *Out of Place*. In this respect, the opening lyric is a return, too, return as reference to a text's other, to one of *Out of Place*'s originary resources, a movement backwards; but it is also a repetition, as the phrase 'estevan poem' will repeat itself, with difference, later on in *Out of Place*, in the form of the actual Estevan poem, 'estevan, 1934.'

That forward movement, which is the movement the reader follows, extends referentiality to include self-referentiality: the opening lyric refers to the poem it is going to become (29), it moves towards its intertextual other. The exterior and interior boundaries of the long poem are dissolved as Mandel's language affirms its materiality. Similarly, the margins that separate the present from the past are erased as well. The enabling power that makes room for the metonymic transposition and double movement illustrates the long poem's heterogeneity. Whereas the transferral works metonymically – Estevan as poem, Estevan as town – the generic contrast of the epic and lyric modes occurs temporally, in their differences in tense. Temporality dissolves the distance that characterizes epic representation without, however, neutralizing the epic impact of the poet's quest. Reflexivity seems to be the trope that resolves the contrasting intents of these genres.

The second lyric poem further emphasizes this reflexivity.

[signs:][18]

        and omens   windows
        facing inward
                        'an ideal
        inserted into the plane
        we call reality'   words
        warning this is the place
        you reach
                    to name
        remember and recite

        the Hebrew alphabet
        Invictus the first three
        lines of Genesis
        the unremembered man who stole
        children from an empty town and
        Latin   heroes in the hills and
        glyphs uncles cousins step-
        grandfather's sons and sisters

        whatever has been hidden here
        remains of speech
                        the town lives
        in its syntax we are ghosts

        look   on the road beyond
        mesas and moonscape
        hoodoos   signs cut in rock

graffiti gods
an indescribable border   (14)

The gravitational pull of grammar tempts the reader to ignore the
colon after the title 'signs' and read 'signs and omens ...' But if we
allow our reading to follow the notation of the poem, we avoid the
ensuing tautology and the semantic problem it poses – although signs
are not always omens, omens remain always signs. So we are left with
'and omens,' a (perhaps ominous) beginning without beginning. 'And,'
as the opening word, is connected to no other words; it is connected
instead to nothingness and its many 'signs,' the plurality of origins that
Out of Place continually asserts.

'And,' then, embodies the same double movement; looking backwards, which is to say towards the preceding substantive its grammar
implies, 'and' sees nothing, a fact that might be interpreted as a 'sign'
of pregnant silence, indeterminacy, unreadability, or utter nothingness; looking forwards, 'and' sees 'omens windows / facing inward.'
The paradox here, also a parodic sign, affirms the self-reflexivity of
the poem. Indeed, the following lines support this forward gaze:
'words / warning this is the place / you reach.' The deictic referentiality of 'this is the place' is yet another 'sign' of self-referentiality
– the place being the blank space trailing in the rest of the line, a
window facing inward, the page, the poem itself. Even if we take the
apostrophic 'you' to refer to Ann, Ann as the writer of the 'Preface'
further asserts the poem's materiality.

The place Mandel reaches after traversing the white space of his
lines is also the tentative space evoked by the infinitives 'to name /
remember and recite.' Naming, a performative act, invents the past
as memories and creates poetry as 'recitation,' again a linguistic act,
that actualizes the past by making it present. The rendering of the
past into the present makes the former accessible by minimizing the
distance that separates us from it. Our only way of knowing the past
is by way of erasing this distance. Mandel, however, does not take this
knowledge of the past for granted.

the endless treachery
that is remembering
there are no definitions   (19)

He is cautious of memories because of the distortion they might incur.

Undue reliance on memories, he seems to be saying, tends to privilege one aspect of reality at the expense of another; obsession with memories threatens to reduce the immediacy and primacy of the present. This is why throughout *Out of Place* he constantly thwarts his own temptation to make his journey of nostos follow a linear track of memories. Simultaneously, he also resists the search for a definite identity. He lets himself instead follow the traces of language – 'whatever has been hidden here / remains of speech.' Memory is found in, and retrieved through, speech. Similarly, locality is defined through language – the town lives / in its syntax we are ghosts.'

Recollection and repetition are what account here for the length of *Out of Place*. They become the generative principle, the cause and effect of the poem. They also direct the trajectory of the reader, who must constantly move back and forth in the poem. The phrase 'signs cut in rock,' for instance, demands that the reader make a leap across the text to 'the double world' to find 'what was written in the rocks' (53). Leaps of this sort are far from being cases of gratuitous self-reflexivity, nor are they meant merely for the reader's pleasure in tracing references. Their primary function is to undo the closure of the individual lyrics *Out of Place* consists of, to stretch the individual short poems beyond themselves and into the textual maze of the long poem. The ragged lines of the poet's and the reader's itineraries mark the 'indescribable border' between the epic and lyric elements in the poem.

The colon that punctuates the titles of the individual poems contributes to the extensive and extending nature of the lyric genre in *Out of Place*. The colon not only establishes a closer rapport between title and poem – almost setting the title out as the opening word of the poem – but also creates a chain of poems-as-events that formally constitutes *Out of Place* as a long poem. Here is how it looks schematically:

preface: ... the return: ... signs: ... doors of perception: ... birthmark: ... souris river: ... badlands: ... etc.

Besides being a pointer of continuity, the link of seemingly disjointed narratives, the colon is also an indicator of prolongation. It functions as a pause announcing the departure from one version of nostos or definition and the arrival at another. Further, it punctuates Mandel's fascination with doubles, and his own double in particular, as it introduces various configurations of the poet's identity. This is evident throughout the whole poem, but is best exemplified in the section called 'The Double' – significantly, the second part of *Out of Place*.

The colon is used in this section as a rhetorical figure of equilibrium with difference: it outlines *and* blurs the differences and similarities of self and place as is the case in 'various kinds of doubles:' (57). This poem is repeated in an inverted form on the preceding and facing page. The inverted double posits itself as the figure of *mise en abyme*, a mirror that reflects identity with difference; it unsettles reflexivity and deflects and delays the reading act by blurring language. The colon, then, acts as a metaphor of the substitution devices Mandel uses as well as a trope of the constant shift of his meaning.

The only exception – a good example of the contradictions inherent in the long poem – to the use of colons in the titles is found in the third section of *Out of Place*, 'A Suite for Ann.' The absence of the colon here marks a shift in the lyric tone. The disjointed attempts towards narrative of the earlier parts of the poem, which the book will resume later, are abandoned for a more authentic lyricism. This shift is marked by the rhetorical modulations employed in 'A Suite for Ann.' The tone is more subjective, the language more abstract, indicating yet another attempt, this time more meditative, to deal with locality. The four poems, 'Fear of Flying,' 'Strange Places,' 'Place,' and 'The Wayfarer,' all concern place, while the ambiguity of the collective title of the section further enhances the complexity of locality.

The first poem opens as an extension of Mandel's encounter with his shadowy self in 'The Double.'

I dream of flying but I fear
I either will or will not fly
or flying will not land or will
or landing will at once arise

waking
    I place my feet on
creaky floors
        you beside me
dream of stairs   climbing
vines
   and wings   (61)

Within the intersubjective self and space of his dream, Mandel moves

beyond his conscious self and geography. But the dreamscape he promises to describe is immediately put under erasure. It suspends itself
within the undetermined mental frame of the poem. The either/or
structure, the give and take of possibilities and action, the hesitation
together with the need for certainty, all these become the rhetorical
modulations that double-speak (contradict and interdict) the poet's trajectory. His search for the precise meaning of his dream is rechannelled
by the antithetical options he locates within the dream itself. Mandel's
questioning of his dream inside this dream (which, of course, is atemporal) is performed through language, which occurs in time. More
than that, his performative act is framed by the present tense, which
makes the dream simultaneous with empirical knowledge. His constant
wavering, however, between this fear of flying and fear of landing is
expressed in the future tense. Thus the present tense, the repetition
of 'will,' and the uneasiness of this stanza's syntax convey the illusion
of mimesis – in accurately recording the dream he shows dramatic
confusion. But these elements also stress that, although the poet can
come to grips with his dream only through discourse, dreams resist
interpretation because of their inherent unreadability.

The differentiation Mandel tries to reach through his dream leads
not to self-definition but to his increasing awareness in the course of
the poem that binaries such as that of the either/or structure in the
dream do not provide concrete answers to his questions. That's why
he constantly shifts away from the stability of fixed meaning towards
the interdeterminacy of signification. The place the poet inhabits is
not the atemporal space of his dream, nor is it the creaky floor on
which he places his feet when he wakes; it is his poem itself, a meta-
place, the writing ground that enables him to engage himself in differentiation, continuing thus his meditation on place.

As soon as Mandel exits from his dream of flying he enters the dream
of Ann sleeping beside him. The line 'you beside me' is the first direct
apostrophe to her. Although the figure of Ann appears frequently
throughout *Out of Place*, the marginality by way of which she has introduced herself is now formally resolved through the rhetorical trope
of apostrophe. Having realized that the desired place can be re-entered
only in writing, and having already dealt with his shadowy self, Mandel
now moves to an encounter with his contra-sexual self. 'A Suite for
Ann,' as the title suggests, is a 'place' clearly delineated 'for Ann,' an
attempt to get hold, through her, of the elusiveness of space. It is the
poetic ground for the writer of the 'Preface.' She appears in this section

through the apostrophe in 'Fear of Flying.' Apostrophe, Culler reminds us, 'is perhaps always an indirect invocation of the muse' (1981, 143). But, as we have seen, between Ann Mandel as the writer of the 'Preface' and the Ann of this section there is a whole range of roles that both support and question the traditional assumptions of the muse figure.

Mandel employs apostrophe to present yet another version of the *I – thou* relationship. To quote Culler again, 'the vocative of apostrophe is a device which the poetic voice uses to establish with an object a relationship which helps constitute him. The object is treated as a subject, an *I* which implies a certain type of *you* in its turn. One who successfully invokes nature is one to whom nature might, in its turn, speak. He makes himself poet, visionary. Thus, invocation is a figure of vocation' (1981, 142). The 'you beside me' in 'Fear of Flying' dramatizes the alienation of the poet's empirical self from his dreaming, poetic self. Ann as 'you,' as the second person, becomes the poet's other that re-establishes his bearings with external reality, that soothes his fear of flying, his uneasiness about the creaky floors. In this respect, the 'you' becomes an allegory of desire; it constitutes what the 'I' lacks.

The apostrophe further dramatizes the way Mandel relates his dream to himself and to Ann. He wills himself to imagine that Ann, as he was himself moments ago, is dreaming. Differentiation occurs in the continuation of his dream in his waking. But the lines 'you beside me / dream of stairs' are syntactically ambiguous. If we take 'dream' to be a noun and not a verb, the apostrophized 'you' may well refer instead to the 'dream of stairs' Mandel imagines. His dream has become now a fiction, a dream imagined. When apostrophe functions as a sign of fiction, it stresses, according to Culler, its optative character. The result is that such an apostrophe does not establish a relationship between the self and the other; instead, it reveals an act of 'radical interiorization and solipsism,' one that either disperses fragments of the self in order to fill the world, or allows the self to internalize what is external. This latter procedure, Culler argues, implies that when the *I* names as a *you* something that cannot possibly be a *you* (i.e. the earth), the *I* 'preempts' the place of the *you* in a gesture of poetic intervention (1981, 146).

The dream as the 'you' of Mandel's apostrophe externalizes, then, what he has interiorized. The dream he refers to in his waking is a recollection of his own dream but with a difference. Ann dreams of 'stairs   climbing / vines / and wings.' Ann's dream and/or the dream that Mandel imagines is a metonymic substitution for his own (real) dream. The difference lies in the syntax and diction he uses when he talks about the two dreams. Mandel translates Ann's dream in a discourse that lacks the abstraction and the syntax, doubling upon itself, that the discourse of his dream had. Whereas he was dreaming of the act of flying as an abstract concept, Ann dreams of things that climb or fly naturally or facilitate flying. The concreteness and the litotes in the discourse of Ann's imagined dream are accomplished primarily by synecdoche, by 'wings' substituting for 'flying.' The function of the apostrophe is nothing else than to translate Mandel's own dream in terms that internalize the positiveness of his female other, that exorcise his fear as he departs from this lyric, donning the wings of its last line.

Thus the apostrophe allows Mandel to leave a space that inspires uneasiness and to concretize his notion of the self. All this is achieved through what Culler calls the 'now' of apostrophe, 'not a moment in a temporal sequence but a *now* of discourse, of writing' (1981, 152). Although there is no narrative sequence in this suite of poems, however, the vocative 'you beside me' prepares the reader for the 'we' of the following lyric, 'Strange Places.' The first stanza of this poem, like the first one in 'Fear of Flying,' has the same lexical repetition and doubling syntax that make the poem turn back upon itself. The 'strangeness' of place marks the poet's estrangement from a monologic self further emphasized by the persistent 'we.' Contradiction, once again, functions as the generative principle both of 'A Suite for Ann' and of the entire long poem.

'Place,' the lyric that follows, in its lean column of no more than two words per line, evokes the separation of self from place, presence and absence, writing and silence. What trails behind the last word/ line of the poem, 'here,' is the deep white silence of the page. 'Here' is empty. Where there are no words, for Mandel, there is no place, or at least no discernible place. And this is by no means an element peculiar to Mandel's poetics. It is one of the elements that characterize the ideology of the long poem at large. The long poem, as a series of conscious acts of writing, is always tempted to identify location with the field of writing. But that connection again opens new crises. Whether location takes the form of the page or of the whole poem, or whether it manages to maintain, to a larger or smaller extent, its geographical entity, place as treated in the long poem cannot contain the poet's self in its plenitude. The desire to get more of the self into place, into writing, while knowing that there is always a part of it left out, is another generative principle of the long poem.

The co-presence in Mandel's work of epic and lyric elements, together with the non-linear narrative of letters and photographs, illustrates the variables of place with which Mandel is concerned. The poet's nostos sets him on a personal journey towards a real place that can be identified geographically. This movement towards real place both affirms the need to understand one's locality and shows how genre and experience interrelate. But the personalized vision of this journey manifests the extent to which the long poem parodies the heroization of the epic tradition. That same vision causes a detour of the epic direction, and it leads Mandel to a space that is identifiable textually. Locality becomes the field of writing. The shift from geography to textual locus has a multiple function. It accentuates, first of all, the difference between place and space, the former delineating the physical boundaries within which an object is contained and by which it is named (i.e., Estevan), whereas the latter indicates the inner boundaries of the containing object (i.e., the location of the poet's self). The emphasis on textuality as locality, far from erasing the referential elements, illustrates how referentiality is constructed by discourse.

One might be tempted at this point to see the shift from geography to textual locus as a metaphor (literally a *metaphora*), with place being the tenor and space being the vehicle. But given the continuous emphasis in *Out of Place* on the impossibility of entering a place of the past and on the need to produce space through language, it would, perhaps, be more accurate to view place and space as an intertextual coupling. Place, having a concrete form and structure, is conducive to mimesis; space, being inner and indeterminate, defies it. This reflects the anti-mimetic intent of the long poem's textuality. Space as writing (the poem as locality) signals to the reader that place, even when it is taken to be the destination of a journey, has to be viewed, inhabited, with difference.

It is the rendering of place into space that partly accounts for Mandel's personal epic journey. He articulates his journey in a parodic epic discourse, thus undoing the epic genre by interspersing it with lyrics, letters, and photographs that enunciate the ways in which inner space becomes external. Ann Mandel's 'Preface' also breaks down the patriarchal ideology of the epic tradition, while the presence of the poet as anti-hero and as his double dismisses the monologic ethos of that tradition. The reliance on tradition and on an absolute past that Bakhtin sees as generic elements of the epic are dismissed too. Mandel affirms the fictionality of linear tradition while prizing the non-linear significance of the genealogical documents in the vault. The epic notion of an absolute past is also parodied as he traces the past of a place in the present of his text. The poet's desire to return home is no longer informed by Bernstein's collective nostos of a tribe. Mandel fails to retrieve his lost origins, but he is at home in the writing he composes.

4

The Self in the Long Poem

Who is this *I* infesting my poems? Is it I hiding behind the Trump type on the page of the book you are reading? Is it a photograph of me on the cover of *Wilson's Bowl*? Is it I? *I* said, *I* say, *I* am saying –

Phyllis Webb, 'Performance'

... I want to fail to understand notation. & the sounds. Aphasia. I love you. My readers. What we are given to understand. What we are given. Begs the question. One question. So I can kiss you. The words kiss & question unconnected until now

Erin Mouré, 'The Jewel'

SELF/IDENTITY/PRONOUN: bpNICHOL

More than any other Canadian long poem, bpNichol's *The Martyrology* illustrates the long poem's plurality of genre. The acknowledged distrust of generic origins in *The Martyrology* declares that the formal plurality of Nichol's poem is grounded in the self and, by implication, in the linguistic utterance on which the self relies for its formulation.

The various generic names attributed to *The Martyrology* indicate Nichol's plural, but simultaneously elliptical, treatment of the self. Kroetsch calls *The Martyrology* a 'life-long poem' (1989, 119), an appellation reiterated by Stephen Scobie: '[i]t has become not just a long poem but a life/long poem; it may even be regarded, after Eli Mandel's punning title, as a "life sentence," from which the author occasionally gets out "on parole"' (1984, 106). Roy Miki points to Japanese linked poetry, and more specifically the utanikki, as one of the main generic paradigms operating in the poem;[1] Nichol himself has called his poem a journal, and a book about the history of saints (1985, 24). One could even call it a meta-long poem because its complexities and inner tensions derive largely from Nichol's anxiety about the act of writing a long poem and of writing about oneself. All these generic names stress the different ways in which Nichol brings together life and poetry. Although the autobiographical impulse pervades *The Martyrology*, however, it would be misleading to argue that the poem is strictly speaking autobiographical. Like other long poems, such as Lola Lemire Tostevin's *Double Standards*, Daphne Marlatt's *How Hug a Stone* and *What Matters*, and George Bowering's *Kerrisdale Elegies*, Nichol's poem flirts with the genre of autobiography: it uses the experientially real as a point of departure for its meanderings in the linguistically real.

Nichol's concern with the self in *The Martyrology* reflects one of the primary features of the contemporary long poem, namely the treatment of a problematic self. The plural form of the long poem never quite fulfils the reader's generic expectations, and, similarly, its treatment of the self never quite shares the self's presumed totality with the reader. The self in the long poem remains elliptical. It *promises* to unveil its truth, but it continues to point away from it; it distances itself not only from the searching reader but from its own meaning as well. Although such a self occasionally creates the impression that it feeds on mystification, it also practises disclosure, because of its ability to engender itself as subject and thematize itself as object.

This double function of the elliptical self, as *The Martyrology* demonstrates, deconstructs the Cartesian ego and its fiction of totality. The Cartesian ego as unary subject celebrates humanism.[2] In contrast, the self in the long poem goes beyond humanistic 'man' and the authorial/authoritative configurations he assumes in his role as singular subject of consciousness. The long poem deals with humanism as a set of aporias derived from a system of totality and the privileging of the self as monologic subject. The self in this kind of poem does not recognize the constancy of the Cartesian ego; its own constancy is invariably that of a missing element located in language.[3] That which is missing inspires *longing* (desire and deferral).

In *The Martyrology* Nichol invents his own origins by creating a cosmology and a genealogy that substantially alter the humanistic ideology that has defined the self. Nichol, contrary to the formal unity by which humanism abides, takes a non-linear approach to the self.

He uses deferrals, detours, surprise techniques, repetitions, and hiatuses in order to disclose the elliptical, but paradoxically abundant, notion of self. And, appropriately, he begins his exploration of the self by questioning the fundamental humanistic notion of origin: the origin (of the self) as textual beginning, but a beginning that doesn't want to begin.

Book 1 of *The Martyrology* begins with a series of textual delays. In the first edition of Book 1 (1972) we find, inserted between the cover and the first blank pages, a leaflet of four pages. On the first page, and above the title *The Martyrology*, we see the iconic figure of St Maria Goretti[4] whose brief life, violent death, and subsequent canonization are reported on the fourth page of the leaflet (together with her photograph) in the journalistic language of the *Toronto Star*. St Maria Goretti announces the recurring theme of martyrology. In the inside pages of the leaflet we read Nichol's own genealogy of saints, a genealogy that parodies both Christian and literary canons alike: 'of those saints we know the listing follows,' the opening line says. What follows is indeed a list of names presented in the discourse of Genesis. This discourse, however, is multilayered, as it evokes such ancient cosmologies and genealogies as Hesiod's and the epic catalogues we find in Homer. These multiple evocations, together with St Maria Goretti, substitute for the invocation to the muse.

The Martyrology begins, then, in the most traditional fashion. But given Nichol's private and invented genealogies, its beginning is one of parodic inversion. We participate in Nichol's parody as readers when we identify in *The Martyrology* traces of the discourse of cosmogonies, genealogies, epic invocations, catalogues, and biblical and canonical texts. But Nichol himself turns parody from a mode of discourse into a theme in itself:

is nothing but a history
brief at best
an end of one thing
beginning of another
premonition of a future time or line we will be writing

(Book 1, leaflet, np)

What we read in the listing of saints is a beginning before the formal beginning of the poem, and a beginning within this beginning: *medias res in medias res*. Nichol's beginnings are tentative and arbitrary. The fact that the above beginning appears in the physical form of a loose leaflet that we can lose or misplace in the text, thus erasing a beginning and/or creating different versions of beginnings illustrates that Nichol overtly engages the reader in the making of his text: the reader has a hand in the poem's intertextuality.[5] The poet's show of allowance towards the reader stresses too how Nichol deconstructs the notion of origin and the certainty with which humanism and specifically the Christian tradition have endowed it.

The fluidity of the beginning[6] situates *The Martyrology* not so much within the world of specific books – although there are plenty of examples of the poem's indebtedness to many sources[7] – as within the tentative boundaries of intertextuality. Nichol has always displayed an interest in the fluidity of texts. His shuffle texts *Transformational Unit* (1983), *Still Water* (1970), and *Continuum* (1984), for instance, exemplify a writing that is, physically and textually, unbound.

'Things I Don't Really Understand about Myself,' one of Nichol's statements about the long poem, is exactly such a shuffle text, dispersed throughout *Open Letter*'s special issue on the long poem (1985). The dissemination of the text does not simply affect the deliberate unravelling of Nichol's shuffle writing; it actualizes the continuous alterations of the self's narrative. For a shuffle text, Davey reminds us, 'may be read in any order' (1985, 152). The undoing of Aristotelian structure, the resistance to thematic unification, the continuous reversals of beginnings and endings, all come the fore in Book 5 of *The Martyrology*. Here, the twelve chains of the text link its different parts in intricate ways, creating a textual labyrinth lacking a centre that defies metaphorically the unity of self. Nichol's writing reads as a continuous series of detours, and this inevitably affects the reader's own movement in the text. The self remains a tantalizing figure, its completeness kept in abeyance.

But to return to Book 1. Following the leaflet, the page with the epigraph from Gertrude Stein,[8] and the title page, we come to yet another beginning: an excerpt 'from *The Chronicle of Knarn*.' The word 'from' suggests a missing beginning and marks these three pages as direct quotations from a text, obviously of Nichol's invention but seemingly situated here as an excerpt from a canonical tradition. The difference between this and the leaflet resides in the point of view. The genealogy is told in the first person plural: 'we know ... we mention

... we will be writing.' The 'we' gives authority to the text – the authority of collective voice, the sacredness of material that has been sanctified by the-Word-become-Flesh. This, besides casting doubt on Nichol's own authorial control of the material, is meant to stress the kind of objectivity and truth that the reader, presumably, cannot question because they directly derive from the Word. In contrast, the 'i' in the fragment 'from *The Chronicle of Knarn*' undermines authority by foregrounding its personal narrative of sorrow and loss. The lower-case pronoun is an immediate deconstruction of the Cartesian 'I,'[9] the erect letter that has inscribed patriarchal tradition and that bears the weight of responsibility for compiling genealogies and history by following solely its own ideology.

The interrelationship between the singular 'i' and the plural 'we' is one of Nichol's primary concerns in *The Martyrology*. The unfolding of the self follows the shift from singularity to plurality in terms both of the quantitative nature of the self and of its perspective. But before Nichol focuses on this shift, he continues his play with beginnings. The multiple beginnings correspond with the multiple 'i's of the poem. As the self resists definition, so the poem amplifies its origins, thus echoing its resistance to the middle and end of its structure.

What subjectivizes further this section is the tentativeness of the discourse of the 'i' – 'i used to love you (i think)' – and the direct expression of its desire – 'wishing i were near you,' 'my arms ache from not holding you.' The tentativeness of love questions the fundamental Christian notion of *agape*, a selfless love devoid of desire for the mortal self and informed by desire for the Other, God.[10] *Agape* is directed towards the symbolic Other lying outside the self, whereas desire returns to the self.

Ironically, the lower-case 'i,' while not expressing a selfless self, implies a centre that absorbs the self. It posits a self conscious of its limitations and relative marginality, as illustrated by the following parenthetical prose stanza:

(a long time ago i thot i knew how this poem
would go, how the figures of the saints would
emerge. now it's covered over by my urge to
write you what lines i can. the sun is dying.
i've heard them say it will go nova before the
year's end. i wanted to send you this letter

(this poem) but now it's too late to say
anything, too early to have anything to send.)   (Book 1)

The title of this section evokes the classic narrative tradition where there is a distance between narrator/singer and hero/character. Nichol, however, does not fulfil the generic expectations the title promises. He not only writes here in a lyric voice, but also collapses the traditional distance by letting the subject sing its own song. This rhetorical trope marks Knarn both as the name of a place and as the name of that rhetorical topos of the self where the narrative gap between subject and object is questioned, if not entirely eliminated. Hence the singer's self-consciousness about his art. Paradoxically, however, the art the singer talks about is not singing – it is writing. Nichol does not locate his 'Chronicle' in the oral tradition but in the tradition of the written word, or more precisely the genealogy of the word being written.

The line 'the language i write is no longer spoken' (Book 1) illustrates that the singer's life and art function on the same plane and are thus inseparable. Moreover, it emphasizes the difference between speech and writing, a difference which, through its Saussurean and Derridean ramifications, questions the placing of the oral tradition as the beginning of literature. The result of this process is that, in de Man's words, literature as a 'humanistic and historical discipline,' and as 'a relatively stable canon of specific texts' gives way to *écriture* (1986, 21).

The artist, Nichol seems to be arguing, cannot divorce art from the life that makes it. The self as a principle engendering art loses its generality, it is particularized. In this respect, autobiography in *The Martyrology* functions not as a genre that seeks to encompass the life of the self by assigning meaning and an ordering shape to it, but as a writing activity that unravels the complexity of the self by exploring its signification. Nichol says in 'Things I Don't Really Understand about Myself' that

the hardest thing about using autobiographical detail in the long poem is to get the reader to accept it as what it is: words in a book revealing exactly the amount of information necessary for that moment of the composition. autobiographical information seems to raise the desire for more such information, as if knowing it would somehow increase one's appreciation of the text when, in fact, the exact opposite happens; the additional information changes our reading of the text & thus distorts it. (1985, 73)

Hence Nichol's a-version to literary beginnings where the self begins to express itself only through the act of writing. That is why the chronicler is not a poet who sings but a poet who writes. Orality, which necessitates presence, creates a support system for the self that lies outside it; writing, harbouring absence, demands that the self be disseminated.

Before we move to the next beginning, it is important to notice that the fragment 'from *The Chronicle of Knarn*' is seemingly presented as direct quotation. Yet there are no quotation marks because 'from' is used as a deictic signifier of an assumed larger text. The last lines of 'from *The Chronicle of Knarn*,' 'my hands turn the words / clumsily,' announce that the turning of the page will reveal yet another beginning, this time a more formal one: the title page with the publishing information.

Following this is an epigraph, another direct quotation, whose source, 'from THE WRITINGS OF SAINT AND,' also reveals it to be a text of Nichol's invention. Again, the title of this missing text thematizes Nichol's play with textual delays. St And reminds the reader that it is necessary to stand by the poet's principle of delays if the text proper is ever to be reached. St And intimates the cumulative principle that characterizes *The Martyrology*.

the precision of openness
is not a vagueness
it is an accumulation
cumulous

(Book 4)

Delay, accretion, and prolongation are three of the most significant principles of composition and structure in *The Martyrology*. Since the textuality of the long poem depends largely on its thematization of structural and formal devices, delay, accretion, and prolongation are also the principles that reveal, gradually, tentatively, and polyvalently, the self.

St And, then, as a sign pointing to the dedication page,[11] again foregrounds the importance of the writing act. But this is not the end of delays. Two brief stanzas precede St And's icon and the title of the first section of Book 1, 'the martyrology of St And':

the breath lies

on mornings like this
you gotta be careful
which way you piss   (Book 1)

The synecdoche of breath brings together Nichol's major concerns in
The Martyrology: speech, logos, spirit, pneuma. Yet breath, Nichol warns
us, is capable of lying. He rejects the pneumatological nature of phon-
ocentricism – the sign always turned towards God, towards a metaphysical presence – and proposes instead his grammatological[12] project, a project in which writing cuts breath short.

Although the poem is filled with speech and sound patterns, Nichol
does not intend speech to overshadow writing. Quite the contrary.
While extending the possibilities of speech towards a graphics of *phoné*
and those of writing towards a phonetics of inscription,[13] he seems to
criticize the Platonic ideology that has valued the former and condemned the latter. The reader recognizes at this point that the textual
delays of beginning in *The Martyrology* have yet another function: to
question speech and the sign, and the ways in which they privilege
the metaphysical concept of self as presence.

The main text of the poem begins to unfold with a line that further
emphasizes the thematization of beginnings and delays:

so many bad beginnings

you promise yourself
you won't start there
again

december 67

the undated poem is
found and
            forgotten

passes[14]   (Book 1)

This 'final' beginning introduces yet another genre, that of the journal,
which further foregrounds the first person, one of the most frequently
used points of view in Nichol's work.

It has become obvious by now that the textual detours that introduce the beginnings of *The Martyrology* are organic to the elliptical self. The layers of genre that Nichol works with – chronicle, oral versus written tradition, genealogy, liturgy, epigraph, journal – depend on the principle of deferral, for deferral works against the intent of traditional autobiography to pursue the totality of a unary subject. Moreover, deferral also deflects linearity, which is one of the fundamental devices employed in traditional autobiography. As Philippe Lejeune argues, '[l]e récit autobiographique traditionnel choisit comme structure principale l'ordre chronologique (avec tout ce qu'il implique d'explication "diachronique" de cause à effet), réduisant l'ordre thématique au rôle de structure secondaire à l'interieur de l'autre' (16). The textual delays beginning *The Martyrology* speak the aleatory nature of the self; the prolongation incurred, then, demonstrates the need to keep addressing the self in an attempt to get hold of its elliptical nature.

The polyphonic beginning of *The Martyrology* announces the poem's formal and thematic plurality. It enhances what Edward Said defines in *Beginnings* as the degrees of self-consciousness characterizing the opening point of a work. 'The search for such points,' Said remarks, 'not only is reflected in language, but is carried out in language and ... is necessary *because of* language. Polytechnical unlike any other human activity, language was discovered to be a suitable vehicle for posing questions of origin for purely linguistic as well as social, moral, or political reasons' (47). Nichol's long poem deals with the politics of the self, the self's wavering between revelation and concealment. If *The Martyrology* is *about* anything in particular, it is about the martyrology of the self and of language, logos being both pursuer and martyr. Logos as the sign of the self warns of the multiple linguistic and narrative structures necessary for the self's expression.

At the risk of reducing the complex notion of self in *The Martyrology*, I will argue that Nichol structures his poem around the tension between self and identity. This is achieved by the employment of the first-person pronoun – the shared ground of self and identity – as a purely linguistic construct, as the performative that actualizes the self's enunciation without assigning any eventuality to the self. Identity, in turn, is the specific configuration the self insists on assuming during its performative acts. The uniqueness of identity inheres in the repetition of compatible performative acts. Whereas the self's signifiers (pronouns, names) shift, the agent of the self's performative act initiating the shifts remains seemingly stable, bearing one name at a time (the signified, identity). The closer the self comes to achieving an identity, the more rigorously do pronouns claim to be the performatives of the self.

Nichol's deconstruction of autobiography begins with the self's zero point of origins.

> it's so far from one end to the other
> sound repeating itself beyond perfect zero
> > (Book 1, 'scenes from the lives of the saints')

The circular figure of 'perfect zero' parodies the erectness and primacy of the Cartesian ego; it points to the non-originary origins of self and language. The zero point that precedes the beginning of a writing activity is, as Said observes, 'a forbidden paradise which literacy [writing] penetrates only at the same critical moment that the paradise is being obliterated' (317–18). Nichol's 'perfect zero' dramatizes the ritual of beginning by exaggerating ritualism and therefore by parodying paradise – the innocence of the blank page. Each beginning, while starting the poem anew, falls behind its previous beginning in a *mise en abyme* configuration that expresses the impossibility of fully stating the self. This zero point of beginnings echoes the lost paradise of Nichol's saints. Paradise cannot be entered, let alone experienced, without a language that can exceed profane knowledge. Paradise is a different name for the language of transcendence and unification, the metaphysical origin of the self. In his attempt to create a genealogy of the self, Nichol employs a discourse that addresses the sacred as the origin of the self.

The poet situates his self in a paradise of a different order, a paradise of words occupying the middle ground between the non-language of transcendence and the language of the body, 'what comes forth from my mouth' (Book 3).

> this time the sky screams   BLUE
> thru a break in the clouds   high above me
> so high i cannot fly there with the mind
> the saints live   & they called it cloud town
> when they fell to earth as strangers
> wide-eyed at all this tumbling green land
> spun thru space towards their falling bodies &   caught them

SKY BLUE   the colour of saint and's eyes
taking in this surprising place he'd come to

if there is a land which is the mind
it is as brown as earth & cool there   (Book 2, 'clouds')

In its inarticulateness, the scream of the sky conveys a tentative, self-doubting meaning. The upper case of BLUE foregrounds its function as linguistic sign situated both in between and apart from the sentence because of the blank space that surrounds it. The reader is reminded of the arbitrary convention that gives the sky the quality of blue, a colour that, by extension, becomes the signifier of things celestial, of purity, sainthood. Nichol salvages language from the 'martyrdom' it has been subjected to and lets language be itself. As he puts it, 'its a good idea, at least from time to time, to let the language speak' ('Things' 132). It has to be brought down from paradise, down to 'earth,' to come into existence as linguistic utterance. Otherwise it remains untenable.

The self in *The Martyrology* is similarly untenable. It is polyphonic, protean. The fact that the 'i' in this poem is the speaking persona of Nichol's many saints, that is to say language, as well as of himself, illustrates that Nichol takes the content of the self to be not anterior to form, style, or linguistic utterance but constructed the moment it enters the field of language.

i want the absolute precision
of fluid definition
the saints learned
long ago
...
there is no definition
where you cannot see the line
of drawing
     writing
        music
the form a focus for us
i wakens from
the dreamed landscape
out of the words' tumble
should meaning separate

when it is the torrent sweeps me
thru the bound beeches   (Book 4)

'i want' asserts the presence of the self but at the same time defines
the self by its lack or the absence it suffers. The oxymoron of 'fluid
definition' locates the self within the realm of desire. The object desire
addresses is language – language as 'the line / of drawing / writing
/ music.' Nichol sees the fluidity of definition in language as graphism,
in the Derridean sense that 'there is no linguistic sign before writing'
(1976, 14). That fluidity of the self's definition delays the writing act,
thereby prolonging *The Martyrology*.[15]

That same fluidity also draws a distinction between the self and the
first-person pronoun. Here is what Nichol says about his use of pronouns:

often when I'm talking about 'I,' I'm talking about the 'I,' that is to say, your
I, his I, her I, so on ... See, to me, pronouns are more universal, that's why
I like them. I think it's harder for a general reader to identify with an 'I,' I
would agree, but I think that we get into that eventually. He, she, we – it's
looser, it isn't named. Naming, though on the one hand it claims, often distances. So in trying to deal with the reality of how we perceive and so on, I
often prefer to use pronouns. In those cases, that shift to the third person
verb is to indicate that type of usage of the word 'I.' 'I' is an interiorized
concept – in short, 'I' is inside. (1985, 41)

Nichol's use of the first-person pronoun with the third-person pred-
icate, as in his line 'i wakens,' displays both his poetics and his attitude
towards language. The 'i' in 'i wakens' does not obviously refer to the
speaking subject; 'i' functions as the name of the self, but at the same
time 'i' also speaks of the naming act that characterizes the performative function of language. 'i' as name comes before, and coincides
with, the self's manifestation, suggesting that the self as concept precedes identity and is harboured in language. In the first person, as
Benveniste says, 'there are both a person involved and a discourse
concerning that person. "I" designates the one who speaks and at the
same time implies an utterance about "I"' (197). The pronoun 'i,' then,
functions as the collective name of all the saints, Nichol himself, and
the other personae that figure in *The Martyrology*. What differentiates
them is the discourse each 'i' employs.

In 'the sorrows of saint orm' (Book 1), the 'i' is distinguished by its writing activity: 'notes in my journals / don't hold true.' The journal as genre that relates in a first-person narrative what comprises the self as an object of knowledge loses its authenticity; it becomes a genre that is defined by the poem's textuality, by the discourse of the 'i.'

> i knew when i headed home tonight
> the whole poem graphed in my mind
> i'll never make it
>
> some things are stronger than words
>
> if i could throw down this pen i never use
> then i could live my life   free of naming
>
> (Book 2, 'book of common prayer')

The break point between the poem as mental 'graph' and as writing act implies a critique of the genre of autobiography. The pen that cannot be discarded – not a pre-thought notion of the self – is what literally marks Nichol's long poem.

This graphic identity of the self is a recurring motif in *The Martyrology*. In Book 4, for instance, we read:

> style's stylus
> the fingers an extension of the mind
> ma 'nd me 'nd
>   personal history

Style inscribes the present self of the writer. It becomes his signature, the present rendering of the self. As Starobinski says, '[i]t is the image of the *stylus* with a sharp point that tends ... to prevail over that of the *hand* moved by the writer's inner spirit' (1980, 76). In this respect, the manuscript facsimiles in *The Martyrology* attract the reader's eye more than the printed pages do, not because of Nichol's writing in longhand, but because they affirm, while casting into doubt, his authorial presence. As Shirley Neuman, extending Starobinski's argument, remarks, '[s]tyle is autobiographically significant because it is attached to the writer's present ... Style carries the "truth" of autobiography' (11). Style in *The Martyrology*, then, brings together signature, mind (ma), the 'i,' and one's personal history, 'ma' (mother).

Style indeed renders as personal what the pronoun 'i' depersonalizes.

The carnivalesque atmosphere of the 'freak show' in 'the martyrology of saint and' (Book 1) accentuates the style of *The Martyrology*'s beginning. The 'maudlin' style of the clownish saints, the 'circus finally grow[ing] old & jaded,' and the poet's own apostrophe to the 'dear funny paper i write upon,' all account for the intricacies of Nichol's saints, and their erratic personalities.

Yet whereas the style of an 'i' at a given point in the poem bespeaks the identity of that 'i,' the proliferation of first-person pronouns in *The Martyrology* reflects Nichol's attempt to disperse the self as entity.

> people how i lose myself in you
> as stein saw it the difference between identity & entity
> it is so much more soothing to live with memory
>
> (Book 2, 'friends as footnotes')

Stein's concept of memory affirms the essentialism of the self, a 'soothing' affirmation in that it contextualizes the self within the already lived. But whereas Stein calls the 'element of remembering ... soothing' (181) – an attribute not to be found in 'existing,' which does not 'have in it any element of remembering' (181) – the methodological function of memory in *The Martyrology* delineates the way the poem remembers itself through its crossing and recrossing of its textual ground. *The Martyrology*'s mnemonic repetitions are far from soothing to the reader, and even less so to the poem's personae. Memory in this poem is a textual activity; it seeks to establish not sameness but labyrinthine echoes that repeat the self with difference. For, while locating the self within the familiar, memory also marks the self's very displacement from familiar territory. 'you' consumes 'i' when 'you' is taken to be a point of mnemonic reference, but 'i' retrieves its textuality when it enunciates itself during its performative act.

Memory, without remedying the essentialism of the self, forecloses the monologism of entity. As the repository of the different stages of the self, memory reveals the self's polyphonic structure. Hence Nichol's 'i' dons a series of identities. As he says,

> we move in threes
> the short statements linked to
> the worlds i live in
> hidden personal one & the same
>
> (Book 2, 'auguries')

The ambiguity of the last line indicates the totality of the self's multiplicity. Sameness does not guarantee identity, nor does it affirm the uniqueness or originality of the self. The plurality inherent in the self brings into focus one of the difficulties in reading *The Martyrology*. The poem, by resisting a unified notion of the self, also resists any reader's attempt at 'figuring' out the different selves and their interrelationships with (their) others. The distinctions Nichol draws among pronouns and his blurring of these distinctions are the reader's index to the concept of self in *The Martyrology*.

Although Nichol for the most part does away with hierarchies and patterns, there is an implicit schema in his treatment of self, that of *self: pronoun: identity*. The self lies both outside any usurping structure and within its specific configurations: the multiple identities in *The Martyrology* relate to the self syntagmatically; the pronouns perform the actions to which the identities refer.

> i am one am many
> the need to be obsesses
> simply as i would i would speak to you   (Book 2, 'auguries')[16]

'the need to be' is nothing other than the need to define one's identity, to ground the self in a singular way. At the same time that Nichol acknowledges that compelling need for definition, he also deconstructs its very intent. The 'being,' or rather the series of 'beings' we encounter in the poem, could not be defined according to ontological and metaphysical traditions; the processual 'being' in *The Martyrology*, as opposed to 'to be,' lacks substance and precision. We get only glimpses of that 'being,' its fleeting figure pointing to a supreme fiction. The 'being' in *The Martyrology* is *en voyage*, destabilized; the poet is a *homo viator*. 'i am one am many' does not leave room for any specific identity to take over. Bordering on the 'father's' sacred discourse – 'you are the one / the unifying / no signifier when we cannot grasp the signified' (Book 3) – 'being' defies immanence precisely because it resides in language. The very length of *The Martyrology* testifies to the self's desire 'to be' (in) language.

Thus, although *The Martyrology* is narrated predominantly in the first person, its point of view does not simply express one identity or one condition of the self. 'i am one am many' is the absent marker, the gap where the war between dissemination (intrinsic to the self) and totalization (extrinsic to the self) takes place. The hiatus between 'i am' and 'am many' connects and separates, delimits and extends the different configurations of the self, thereby showing how *The Martyrology* privileges the self while subverting it. This resistance to a reified self operates against the autobiographical impulse in *The Martyrology*. If the traditional notion of autobiography as genre takes for granted the existence of a single identity, its aim, then, as measure of its success, is to put together the disparate identities of the self. *The Martyrology* defies the unified self as well as the pure genre.

Because no speaker, no writer – or reader, for that matter – can do away with the pronoun 'i,' Nichol recognizes the necessity to expand its function. His constant shifts from 'i' to other pronouns are meant to elaborate the operations of the 'i.'

> saint of no-names
> king of fools
> the days are spent in piecing things together
> the night's strewn with pages you do not remember writing
> third person to first person
> am i the fool
> sick of everything i've written
> fascinated by my own distaste
> keep placing one letter in front of another
> pacing my disillusionment   (Book 3)

No matter what pronoun for the moment Nichol privileges, he cannot get away from discourse, nor can he ever as writer and speaker get rid of the 'i.' His fascination with and distaste for the writing 'i' are not mutually exclusive. By measuring his writing process through the rearrangement of the arbitrary order of the alphabet into a series of letters that signify by themselves, he realizes that the materiality of language composes the narrative of his 'i.'[17]

The apostrophic mode of *The Martyrology* is one of the primary rhetorical tropes Nichol employs in order to establish the economy of his language and to counter the monologic 'i.' Whether the 'i' addresses its other as 'you,' or whether it addresses a 'you' other than itself, its rhetoric of apostrophe marks, as Culler would say, the 'proximity and distance' (1981, 137) that inform the self's reflexivity and referentiality. As Benveniste observes, 'one characteristic of the persons "I" and "you" is their specific "oneness": the "I" who states, the "you" to whom "I" addresses himself are unique each time ... A second characteristic is that "I" and "you" are reversible: the one whom "I" defines by "you" thinks of himself as "I" and can be inverted into "I," and "I" becomes a "you"' (199). The intersubjectivity of the 'i' illuminates Nichol's interplay of identities. The reversibility of 'i' and 'you' points to the self's intertextuality. Intertextuality preempts the 'i,' and dispossesses it of its constitutive identity by continuously recontextualizing it. Hence the ensuing reversibility of the functions of the 'you': 'i fear you think me strange / you lacks meaning for me / becoming them' (Book 3). Here, 'you' serves as the decoder of the apostrophic act; but it also ceases to be the second person. It becomes the third party that is being discussed, what 'lacks meaning' and reference, and therefore what puts the utterance of the 'i' under erasure.

The early stages of the self in *The Martyrology* are those of a self realized and questioned through mirrors. The mirror as a 'figure' stands in the middle ground, between self and identity.

> the part of yourself least recognized
> merges with the mirror
> your fingers do not know your skin   (Book 2, 'auguries')

The fingers' own unfamiliar skin suggests that there is nothing in the mirror to be fully grasped or recognized, that there is an alienating element innate in the self. The mirror images does not provide an instance of *déjà vu*; it draws a figure of the self's other, which spells out the self's continuous defacement.[18]

> i remember now that i remember nothing ...
>
> who takes me as i am
> not this self confronts me in the mirror   (Book 2, 'auguries')

Nichol's mirror, unlike the Lacanian mirror, does not offer 'recognition.' Lacan's 'mirror stage,' during which the child experiences 'in a flutter of jubilant activity' a 'transformation' that helps it identify itself as a co-ordinated being, is clearly not in operation here (1977, 1–2). In Nichol's poem, mirrors are not a source of jubilation, for the specular image the self sees in them results in no recognition of itself or its other. When the specular image unveils an otherness that terrifies, as in 'look in the mirror / knowing you have found the beast' (Book 2, 'auguries'), it becomes clear that mirrors in *The Martyrology* parody the unity of the self. They reveal the other as beast, what Lacan calls *méconnaissance*. But, according to Lacan, *méconnaissance* ('failure to recognize,' 'misconstruction') is always related to *connaissance* ('knowledge') (1977, x–xi).

'auguries' of Book 2 focuses exactly on that tension between the certainty and doubt self-knowledge provides. All the occurrences of 'now' and 'know' in this section engage in battle. The 'now,' which represents the tense of the poem's grammar, works against an achronic, absolute point of self-knowledge. The seriality of knowledge to which 'now' points designates the seriality of the self. The poet's imperative is: 'live in the present / it is all around you.'

> of those things we understand this is the greatest mystery
> knowledge deceives us
> believing we move in our lostness purposefully
> discover new worlds as and did
> knowing nothing he came to that place saint rike now lives in
>
> > (Book 2, 'auguries')

The phonetic proximity of 'now' and 'know,' amplified by the alliteration of 'new' and 'nothing,' dramatizes the impossibility of fully 'knowing ... now,' thereby announcing that the self is unreadable; 'knowledge deceives us,' the speaker reminds us. The 'now' dissolves the power with which knowledge fixes on the self. The moment-by-moment construction and deconstruction of self puts forward a lack of identity: 'you are the mirror of what you deny' (Book 2, 'sons and divinations'). The gap between mirror and self, that physical distance necessary for the mirrored image, conveys the unnameability of the self. The specular image in the mirror accentuates the self's dispersal and further emphasizes this lack.

But Nichol does not stop at this; he also questions the medium of dispersal, the speculum itself.

> I preferred St And a clown
> human & vulnerable
> critical of stupid posturing
> absurd hierarchies he'd left behind ...
> lived on

```
isolate among the many
his face mirrored in the air
he gazed into & fell
self into self
narcosis of narcissus
wandered then
lost among men
the full pain of his loss haunting him                    (Book 4)
```

St And, his name a signifier of the connecting ground he occupies, experiences only disconnection. His public and symbolic roles as saint do not help him to stand opposite or beside himself. For him there is no other to look at. When he gazes at the ethereal mirror, it is not self-love he feels; rather, the specular image he looks at is one of emptiness and loss, the figure of the abyss itself. The other as the object of self-love recedes into slumber. The self resists its own reflexivity and refers to its inexactness, its desire to proliferate beyond a single other.

Consequently, the mirror in *The Martyrology*, far from offering illusions of identity, emphatically presents recognition as a kind of blindness and reductiveness – 'the thinner man confronts you in the mirror' (Book 2, 'sons and divinations'). The mirror fails to fulfil its function as locus for a precise figuration of the self; instead of offering a space that inspires and contains representation, it reflects the tentative – and temporal – nature of identity. It becomes the rhetorical ground within which *The Martyrology* explores the multiplicity of the self.

We can trace the plural nature of the self in the linear and jagged patterns of Nichol's writing process:

```
(i moved during the course of this writing, interrupting the patterns,
jarring at first because i found myself, ten years later, back in the same
house i'd lived in during the writing of 1335 Comox (poem that began
JOURNEYING & THE RETURNS (whose form was perceived after i moved
away from there (from here))) the dilemma being i found myself caught
up in a) mirror image                                      (Book 4)
```

Nichol maps out his writing process by situating it within the layers of his past and present. The open structure of his poem tentatively establishes patterns of repetition – designedly recurring with difference in all volumes of *The Martyrology* – and also mirrors the self's dissemination. Yet Nichol gazes at these mirrors only fleetingly. His act of writing, while displacing the speculum as well as what the speculum momentarily images, becomes the parameter by which he can 'find himself.' The writer as his own reader – his first reader, indeed – creates instead a textual mirror, ribbon-shaped, that scrolls the self. The mirror image of Nichol's writing and reading activities lies outside the bracketing of self-recognition: 'from there (from here))).' Thus mirror and text function as both content and context of the self, but they never present the self in its totality.

Nichol's own 'i' in *The Martyrology* undergoes the harshest questioning, the most relentless displacement:

> this poem becomes a diary of a journey
> personal it evolved impersonally
> a longing as i will say must say please
> saint rand stranded in that strange place
> how would you call it
> 'a problem of resolution'?
> as tho the 'i' the writer of these poems
> controlled your destiny   (Book 2, 'sons and divinations')

The impersonality of Nichol's 'i' corresponds to the formal tension between his personal journey and his impersonal rendering of it, thereby foregrounding the compositional principles of his poem. Self and genre are intertextually related. Nichol's questioning of the 'i' inadvertently destabilizes genre as well as his own authorial/authoritative intrusions. To remedy the monologic 'i' Nichol moves to the pronoun 'we.'

> we's a long way away some days
> there's so much i
> you rise from bed aware of your collectivity
> no sense of one to move towards we from
> carry yourself over water
> forgetting it is your own bones you sail upon
> settle the shores of lakes
> we do forget we   (Book 3)

Nichol's propensity for the 'we' can be partly explained by its stronger rhetorical, and therefore persuasive, function. 'so much i' names the self in relation to 'we.' By evoking Christ as the (absent) name of 'we,'

Nichol establishes the universality and spiritual locus of the 'we' while erasing the distance between Christ's godly and human sides: '*forgetting it is your own bones you sail upon*' (my emphases).[19] As the conscious and unconscious context of 'i,' 'we' puts a halt to the claim for sovereignty made by the 'i.'

> the i is always
> clear it's just the we
> forcing a retreat to memory
> i define myself too often by what went before
>
> (Book 2, 'friends as footnotes')

Memory as the collective context of 'we' disseminates the self, thus revising its singularity and making 'clear' its plural nature. 'this is how the false "i" ends' (Book 3), Nichol says, referring to the 'we' threatening to dissolve the frames the 'i' draws.

Yet Nichol's deconstruction of 'i' does not simply rely on the universality implicit in 'we.'

> no 'i' stands alone
> its base is 'we'
> all the universe embodied in that term   (Book 3)

The universe embodied here is not just humanity, although it includes that. More specifically, it is the uni-verse, writing and its intertextuality. Nichol reverses the constitutive structure of 'we' as Benveniste defines it: '[t]he presence of "I" is constitutive of "we"' (202). Nichol argues instead that 'we,' besides functioning as the context for 'i,' is in fact what constitutes 'i.' The relationship between the 'i' and 'we' is no longer one of extension and accretion, for the plurality of 'we' does not consist exclusively of a series of 'i's. For Nichol, 'we' is not what Derrida calls 'the human *genre*, a genre of all that is in general' (1980, 56). The 'i' participates in 'we' but is not absorbed by it.

The difference of the 'i' resides in the id of identity. The 'i,' being both intrinsic and extrinsic to the 'we,' often becomes in *The Martyrology* a formless form, a pronoun without a person, thus engendering a genre without a genre.

> i am afraid of writing something which does not end
>   as we does not

> only the link which is i
> to be replaced
> other i's to see thru   (Book 3)

The incompleteness of the 'we,' its limitless content, is both liberating and terrifying. The 'i' is only a link to the textuality of 'we,' a boundary without a frame. The 'something' Nichol is 'afraid of' is precisely the martyrology of the self, inclusive and inconclusive at the same time as its namesake poem is.

The 'we,' then, marks the palindromic movement of the self in the poem:

> there is a we
>   different   the same
> link us in the law language comprehends
> i have to trust to carry me thru into somewhere
> ...
>
>   a we that lacks connections   (Book 3)

Because of the difference and sameness of what makes *The Martyrology* both reflexive and referential, the poem's elongation establishes an inward and, at the same time, an outward unfolding. Outwardly, *The Martyrology* extends to encompass everything that constitutes the self, incorporating within its body those genres conducive to the self, such as the journal and hagiography. Inwardly, it spirals within its textual locus as it follows 'the law' of language, a law that is being constituted simultaneously with the poem's composition.

These two intertextually related movements illustrate that the genre of this long poem is not 'something' arbitrarily assigned to it, or designed independently from it. Genre in *The Martyrology* is not just a formal matter. As Derrida says, genre 'covers the motif of the law in general, of generation in the natural and symbolic senses, of birth in the natural and symbolic senses, of the generation difference, sexual difference between the feminine and masculine genre/gender, of the hymen between the two, of a relationless relation between the two, of an identity and difference between the feminine and masculine' (1980, 74). Self and genre in *The Martyrology* often figure as each other's substitutes and supplements. In Nichol's words, 'it is the parallels & not the differences confuse us' (Book 3). The elliptical grammar of this sentence/line marks the impossibility of fully delineating self and genre as a couple graphing the same line.

Gender and self, genre and identity, genealogy and history are interwoven with the linguistic signs of *The Martyrology*. Self and genre, the 'i' and *The Martyrology* as a long poem, are bound by a paradoxical logic that the reader cannot subvert. To subvert it would mean to evoke the law of logos, to make sense out of the senseless.

<pre>
                 a complete thot
       born from the dialogue between you
       or what comes forth from my mouth
       born from the woman in me
       handed down thru my grandma ma & lea
       is what marks me most a man
       that i am finally this we
       this one & simple thing
       my father Leo
       my mother Cancer
                        she births herself
       the twin mouths of women
                          w's omen
       it turns over & reverses itself
       the mirrors cannot trick us
       our words are spun within the signs our fathers left
       the sibilance of s
                      the cross of t
       ...
                    the sign complete
       the w & the circle   turning
       add the E
                    the three levels
       linked by line
                        or the two fold vision
       H to I
              the saints returned to this plane
</pre>

(Book 3)

Nichol locates the self in his poem as a centre that constantly teases its own centrality, and as an origin that blurs origins and originality. This double position, an indication of desire, is the only absolute sign in *The Martyrology*: a 'poem of / perfect movement / containment of / the flux' (Book 4).

RE-SIGNING THE POEM: GEORGE BOWERING AND DENNIS COOLEY

Whereas *The Martyrology* refutes the self as presence, in George Bowering's *Kerrisdale Elegies* and Dennis Cooley's *Bloody Jack* the self is present as signature. More than a signed name, signature relates to the operations between proper names and common nouns, between words and things.[20] As the author is written into the text she or he writes, so signature functions as a sign that oscillates between the author's presence and absence in the text. Signing, then, records the various ways in which an author is inscribed in a text; it also accounts for the author's use of, and departure from, traditional genres. The authorial signature in *Kerrisdale Elegies* and *Bloody Jack* has a transgressive function that interrelates to the various generic modes the poets employ. Bowering and Cooley's writing is both an imitation of existing genres and a transgression of their principles. This parallel writing act is accomplished by interrupting the continuity that validates genre, by apostrophizing what the poets imitate. Their apostrophes, performed at the level of authorial signature, refer to the authors themselves as well as to the cultural and literary texts they parody.

Given the long poem's resistance to definition, there is a certain appropriateness in the fact that the covers of both *Kerrisdale Elegies* and *Bloody Jack* show facial images creating illusions of proximity. In *Kerrisdale Elegies* the cover image is the face of the author wearing dark glasses. The ragged edges of its frame simulate the double texture of a torn photograph, the texture of glossy and rough paper (a manuscript page of writing?). The torn top of the photograph exceeds its margin, threatening to erase Bowering's name: the author's visage is foregrounded; his name is held in disbelief. The reader is faced with the double bind of signature, the naming of an absent presence.

Cooley wanted a 'stylized icon' of himself on the cover of his book,[21] but his publishers did not go along with that. What we see is an indistinct face – the 'pale spectacle' of historical Krafchenko taken from a newspaper photograph, a dissolved identity becoming an anonymous icon. It is a face that is more of an outline than a concrete image in which 'we can read / inklings of' the author,[22] the surface of a palimpsest where both character and poet blend into each other. A face in a stage of collapsing, receding into the poem, 'a book by Dennis Cooley.'

While both authors hold a pose, their long poems sign themselves on the covers as specific instances of different genres: that of the elegy and that of the book. Yet, as is the case in many long poems, the readily identifiable genres of the elegy and the book are not the sole parameters designating the generic character of *Kerrisdale Elegies* and *Bloody Jack*. The reader can take for granted only a number of elements when dealing with these poems. Two books (two faces): two long poems ('an encyclopedia of genres'[23]): one reader (the viewer). The reader of these two poems finds herself caught in the perennial triangle of the story of desire. Each face presents me with the 'organ' I need in order to see it, to touch it; they give me the 'eye' and the 'ear' through which I can read them.[24] These facial images, the textual masks of the poets, initiate a series of paradoxes between themselves and their referentiality. Beginning with their parodic self-portraits on the covers, Bowering and Cooley imitate the tropes of the genres they employ; but at the same time they practise a mimesis that unwrites the style of these tropes. The intertextuality of the generic interplay in the two poems points to an erotics of reading: the poets as faithful or adulterous readers – reading, misreading, plagiarizing.[25] What reconciles the heterogeneous activities within these long poems is the intertextuality of the authors' signatures. If these authors' fixed images fail to seduce me, the translation of the authorial image into signature does not.

The authorial signature in *Kerrisdale Elegies* and *Bloody Jack* that begins to assert itself on the covers supplements the dialogue of genres in these long poems. The signature not only authorizes the deployment of diverse genres; it thematizes genre while presenting signing as yet another form of writing. '*How can one cite a signature?*' Derrida asks; '[*t*]*he signature spreads over everything, but is stripped off or makes itself take off* ...' (1984, 150). Through the authorial signature writing becomes rewriting, autographing, a constant revising (reviewing) of the long poem's discursive field. It allows digressions; it changes the direction of our reading, as Gregory L. Ulmer says, between 'the author-text relation' thus 'allowing contamination between the inside and outside' (21, 63). The authorial signature, in other words, disseminates in these poems not only the poets' presence but also their act of writing.

This multiple signing enables Bowering and Cooley to play hide-and-seek with their readers. They make brief appearances: the poet as flesh, as desire incarnate, as the one who enters where I as a reader, to 'misquote' Bowering, 'have been but can never enter' (43). The reader is invited to share a slice of life, those fragments that become poetry. The authorial signature foregrounds the presence of the reader in the text while, at the same time, putting this presence under erasure. I'm there, in the text, but at the same time I'm constantly put on hold.

Bowering:

> If I did complain, who among my friends
> would hear?
>   If one of them
> amazed me with an embrace
> he would find his arms empty, his own face
> staring from a mirror.   (9)

Love me / love me not, says Bowering's picture. Love my text, the flesh of my life.

> Beauty is the first prod of fear,
>   we must
> live our lives in.
>   We reach for her,
> we think we love her, because she holds the knife
> a knife-edge from our throat.
>   Every fair heart
> is frightful.
>   Every rose petal
> exudes poison in bright sunlight.   (9)

Love the terror of beauty, the image says; make a home for yourself, reader, at this knife-edge space.

>   She says
> I've got you under my skin, yes, she says
> you walk with me wherever I go,
>   you are
> the weather.

>   I reply with a call for help,
> I'm disappearing,
>   there's a change in the weather.   (25)

Love me if you can, if you can really afford it, it says. I nearly can.
I can only if I let 'you' steal my subjectivity, my strategies as reader.
Only if I steal 'your' glasses covering what is already hiding within
the pages of the book. Only if I let the mirror image ('his face') erase
my gender, become the neutral reader who objectifies these textual
slices of life. It is the 'I' of the cover image speaking – not the author
– its life assuming the physical reality of language, being affirmed by
the signature of the writer. Bowering threatens to disappear when the
weather changes, when the reader threatens to get too close.

Although Bowering remains nameless in the poem, his signature is
disseminated by place names and images: Kerrisdale is the name of
his Vancouver neighbourhood; street references are to the same area;
he has been in Duino and some of the other Italian locations he refers
to; he is a baseball fan and has written about baseball, both in his
poetry and in his fiction; there are allusions to some of his favourite
poets, such as Shelley, H.D., Robin Blaser, and Jack Spicer,[26] as well
as references to his own *A Short Sad Book* (1977). The signature is no
longer the author's proper name but has become a metonymy. As
Derrida observes, '[t]he *rebus* signature, the metonymic or anagram-
matic signature, these are the condition of possibility and impossibility.
The *double bind* of a signature event. As if the thing (or the common
name of the thing), ought to absorb the proper, to drink it and to
retain it in order to keep it. But, in the same stroke, by keeping,
drinking, and absorbing it, it is as if the thing (or its name) lost or
soiled the proper name' (1984, 64). The signature as common name
writes the poet into his text while also marking his departure from it,
becoming thus a countersignature. The writer's departure – his de-
composition that erases the strictures of the dialectic presence/absence
– is one of the markers of the elegiac tone of the poem.

>   God, there goes another breath,
> and I go with it,
>   I was further from my grave
> two stanzas back, I'm human.
>   Will the universe
> notice my unattached molecules drifting thru?

Will the dead poets notice our lines appearing among them,
or are their ears filled with their own music?   (26–7)

When the author-in-the-text asserts he is dead, when his friends' arms
reach towards him to embrace only air, when his lines appear written
over and in between the lines of a dead poet, Rainer Maria Rilke, it
is his signature that survives this death incurred in language, that post-
humously, postwriterly, keeps him absorbed as a non-proper name in
the text.

The translation of Bowering's signature into countersignature is the
first marker that designates *Kerrisdale Elegies* as a counterfeit of Rilke's
Duino Elegies. And it is not only the title of Bowering's poem that points
to *Duino Elegies*. A comparison of Bowering's text to any English translation of Rilke's *Elegies* will testify that Bowering's long poem is a palimpsest, his own text superimposed on Rilke's text. It doesn't really
matter what specific translations Bowering used.[27] What matter are
the ways in which Rilke is re-cited, countersigned, in the site of Bowering's text. Here is an example from the fourth elegy.
Rilke:

Even when fully intent on one thing,
we feel another's costly tug. Hostility
is second nature to us. Having promised
one another distance, hunting, and home,
don't lovers always cross each other's boundaries?   (Rilke 1977, 27)

Bowering:

I follow one scent,
                    sure of my appetite,
but am distracted by a crossing spoor.
                                        My nature
is torn,
        I am a trespasser,
                            I promised to
steer clear,
            stay in my own territory,
                                        but love
makes intruders,
                I am not I here,

                              but the burglar
of your past.   (52)

There is as much sameness as there is difference between these two
texts. The sameness violates the distance that is traditionally promised
between an original source and a text derived from it. But this sameness is 'translated' into difference as misrepresentation when Bowering
alters *Duino Elegies* in ways that thematize his misappropriation of Rilke's
text. *Duino Elegies* is also violated by the form of Bowering's text –
that is, the visual rendering of Rilke's *Elegies* in *Kerrisdale Elegies*. Nonetheless, Bowering does not intend to erase Rilke's signature from the
Elegies,[28] for his long poem is inscribed by the games of textual desire:
the mating of text with stolen text; the mating of poet with poet. The
poet, then, as thief of words. He is a thief created by the object that
inspires the theft – the poem that expropriates itself from the singularity of authorship, that liberates itself from monologic existence;
a thief exonerating himself for the stealing of text by using his signature – a double signature at that; a thief appropriating origins and
mocking originality by stealing in the name of writing.

The games Bowering plays with origins point to an erotics of intertextuality. *Kerrisdale Elegies* identifies itself with *Duino Elegies*, but
this is an identification that has to be perceived with critical difference.
Yet the intertextuality observed here is one that involves not merely
allusion or transference of certain signifying forces from one text into
another but mimesis as translation and simultaneous alteration of these
forces.[29] The presence of authorial signature reminds the reader of
the dynamics that gravitate Bowering's text towards Rilke's and that
determine the extent of influence, namely the interdependence of these
texts as well as their autonomy. The intertextual movement is accomplished through transference by alteration and variation, a transference based on sameness as well as difference; it signals the dialogue
between these texts and the respective genres they employ with greater
precision, while its emerging semantic configurations evoke the diversity of the dialogic play at work. This kind of intertextuality designedly indicates an exchange (expropriation), the otherness of text,
the shifting of text in alternating contexts, a shift and change that
often involve corruption of origins, deviation from an original/ori-
ginary point.

Bowering's deviations from Rilke's text do not erase the original;
they alter it while maintaining the 'crossing spoors' that affirm not

only the sameness that binds the two poems but also Bowering's writing steps that make his own poem differ from Rilke's. The intertextual construction that informs Bowering's writing act produces a text of marginal differences, a text of *differance*. For if *Kerrisdale Elegies* is a 'translation,' it is an annotated 'translation,' the annotations being Bowering's appropriation of the marginal space and the space between the lines of *Duino Elegies*.

The infidelities that the reader notices in Bowering's 'translation' of *Duino Elegies* operate exactly on the level of intertextual expropriation: he remains faithful to the fundamental structure, imagery, and ideas of *Duino Elegies* by stealing and appropriating them in his own text through rewriting. One could, of course, explain this appropriation by pointing out that Bowering relocates *Duino Elegies* in Vancouver; yet the changes incurred by this relocation do not account for *Kerrisdale Elegies*' composition. For Bowering alters (adulterates) the form, the language, and many of Rilke's allusions. Linos, for instance, to whom Rilke refers in the end of the first elegy, is translated in *Kerrisdale Elegies* as Marilyn Monroe. Bowering maintains the mythological allusion but translates it in contemporary terms. From the myth about a pagan figure we move to the stardom of Hollywood, to Marilyn who is, as Bowering says, 'the stuff our words are made from' (20). Linos in Rilke's poem is a double signature: it stands for a mournful song; it is also the name of a young man whose life assumes three mythic configurations, two of them related to Apollo – Apollo as Linos' father avenging the death of his son, and Apollo as the god of song punishing Linos for transgressing his human limits as singer.[30] Both signatures of Linos identify the genre of the poem as elegy and raise questions regarding the nature of origins and transgression. Marilyn Monroe's life has similarly evolved into a myth that is still being rewritten.

Bowering's compositional strategies rely on parallelism, the setting side by side of two poems, thus further enunciating the degree of sameness and difference between *Kerrisdale Elegies* and *Duino Elegies*. His writing is an act of mimesis – mimesis, however, in Gérard Genette's sense of forgery: 'la forgerie est l'imitation en régime sérieux, dont la fonction dominante est la poursuite ou l'extension d'un accomplissement littéraire préexistant' (1982, 92). During this mimetic act as 'forgery,' Bowering also imitates (writes into the poem) the writing process he is engaged in. The poet as trespasser is, again, the common name as signature, but this time it is a signature that thematizes the question of genre in this long poem. But if plagiarizing Rilke's text is an aesthetic si(g)n that stigmatizes *Kerrisdale Elegies* with the double signatures of Rilke and Bowering, it is a si(g)n that Bowering is far from ignoring. '[B]ut love / makes intruders, 'he says; 'I am not I here, / but the burglar / of your past' (52). Bowering's apostrophe is to the figure of the lover; but, given the erotics of intertextuality in his poem, his apostrophe may also be directed towards Rilke. Love effaces the writing poet as origin, as the single maker of the poem; it presents the poet as his intertextual (other) self, as a 'burglar' who cannot extract himself from the tradition. He is 'playing house with' (12) the textuality of writing. '[T]hrowing' his proper 'name away' (18), writing himself over (making love to) Rilke's poem, the poet as lover and thief emerges from within the text of another poet in the car-nivalesque paradise of his own text: 'Upstairs with my toys – a pen, some lined paper, / my books open around me' (58). Bowering's sig-nature and countersignature present his long poem as the hiatus of text as source and text as the intertextual other of that source.

The same principle of mimesis as forgery operates in Dennis Cooley's poem.

you have my word

        periodically
they think
they have me
where they want me
that theyve got me
typed ...
lines laid out

...

but i dont
pause dont even
hesitate where they
make the signs

...

... i live in the gaps beneath thot
believe in the invisible gasps under print
i learn to hold my breath

hold my breath
in envelopes of air
refuse to be taken in
i am guerrilla of brackets
you cant see me on the page
whited out in your eyes
...

if you dont keep watch
i will surface under your faces
...

from the edges where you
would gloss me over
write me out of existence
i will shout
to you hard
of hearing
...

that is why
to find me
you must read be
tween the lines   (16–18)

'You have my word,' the poet says, hiding behind his words, talking himself out of the text, inside the text, bracketing his presence, making the reader an accomplice of this war between presence and absence. You have my word, the poet says, and he breaks his promise, breaks away from the reader's hold, as he translates his words into plural meaning, warding off definition. And he surfaces under my face: he translates his act of writing into the reading act, reading under his own face, under my nose, delaying the performance of my own reading by stealing my privilege as reader, by inscribing my reading in his text.

Dennis Cooley's transgression of his writing role breaks the laws that control aesthetic decorum. He's 'laying down the law' (52) that there are no limits for the writing and reading acts alike. It is a law signed by him in script, 'yes truly Dennis Cooley' (146), countersigned by his main character, the Ukrainian outlaw Krafchenko, signed repeatedly by the poet's own inventions of himself. 'For the law as it stands neither you nor I have any responsibility' (49). This lawless law informs the design of the whole book. *Bloody Jack* could be described as a documentary poem about a Ukrainian bandit, persecuted by the Winnipeg police force and loved by the Ukrainian community in Winnipeg in the 1910s. Cooley gives his primary sources in the beginning of the poem. Yet he supersedes the documents at hand and meanders through a web of genres, and of authentic and forged documents. One of his epigraphs is by Julia Kristeva talking about Menippean satire, which she defines as an 'all-inclusive genre.'[31] This sums up the documentary nature of *Bloody Jack*. Far from being a document about a specific criminal – whom some of the public nevertheless saw as a Robin Hood figure thus parodying the law – *Bloody Jack* becomes a document of the generic interplay that characterizes the long poem. One might argue that *Bloody Jack* is about the poet's dream of living in the margins: the lover and poet as outlaw.

The lawlessness that Cooley advocates is primarily realized by *Bloody Jack*'s encompassing genre, that of the book. The main intent of *Bloody Jack* as a book is to foreground the material – language – it is made of. '*Jack's dictionary of cunning linguists*' gives a clear sense of how Cooley uses language:

radical: in a hot bed of activity ...
marginal: involved in split decisions ...
thorough: doesn't want to leave anything out ...
optimistic: believes s/he is making head way ...
reformed: gets a weight off his shoulders ...
divine: she brings down the world on his head ...
promiscuous: has a loose tongue ...
traditional: is above that sort of thing ...   (118–19)

The body of language as the mat(t)er of the book is in constant dialogue with the author who fathers the book. The semantic distortions of the words, while affirming Cooley's playfulness and the erotics of his writing, challenge the concept of definition itself. *Bloody Jack* is presented as a book both in an empirical and a generic sense, but it is a book that defines its bookness intertextually. If the book, as Maurice Blanchot says, is a 'vehicle of knowledge ... [that] receives and gathers a given determinate form of knowledge' (1981, 146), then *Bloody Jack* as a book – dedicated 'to Penny,' a fictional character and a muse / writing figure – becomes its other, what Blanchot calls 'the absence of the book.' '*The absence of the book* revokes all continuity of presence, just as it evades the questioning conveyed by the book. It is not the interiority of the book, nor its continuously evaded Meaning. Rather it is outside the book, though it is enclosed in it, not so much its exterior as a reference to an outside that does not concern the book' (1981, 147). *Bloody Jack* foregrounds itself as an empirical book, complete with an 'appendix.' This is its last paragraph:

> Perhaps, dear reader, you would like to remove this appendix. Go ahead, just cut it out. You always wanted to be a doctor, here's your chance. Be careful to cut neatly so the body will not be mutilated and the scar will not be conspicuous enough to affect the resale value of the book or to ruin your practice. Perhaps, if you are lucky, you will nick Cooley's conscience, his mind there on the margins, in the gutter. Go ahead, take it out on him.   (237)

The book as an empirical artifice seeks to undo its own physicality, talks about itself as if it were an other, seeks to meet with its absence. It is the author, however – or more precisely his signature – that is implicated in the book's death wish.

Bloody Jack in order to be sustained as a book needs its author's name. But the name of the author loses its authority as it becomes a deictic signifier on the book's cover designating the title: 'a book by Dennis Cooley: *Bloody Jack*.' The author does not present himself here: he is presented instead by the (his) writing act; he is positioned in the third person. Benveniste tells us that 'the "third person" is not a "person"; it is really the verbal form whose function is to express the *non-person* ... Indeed, it is always used when the person is not designated and especially in the expression called impersonal' (198, 199). In this respect, while the book appropriates Cooley's signature, the author remains absent as a person – his presence being further neutralized by the passive context of the third person, 'a book *by* Dennis Cooley.' The book and the author become each other's metonymies, two figures existing only through the effects of signature. The book reaches out beyond its margins and its physical body towards its absent other, whereas the author disappears as a person in order to reappear as a character with the same name, a character who both reflects and deflects the author. The destabilization of the author's presence is primarily announced by the single occurrence of his actual signature in the context of which the conventional 'yours truly ...' is inscribed in longhand in such a way that it can also be read as 'yes truly ...' (146).

Signing as writing, while destabilizing language and its signification by virtue of the individual configurations of handwriting, becomes an affirmation of the positioning of the 'I' – 'yes truly Dennis Cooley' – a 'yes,' however, that deconstructs the logocentric positions of language and self as well as the logocentrism of interpretation.

In '*high drama*,' for example, a playwright with the name Dennis Cooley has a hard time making his characters/actors follow the script he has composed for them:

> COOLEY (*to you, dear reader*) Why don't they make love? (*to them*) Hay!
> What are you doing? (*they look up, discovered*) I want you to make love.
> I'm pretty disappointed in you characters, especially you Krafchenko ...
> KRAFCHENKO (*recovered*) Butt out buddy. It's none of your business.
> (*Kraf & Penny begin to kiss. Defiant, then lost in it. Cooley looks angry & impatient.*)
> COOLEY ... According to the script, Kraf, you get yr ass outa here.
> Then Penny is supposed to make a play for me. I wrote it that way. A clear case of textual authority. Of my authority. My authorization ...
>
> (222)

By dramatizing the relationship between signing and writing (penning), Cooley as a writer playing with language both affirms and undoes his authority. In another instance, in '*the obligatorylongawaited poem in which the hero | speaks from the grave thots thick with gumbo*,' it is Krafchenko himself who talks about the writer's authority and who foregrounds the self-conscious use of genre:

> yes yes well i spose cooley
> was a grave robber all along
> wasnt he
>
> this comes from
> knowing Foucault
> I told him so myself
>
> & I spose I wulnt [*sic*] even get a peep in here if cooley
> wasnt interested in some kind of parody ...   (231)

These references to Dennis Cooley as *play*wright and as poet still maintain the proper name of the author as person but they are not to be considered autobiographical. This illustrates what Ulmer calls autography, a form of writing that 'transforms the proper name into a thing, into a rebus' (132). Autography in *Bloody Jack* points to the deconstruction and the dissemination of the authorial self. The author's signature is the centre of the book's puzzle, but it is a centre lying off-centre, refusing to be given a single configuration, a definitive interpretation. The signature in the text imitates the subject of the proper name, inscribing the author within his own inscription.

It is this same function of the signature, together with the multiple genres that Cooley uses and his excessive use of punning, that brings *Bloody Jack* as a book closer to its absent other. *Bloody Jack* falls apart, disorders itself, and pre(post)scribes into its body the responses it expects to generate as a published book: 'Dear Editor, I for one am not in the least amused by Dennis Cooley's writings. And I know from talking to others that they have had it up to here with all this filthy language,' says a Mrs Agnes Klassen (89). The book outdistances itself; it denounces its bookness by taking over its own margins. As Blanchot says, '[s]eul importe le livre, tel qu'il est, loin des genres, en dehors des rubriques, prose, poésie, roman, témoignage, sous lesquelles il refuse de se ranger et auxquelles il dénie le pouvoir de lui fixer sa place et de déterminer sa forme. Un livre n'appartient plus à un genre' (1959, 243–4). *Bloody Jack* as a book explodes its frame by displaying its anatomy. 'Have you no sense of anatomy?' the 'cunning linguist' asks (84). But the genreless genre of *Bloody Jack*, its deconstructed anatomy, offers only intimations of its absent other. Blanchot remarks: 'How long will it last – this lack that is sustained by the book and that expels the book from itself as book? Produce the book, then, so that it will detach itself, disengage itself as it scatters: this will not mean that you have produced *the absence of the book*' (1981, 149). Dennis Cooley does not produce 'the absence of the book,' but internalizes in his discourse the absence that he cannot write in. His signature as proper name and as the name behind his exaggerating use of puns countersigns this absence. *Bloody Jack*'s content is, ultimately, what it cannot contain.

Both in Bowering's *Kerrisdale Elegies* and Cooley's *Bloody Jack*, the authorial signature validates the act of stealing, the appropriation of other texts and genres. Stealing in the open from another text or within the author's own text is to be seen as an act of denying originality, of merging the beginning of a poem with the beginning of poetry, of dissolving the frame of a book. It is the poet as thief – as criminal – who can immerse himself totally in writing and can marginalize his own book. The admixture of diverse genres in the long poem is a double signal: it challenges the classic law that argues for the purity of genre, and it recommends what Derrida calls 'the limitless field of general textuality' (1980, 210). If this 'general textuality' creates the impression of generic or formal chaos, it is the chaos of carnival we find in bpNichol's cloudtown, in the escapades of Cooley (alias Krafchenko). The authorial signature, the proper name as frame of property and agent of interruptions, validates these long poems as rites both affirming and questioning the tradition. The coming together of self and genre discloses the self's susceptibility to the play of rhetoric, draws the ineluctable limits of its subjectivity, and intercepts its epistemology.

5

Outlawed Narrative:
Michael Ondaatje

Now we've discovered the true newness
of the broken world
of discourse ...

Sharon Thesen, *The Beginning of the Long Dash*

'For life,' he said, 'I am a page of writing. Just
as death is, for me, the page I read.
'Hence writing is both death's reckoning and
death's recklessness.
'You read what you have been. You make others
read your future.
'In the book, then, life is but the passage from
unreadable to readable and lost the very
moment it is achieved.'
He added: 'Life is called, death chosen.
'Their secret dialogue goes on, ever more dis-
tressingly inaudible, in our inaccessible heart of
hearts.'

Edmond Jabès, *The Book of Dialogue*

WHITE MYTHOLOGY

On opening Michael Ondaatje's *The Collected Works of Billy the Kid: Left
Handed Poems*, we encounter a blank square, perhaps the frame of an
absent photographic image. Ondaatje's opening device foregrounds a

beginning that is both there and not there. If this frame enframing nothing is supposed to be the beginning of the poem's narrative, then the narrative in question bears no signs of inscription except the four geometric lines drawn to form the empty square. The white space becomes the figure of a narrative that is both present and absent, a discourse without subject. It is a gap for the reader to fill. Only when the reader's eyes move past the white space and begin reading the text that follows do we infer the meaning of the empty frame. From that frame of nothingness, Ondaatje moves to a quotation by Western photographer L.A. Huffman.

> *I send you a picture of Billy made with the Perry shutter as quick as it can be worked – Pyro and soda developer. I am making daily experiments now and find I am able to take passing horses at a lively trot square across the line of fire – bits of snow in the air – spokes well defined – some blur on top of wheel but sharp in the main – men walking are no trick – I will send you proofs sometime. I shall show you what can be done from the saddle without ground glass or tripod – please notice when you get the specimens that they were made with the lens wide open and many of the best exposed when my horse was in motion.* (5)

This quotation emphasizes the historical referentiality of the poem, a referentiality, however, which, as we will see, plays with and against history. Moreover, the quotation invites the reader to abandon a linear reading of the text. Before moving on, the reader is tempted to go back to the empty frame, to reread its signifying emptiness. This reading detour reveals that the empty frame is no longer empty. In fact, we rename it: we see it as a specific photograph. A photograph, though, without an image; a photograph of whiteness, of what leaves no graph, no mark when printed. It announces Billy the Kid's 'white mythologies,'[1] the true and legendary stories that compose his portrait. The absent portrait of Billy also announces the 'negative' of narration. It becomes, in Derrida's words, an *exergue* – what lies 'outside the work,' 'inscription,' 'epigraph' (1982, 209). It suggests that Billy lies outside the poem, cannot be contained in a single frame. He evades the poem as he will evade all the attempts to capture him, in fact or word. The discourse of this emptiness has no precise subject or origin; it becomes the discourse of language itself, a discourse that speaks hesitancy.

The rereading of the poem's opening illustrates how Ondaatje prolongs the beginning of his long poem. Beyond this, the quotation from Huffman's text introduces narrative as a story already begun – begun, that is, outside the poem itself. We are reminded of how narrative is essentially a referential system, but also of the extent to which referentiality is textual. Not only Huffman's quotation but the other sources Ondaatje acknowledges at the end of *Billy the Kid* affirm the textuality of the long poem. I am going to leap for a moment to that last page, and create a hiatus in my reading, because what happens there is, I think, the index to the poem's outlawed narrative.

On the very last page of *The Collected Works of Billy the Kid*, following the dedication and the publishing data, Ondaatje cites the sources he used in the making of this long poem. He concludes his list of references by saying: '[w]ith these basic sources I have edited, rephrased, and slightly reworked the originals. But the emotions belong to their authors' (110). Ondaatje denies himself the authority of the author; instead, he foregrounds his role as reader, a reader of found narratives, a reader who becomes a writer. This exchange of roles becomes an integral part of Ondaatje's literary signature. It dramatizes the degree to which he posits both his reading act and his found material as being the generative forces of his poem. The assumed authorial control of that material gives way to inscription, to the act of recording the 'emotions belong[ing] to their authors.' Accordingly, the readers' expectations of originality are replaced by their search for authenticity, their desire to measure the extent to which Ondaatje departs from, or distorts, his sources.

Ondaatje's ambivalent distance from his documents has given rise to a number of interpretations that tend to privilege the documentary material at the expense of the textual evidence provided in the poem. Some of these critics focus more on the historical and legendary narratives of Billy's life and less on the telling of the story itself. The quotations, paraphrases, and photographs that we find in *The Collected Works of Billy the Kid*, as the title of the poem indicates, are not elements of a found narrative but signs of literariness.[2] Ondaatje's credits are meant to acknowledge not history but the making of literature out of history.

Yet, in spite of his claims, Ondaatje does not free himself from this referential context. As reader and writer, he resides inside the referential system of the documents he employs. *The Collected Works of Billy the Kid* is a *collection*, an accumulation of sources, including the textuality Ondaatje has woven in his own game with the reader. The result is a book recording the testimonies of characters, Ondaatje's reading of and selection from his sources, the telling of the reading act – a telling that becomes the writing down of reading and story-telling alike. The narrative figure emerging from this collection has no precise origin; or, to put it another way, has no origin other than in language.

Perhaps this is one of the reasons that prompts Ondaatje to disclaim control over his characters' emotions. The narrative of the poem, acted out as a juxtaposition of dramatic monologues, does not acknowledge him as its master. A narrative without master is a narrative without grammar, the grammar that structuralists like Todorov read into literary works. This is particularly true in the long poem. Its verse constantly re-verses the process of narration. This reversal accounts for what elongates the form of the long poem and articulates the ungrammaticality of its poetic narrative. The long poem does away with the sentence, the central grammatical and narrative unit, in order to follow its own line of unfolding.

Ondaatje's sources, whether cited accurately or imaginatively appropriated, are not meant to recreate in *Billy the Kid* the sequence of the historical Billy's experiences and actions. Ondaatje is not interested, as his ludic use of documents indicates, in narrative as a sequence of actions. Yet most criticism of *Billy* is characterized by a search the critics have in common, the search for narrative.

Judith Owens, for instance, opens her essay on the poem by stating that '[t]he reader finds in Ondaatje's Billy a strong desire for order, a rage for order' (117), and concludes that 'the narrative line, which has progressed only fitfully to this point in the volume [76], moves rapidly and fairly straightforwardly to its *conclusion in Billy's death* ... draw[ing] attention once again to the relationship between "order" and "death"' (139; my emphasis). Owens relies heavily in her interpretation on Ondaatje's placing of Billy's death at the end of the long poem. In a seemingly similar way, Scobie observes that the poem's 'material may be seen as a narrative with two main strands: the conflict between Billy and Pat Garrett, *culminating in the manhunt and the deaths* of Tom O'Folliard, Charlie Bowdre, and Billy himself; and the opposite of conflict, the scenes of peace and companionship, centring on Miss Angela D. and the Chisum ranch. Underlying these two narrative strands is the central theme of violence, as it erupts in both outlaw and artist' (1972, 45; my emphasis). Scobie is correct in outlining the action of the poem, but his 'may' is, I think, more forceful than he intends it to be. Although Scobie is primarily interested in the historical aspect of Billy and in how Billy has been mythologized, he structures his reading around his binary arrangement of Ondaatje's material.[3]

Although Ondaatje's critics such as Owens, Sam Solecki, Perry Nodelman, and Dennis Lee delight in the artist's aesthetic violence, they also attempt to set him straight.[4] But Ondaatje's disjointed presentation of action is meant to remain this way. The lack of surface narrative does not necessarily imply that there is a deep structure to be discovered or, worse, invented by the reader, as I think Dennis Lee insists.[5] Ondaatje displays an interest in discourse, in the way these actions are reported by language and become known as verbal acts. Discourse does not, as Barbara Herrnstein Smith puts it, 'consis[t] of sets of discrete signs which, in some way, *correspond to* (depict, encode, denote, refer to, and so forth) sets of discrete and specific ideas, objects, or events' (225). This holds all the more for so self-regarding a construct as the long poem. Discourse in the long poem resides in the series of verbal acts that actualize the performative function of language.

To return to the beginning of the poem, the citation from Huffman's book not only frustrates narrative order but also illustrates the many levels of discourse operating in the poem. The prose paragraph takes the reader from a discourse degree zero – the vacant frame written in white ink – to a discourse that is already double-coded. Challenging the norm is for Huffman a 'daily experiment.' His lens remains 'wide open,' an instruction to the reader to keep her or his reading perspective open too. Beyond this, Huffman's discourse is technical – the Perry shutter, Pyro and soda developer, the proofs, the ground glass or tripod – asserting the particular referents of textuality.

Yet, despite this specialist's vocabulary, the reader is drawn into the poem by Huffman's apostrophe. Since Huffman is quoted out of context, the 'you' he addresses remains undetermined. That 'you,' however, at the same time that it addresses Huffman's reader or addressee, also apostrophizes Ondaatje and his own reader who are overhearing or, more precisely, overreading Huffman's discourse. This direct address marks the first apostrophe in a long series of apostrophes throughout the poem. Apostrophe is indeed the primary rhetorical trope of the poem's self-referentiality, for it establishes the priority of discourse over narrative.

THANATOGRAPHY

The Collected Works of Billy the Kid may be about Billy, but the numerous accounts about him and by him do not add up to a traditional narrative. Ondaatje has structured his poem as a series of dramatic monologues, prose fragments, and lyrics that interweave with each other and lead in different directions. Indeed, it is the use of dramatic monologue rather than narrative that foregrounds discourse as the poem's movement. Ondaatje, relying on the drive and immediacy of discourse, composes his poem as a chorus of voices. Discourse, Barthes reminds us, is '[*d*]*is-cursus* – originally the action of running here and there, comings and goings, measures taken, "plots and plans"' (1979, 3). The dramatic monologue as a specific mode of discourse and the 'I' as the vehicle of its utterance choreograph the movement and texture of the poem's voices. Some are cacophonous and discordant, others elegaic, parodic, or lyrical; all dramatize Billy's persona.

Billy, as we have seen, is introduced as a figure drawn in white ink, invisible inside the frame of Huffman's photograph. This absence, although initially puzzling, is immediately explained on the page following the poem's first photograph. The list of the dead given by Billy himself is the index to the structure and discourse of the poem. Like an epic catalogue, and in the epic fashion of conflict,[6] Billy gives us two separate lists of 'the killed' (6), those killed '(By me)' and those killed '(By them).' Sheila Watson rightly observes about the list that it 'paradoxically includes the name of the sheriff Garrett, who survived to record the experience in print' (157). The paradox affirms the fictionality of the world Ondaatje creates and, beyond this, points out the extent to which textuality determines its own referents.

But there is yet another paradox, one that Watson doesn't comment on. The last of the killed mentioned in the list is Billy himself.

> and Pat Garrett
> sliced off my head.
> Blood a necklace on me all my life. (6)

Although dead, Billy is the speaker of this monologue, and of all the other monologues he presumably delivers in the poem. We see now that the absence in the opening photograph speaks of his death. This absence, his death, is further emphasized by the fact that Billy's list of the killed is framed exactly by the lines of the empty frame on the opposite side of the page (5). The poem's discourse, then, is largely uttered by a dead subject. It is this paradox that defies most critics' attempts to identify the narrative pattern that leads to Billy's death. Billy does not die in the poem. He is already dead when he utters his first monologue. This death is the real *exergue* in the poem. It is the 'work' that cannot be collected in *The Collected Works of Billy the Kid*. Billy's last monologue, uttered as he lies dying (95), is not a performative but a constative act of language: nothing happens under the reader's eyes but the very acting out of language.

Billy's dead voice demarcates itself by leaving on the poem's text the marks of its genre. White voice. Black marks. Red necklace. Discourse with and without subject. As the 'I' of his discourse, Billy is dead but living, the subject of paradox itself, for he does not remain speechless. 'A discourse on life/death,' Derrida remarks, 'must occupy a certain space between *logos* and *gramme*, analogy and program, as well as between the differing senses of program and reproduction. And since life is on the line, the trait that relates the logical to the graphical must also be working between the biological and biographical, the thanatological and thanatographical' (1985, 4–5). One could argue, then, that the rhetoric of Billy's monologues is that of thanatography, a writing that emerges from death, a writing that seeks to cancel the finality we usually ascribe to death.

Although a dead subject, Billy displays volatility, as the following monologue shows:

Am the dartboard
for your midnight blood
the bones' moment
of perfect movement
that waits to be thrown
magnetic into combat

a pencil
harnessing my face
goes stumbling into dots   (85)

The dartboard is one of the many masks Billy puts on. The metonymy 'Am the dartboard' eliminates the 'I' (he doesn't say 'I am the dartboard'). The dartboard itself becomes the space of utterance where the combat between life and death occurs. Life is on the line of the 'perfect movement,' but it is a *gramme* (line) already become *gramma* (letter), inscribed by 'midnight blood.' The red of blood is the colour of thanatographical inscription, the colour of death. Playing darts is almost synonymous with the game of writing. Billy's discourse oscillates between violence as game and violence as reality. His writing, a writing of loss, progresses towards the 'bones' moment,' the moment of death. The dartboard figures as a 'magnetic' field where biography and thanatography overlap, where scriptor and reader meet: 'a pencil / harnessing my face / goes stumbling into dots.' Writing posits itself as torture, turns the dartboard metonymy upside down. So when Billy shows his face at the end of this monologue, marked with dots, signs of torture and language, the face is nothing less than the text itself, the face of Billy's other. Death here refers not only to Billy but to the drama of death incurred by language.

But the main drama in Billy's monologues is his return from death as subject of discourse and as the subject of his namesake text, *Billy the Kid*. Billy plays against the logos of narrative.

> Not a story about me through their eyes then. Find the beginning, the slight silver key to unlock it, to dig it out. Here then is a maze to begin, be in.

> Two years ago Charlie Bowdre and I criss-crossed the Canadian border. Ten miles north of it ten miles south. Our horses stepped from country to country, across low rivers, through different colours of tree green. The two of us, our criss-cross like a whip in slow motion, *the ridge of action rising and falling*, getting narrower in radius till it ended and we drifted down to Mexico and old heat. That there is nothing of depth, of significant accuracy, of wealth in the image, I know. It is there for a beginning. (20; my emphasis)

Billy's knowledge challenges the reader's epistemology because he speaks from within that ultimate knowledge ensuing from death, a knowledge located on the borderline of impossibility. Like the Canadian border, Ondaatje's authorial signature, this borderline is both signed and signed off. From Billy's vantage point, borders cease to mean, to demarcate difference. Billy's movement from country to country becomes the symbolic movement of his return from the dead. It echoes parodically Dante's journey with Virgil through inferno, purgatorio, and paradiso. But the order of Dante's pauses on the planes of death and afterlife is here diffused, for Billy ends up in the 'old heat' of Mexico and returns to us after seeing not Dante's *candida rosa* but 'the sun turned into a pair of hands' (76).

The only knowledge Billy can convey to the reader is that 'there is nothing of depth, of significant accuracy, of wealth in the image,' and that the reader is already inside the 'maze' of narrative Billy alludes to. A 'maze to begin, be in.' The typographical gap between 'be' and 'in' is the glyph of *g* in 'begin.' The maze is engendered by the alliteration in Billy's discourse; the repeated sounds (begin, be in) echo the labyrinth of language. Billy's appeal to the reader is not simply to begin, but to admit the fact that the very act of reading implicates the reader's presence in the maze of discourse. Billy talks about re-beginning 'here,' on the page, in the text.

The interval between absence and presence, that is, between death and the materiality of Billy's language, becomes the pivotal figure in the poem. 'The others, I know, did not see the wounds appearing in the sky, in the air' (10). The difference between Billy and the 'others' is his own otherness. Billy is both within and on the far side of language. It is not so much the reader who overhears his monologues, as it is Billy who overhears the reader. Hence his warning that the narrative image is there only 'for a beginning.'

Billy's existence becomes an event sustained solely by discourse. His discourse occasionally assumes a visionary style, when he talks about animals and, especially, stars:

I have seen pictures of great stars,
drawings which show them straining to the centre
that would explode their white
if temperature and the speed they moved at
shifted one degree.

Or in the East have seen
the dark grey yards where trains are fitted
and the clean speed of machines
that make machines, their
red golden pouring which when cooled
mists out to rust or grey.

The beautiful machines pivoting on themselves
sealing and fusing to others

and men throwing levers like coins at them.
And there is there the same stress as with stars,
the one altered move that will make them maniac.   (41)

Billy's view of the stars, although he is on the other side of life's border,
is uttered in the conditional mode, but affirmed by the hindsight that
pervades his discourse as a dead subject. His discourse echoes, on a
purely textual level, Dante's description of the stars in Canto II of
'Paradiso,' a description relying on knowledge current during his time
as well as on what the deified Beatrice explains. Like life and death,
the beauty and stress of the 'machines pivoting on themselves,' anal-
ogous to the beauty and stress of the 'great stars,' are defined by 'the
one altered move that will make them maniac.' That move points to
the alterity of identity. It is effected by Billy's 'manic' desire to be in
a state of otherness.

The same manic desire is the impetus behind Billy's actions. Billy
does not act out of 'fear of mortality,' as Owens argues (120), for, being
dead, he is already outlawed from the world of mortals. What activates
his discourse is a desire to be impervious to motion, a wish that explains
a seeming distancing from emotions that Nodelman finds in Billy (69).
Desire for Billy points to the radical place that is both inside and outside, life and death, earth and the 'great stars.' This is the topos of
his discourse, a place of paradox. Death does not stifle language. Instead it imports into narrative the strangeness of discourse, the same
strangeness that characterizes Billy's relationship with Angela Dickinson.

THE EROTICS OF RHETORIC

Angela D. figures in the poem as a series of prosopopoeias. In many
respects, Angela is an allegory of the erotic.[7] The fact that she is usually
referred to as Angela D. and not as Angela Dickinson points, I think,
to her signifying the other that desire yearns for. She is an apostle of
Desire itself, a desire that occurs on the edge of Billy's textual life.
Unlike Sallie who 'slowly lean[s] up to find her body' 'when the sun
eventually reach[es] the bed and slid[es] over her eyes' (32), Angela
never loses her body and is always in tune with its desires. Because
of this she is a reminder of the pleasure, fears, and violence the life
of the body entails. As a woman who shamelessly puts forward her
body, she teases the reader as a whore; as the first woman to shave

her legs 'hairless' (25), she is a suffragette; and she also cuts a courageous and passionate figure as Billy's lover. She is, in other words, the prosopopoeia of paradox itself. That's why Billy both resists and adores her.

Angela's supple body cannot be contained within frames, and she thus becomes a prosopopoeia of the edge. 'The edge of the pillow in her mouth, her hip a mountain further down the bed'; 'over the edge of the bed like a peninsula rich with veins and cooler than the rest of her for it has been in the path of the window's wind all night' (71). She is a woman of edges, edges that reveal yet another layer of prosopopoeia, the edges of earth formations, the borderline marking low and high, warm and cold, the difference of elements. Edges are what Angela D. and Billy primarily share. Billy stays 'at the edge of a farm' (17), sees 'the sun [as] a flashy hawk / on the edge of' the river (26), is aware of 'the edge of the dark empty desert' (62), finds himself 'on the edge of the cold dark,' 'on the edge of sun' (74). But Angela D. outdoes Billy in her capacity to be a figure of edges, and she does so in a way that forces him to confront his thanatographical discourse.

During one of their most powerful and evocative encounters, Angela D. shows her true face.

She leans against the door, holds
her left hand at the elbow
with her right, looks at the bed

on my sheets – oranges
peeled half peeled
bright as hidden coins against the pillow

she walks slow to the window
lifts the sackcloth
and jams it horizontal on a nail
so the bent oblong of sun
hoists itself across the room
framing the bed the white flesh
of my arm

she is crossing the sun
sits on her leg here
sweeping off the peels

traces the thin bones on me
turns toppling slow back to the pillow
Bonney Bonney

I am very still
I take in all the angles of the room   (21)

This monologue articulates the drama of Billy's life and death, his
move away from narrative and towards discourse. From being a figure
of desire, Angela D. figures now as the angel of Death. Desire for the
other reaches here its ultimate edge; it 'topples' over the border of
life. The rhetoric of Billy's discourse renders the love scene as a scene
during which the female lover, the woman of edges, administers the
rites of death. The peeled oranges 'as hidden coins' mark the economy
in Billy's discourse. It is an economy that deflates Angela Dickinson
as character, but also inflates Angela D. as rhetorical persona.

Beyond this, through the same economy of rhetoric the sun emerges
not as the intruder let into the room by Angela but as the element
conflating the physical time of heavenly bodies with the biological time
of mortal bodies. Angela is able to cross the sun and sweep off the
orange peels in the same stanza, for she, the woman of edges, belongs
to both temporal dimensions as they are actualized in the monologue.
In the present tense of Billy's discourse, the bed sheets serve as a
euphemism for shroud. Angela D. is 'tracing' Billy's 'thin bones' while
calling him 'Bonney Bonney.' This testifies to Billy's rhetorical death.
Apostrophizing him in his last name does not suggest a psychological
distance between the two lovers, as Owens argues. Quite the contrary.
It is not the first time Angela calls him Bonney. To use someone's
last name frequently signals a kind of intimacy, as it does when Angela,
after she is shot in the hand by Billy's enemies, shouts to Billy: 'O
Bonney you bastard Bonney / kill him Bonney kill him' (66). The
family name in this instance, accompanied by the exclamatories 'O'
and 'bastard,' expresses her pain and rage. In both cases, the last name
functions as a double signature referring not merely to the named one
but to the caller's choice of name as well. Since the use of 'Bonney'
both times connects with death, we surmise that Angela mediates between Billy and death. We are reminded that the bullet that wounded
her hand was meant for Billy, and, although she does not die, he
includes her in the list of those killed 'by them.' Whether angel of

Death or guardian angel, Angela D. herself remains immune to the ordinary concept of mortality.

The *mise en scène* in this monologue involves both *thanatos* and *eros*. Thus while Angela's fingers feel the thin bones under Billy's white flesh in a gesture of desire, his stillness marks his readiness to delay his orgasm, the 'little death.' Her loving fingers make of 'phallus' a double signifier, one that brings together sexuality and death. The proper name 'Bonney,' because of its phonetic variations, reclaims its thingness: bone; skeleton; phallus. That same name designates that Billy is a 'bony' man, and it becomes a 'bonny' thing because it reveals the textuality of its signification, the multiple desire contained in language. Although it is Billy who is the speaker of this monologue, it is Angela D. who makes the poem turn around rhetorically. Angela is 'all the *angles* of the room' (my emphasis) Billy takes in, the anagram (Angela/angles) of the multiple perspectives the reader discovers in this long poem.

Despite the game of life and death Angela plays, Billy's discourse does not insinuate any resentment towards her. Instead he intuits that he has been 'framed' by the sun, and shares this with the reader in an almost nonchalant way. The sun, one of the most frequently recurring images in *The Collected Works*, 'crosses' Billy. Hatless, his 'legs handcuffed,' his 'hands bound' to his horse's bridle, Billy goes 'mad from saddle pain' and the merciless heat of the sun as Garrett leads him and his two buddies, Wilson and Rudabaugh, to face the law (76). Billy's delirium begins with a prosopopoeia of the sun: 'the sun turned into a pair of hands' (76). This personification foregrounds the nonpresence of a thing, creating, that is, as do all rhetorical tropes, a figure through the materiality of language.

Once the distant sun is brought down and endowed with hands, it begins torturing Billy. 'It used a fingernail and scratched a knife line from front to back on the skin'; 'with very thin careful fingers it began to unfold my head drawing back each layer of skin and letting it flap over my ears' (76). The scratched and peeled head of Billy (metonymically related to the peeled oranges and the sun itself) is also marked by the sun's unreadable signifiers. The violent 'unfolding' of the skin suggests the turns of Billy's discourse. We thereby encounter the same texture of language when Billy muses about the fatal shot he receives from Garrett. His delirium, now one of physical death, conjures up images 'of lovely perfect sun balls / breaking at each other click,' 'oranges reeling across the room ... / it is my brain coming out like red grass / this breaking where red things wade' (95). Billy goes *out* of his mind. The slippage of time in this passage, with Billy 'wading' both in physical and biological time, suggests that perception and discourse are equally constituted by language.

The specular and graphic elements of Billy's torture are not just here for the sake of sensational emphasis; they are meant to accentuate the theatre of torture, the inscription of pain on the body: Billy embodies the theatre itself. 'The brain juice began to swell up. You could see the bones and grey now. The sun sat back and watched while the juice evaporated' (76). The merciless sun, both inside and outside the performance, figures as the god of torture. Its role as a viewer sitting back to watch Billy may be seen as a metaphor of the reading act: the god of torture is busy reading the work of cruelty it has created.

The theatre of cruelty continues, and the personification of the sun seems to be completed when the neutral 'it' that has so far carried the personification is replaced by the male personal pronoun. 'When he touched the bone with his fingers it was like brushing raw nerves. He took a thin cold hand and sank it into my head down past the roof of my mouth and washed his fingers in my tongue' (76). The personification elicits now a double disfiguration: Billy is disfigured by the sun but the sun is also disfigured by the new pronoun that now defines it.

Yet the personification in this passage never reaches complete maturation. The sun remains effaced; 'he' never assumes a face, not even what we might call a body. He is all hands, hands touching Billy's bones, hands penetrating his skull. 'Down the long cool hand went scratching the freckles and warts in my throat ... with his wrist, down he went the liquid yellow from my busted brain finally vanishing ... the long cool hand going down brushing cobwebs of nerves the horizontal pain pits ... the cool precise fingers went into the cistern of bladder down the last hundred miles' (76–7). The visceral details in this monologue point to Billy's cannibalistic discourse. The sun untexts Billy. His tortured body becomes the text, but a text that is dissected mercilessly and with great, almost scientific, precision. His textual body, with loose nerves and a brain full of fissures, has been unbound.

Billy's bodily and textual dissection bears signs of mysticism. His body is transverberated. '[I]n a jerk breaking through my sacs of sperm got my cock in the cool fingers pulled it back up and carried it pulling pulling flabby as smoke up the path his arm had rested in and widened.

He brought it up fast half tearing the roots off up the coloured bridges of fibres again ... locked in his fingers up the now bleeding throat up squeezed it through the skull bones, so there I was, my cock standing out of my head' (77). Billy's experience in this scene borders on death and orgasm. 'Ive been fuckd [sic] Ive been fucked by Christ almighty god Ive been good and fucked by Christ,' he yells to Garrett (78). But this ecstatic cry does not elucidate the experience Billy describes in this monologue. Although it is an utterance seemingly affirming Billy's apotheosis, it raises more questions than it resolves. The beginning of Billy's description of his torture suggests a narrative movement towards rape, and perhaps castration, but the tone of his exclamatory utterance is certainly problematic.

In the double context of torture and mysticism, the passive voice of the utterance creates ambiguity. 'Ive been fucked by Christ' might suggest rape or castration, the eradication of the phallus as sexual organ and as the privileged signifier. Billy's hallucination during his sunstroke, instead of belying the reality of his experience, affirms both his desire for the other and his desire to erase his otherness – an expression of his death drive. Thus we can hear Billy's utterance as a cry of rage barely released from the agony of his pain; but we can also hear a voice of jubilation – 'Ive been good and fucked by Christ.' Whether what we hear is agony or jubilation, or both at the same time, the ambiguity is in keeping with Billy's mystical experience.

Knowing that Billy's voice tastes of death, we cannot afford to read his ecstasy about being 'fucked by Christ' as an affirmation of religious faith, for it is devoid of any metaphysical import. Instead, dwelling as he does in the realm of rhetoric, his ecstasy celebrates not faith but his knowledge of the lack of a supreme God. God as someone who 'fucks' so furtively and so violently an outlaw figure is, to say the least, not the image of the Christian God. God is himself outlawed. He becomes a 'dark AMATEUR,' a figure loved and feared, inspiring the same vacillation of emotions as Garrett (and also to some extent Angela) does (53). As a dark amateur the sun assumes the double configuration of the Beloved Son and the Infidel. Billy's week-long ride across the desert, with its biblical allusions, is not affirmative but parodic in its function. He speaks through Angela's 'mouth [which] is an outlaw' (64).

The sun become Christ is, of course, hardly surprising when seen within the conventional configuration of the source of life. This interpretation centres not on metonymy but on the presence or absence of the male sexual organ. As the sun/Christ in its/his personification is not given a face (or rather as it/he has a face neither Billy nor the reader can risk looking at directly), nor is it/he given a penis. Thus Billy has not been 'fucked' at all, or at least he has not been 'fucked' by a penis. His reference to his own 'cock' becomes narratively redundant because it is implied by the homologous gender relation between himself and the sun/Christ. The homoerotic component in Billy's delirium suggests that he has reached his other, a male other metonymically related to Christ. Again, sexuality and mysticism overlap. His torture, in this respect, can be seen as his 'passion,' the same passion alluded to by the nails and the cross and the sackcloth and the sun hoisting itself in the monologue about Angela and Billy.

We are left then with Billy's words, his words now speaking of the 'long cool hands.' Words and hands brought together here become a sign of inscription affirming Billy's discourse, namely his role as an artist who 'tricks' death.[8] Thus the icy coolness of the sun's hands, contrasted to the sun's intense heat, grounds Billy's delirium in his ride across the desert and in his desire to reverse the circumstances. But the text does not instruct the reader to interpret the hands metaphorically, and certainly the repetitive references to hands in this prose monologue further reinforce their tangible presence.

After Billy's penis is spirited away, 'standing out' of his head like the fire of the Holy Ghost, the sun's hands continue to gesture in a way that adds yet another layer of interpretation of Billy's discourse.

Then he brought his other hand into play I could feel the cool shadow now as he bent over me both his hands tapering into beautiful cool fingers, one hand white as new smelling paper the other 40 colours ochres blues silver from my lung gold and tangerine from the burst ear canals all that clung to him as he went in and came out.

The hands were cold as porcelain, one was silver old bone stripped oak white eastern cigarettes white sky the eye core of sun. Two hands, one dead, one born from me, one like crystal, one like shell of snake found in spring. Burning me like dry ice.

They picked up the fold of foreskin one hand on each side and began the slow pull back back back back *down* like a cap with ear winter muffs like a pair of trousers down boots and then he let go. The wind picked up, I was drowned, locked inside my skin sensitive ...   (77)

The hands' motion suggests masturbation, not exactly what Billy means by 'fucking,' but this sexual act, too, since Billy's hands are bound, is one of homoeroticism, reinforcing his experience of otherness.

If this passage is the pivotal place in the poem where Billy achieves a state of otherness through an ecstatic experience, it is by no means the only place where Billy pays attention to hands. Hands are generally important to Billy. They can be both self-loving and destructive instruments, as when, while 'cross[ing] a crooked river / loving in my head,' he shot a 'crooked bird / Held it in my fingers' (14). The pun on bird, together with the references in this lyric to riding and yelling, and to eyes, refers to the same movement that we saw above, violent death and sexuality come together. The cross-references do not stop here. They all emphasize the poem's textuality, which keeps unfolding like Billy's skin, in his hand – under his hand, his signature. Hands are instrumental in this unfolding: they make love and kill, but they are also deictic signifiers, markers pointing the reader to the multiple directions of Billy's discourse.

Similarly, the recurrence of bones and hands brings the sun and Angela together, a rapport that could be extended to include other characters such as Garrett or Maxwell. For example, the 'first time' Billy makes love with Angela he uses the same narrative of hand imagery we see in his delirium:

my hand locked
her body nearly breaking off my fingers
pivoting like machines in final speed

later my hands cracked in love juice
fingers paralyzed by it arthritic
these beautiful fingers I couldnt move
faster than a crippled witch now   (16)

The self-amatory 'beautiful' is the same adjective Billy uses when referring to the sun's fingers. Yet the connections between all these hands remain discursive; they do not function as codes prescribing meaning and narrative order. What they accomplish instead is a sequence of images and occurrences that is assigned significance by the reader. The order of reading replaces narrative.

The Collected Works of Billy the Kid outlaws narrative. The figure of this outlawed narrative is never fully drawn, however, because On-daatje ends the poem by using a series of delay devices, similar to the ones he employed in opening the poem. Towards the end of the poem, the prose monologue that appears immediately before Billy's picture, which is the cover illustration of the 'Wide Awake Library' series on Billy, is uttered in the conditional; it apostrophizes the reader or an even more indefinite 'you,' and carries no 'I' to designate the speaker's signature. The missing 'I' speculates about what would happen 'if you dug him [Billy] up and brought him out' (97). The 'ifness' of this anon-ymous discourse is seeking traces, '[p]erhaps Garrett's bullet,' 'the sil-ver from the toe of each boot' (97). But these traces are already erased not only by the conditional mode but by this outrageous act of imag-ining. For a moment, the anonymous speaker of the passage (perhaps the informant Paulita Maxwell, or Ondaatje himself) desires to find Billy not in the present tense of his monologues but in his grave, in a past that defies reading. Since the only traces the anonymous 'I' can find are those of Billy's own inscription, this discourse concludes in-conclusively: '[h]is legend a jungle sleep' (97).

This prose fragment is followed in the poem by the device appearing in both the beginning and the conclusion of *Billy the Kid*, that of the frame. The blank frame of Billy's photograph reappears now as a frame where we find embedded a parodic version of the narrative the poem has outlawed. I am referring, of course, to the narrative of the comic-book legend, *Billy the Kid and the Princess*. The reason this hilarious story is quoted in the poem within a frame is partly because it fulfils, while parodying, the norms of traditional narrative, especially those of the romance. Billy the Kid, a figure that eludes narrative, becomes in this story Billy the Gringo, the gallant cowboy who saves La Prin-cessa Marguerita's life and who doesn't quite know how to protect himself from her amorous advances. This story illustrates how Billy's life defies the beginning, middle, and end of life's narrative.

Finally, in the last frame of the book, we find embedded a small photograph of a boy dressed as a cowboy (107). It is a picture of young Ondaatje himself. Billy the Kid has become Mike the Kid. These frames, embedded as they are in the poem, reinforce the breakdown of linear narrative and also the breakdown between life and death. The author appropriates his character's place in the photograph as the character himself has appropriated the author's language.

Billy's voice, although it speaks from beyond death, does not speak the death of the author. It is a voice of ambiguity and uncertainty, as the last brief dialogue in the poem illustrates:

'Pat,' replied Poe, 'I believe you have killed the wrong man.'

'I'm sure it was the Kid,' responded Garrett, 'for I knew his voice and could not have been mistaken.'

(103)

Billy's voice is the equivocal witness of his life as well as his death. What his voice speaks of, be it the voice of a dead or living person, is the enabling power of discourse. Discourse shows him to be capable not only of self-description but also of (re)reading a context where he is the object of someone else's verbal act. Michael Ondaatje, in the guise of Mike the Kid, evidently does not want to interfere with Billy's 'manic' discourse. Billy's discourse remains at the end of the poem powerful and evocative exactly because he is narratively dead. It affirms the poetics of the present tense.

Conclusion

... how to avoid becoming too comfortable in
the abyss.

Barbara Johnson, *A World of Difference*

Endings are a kind of death, the end of discourse; but endings are not
always closures. Only upon reaching the moment of concluding this
book did I realize that the last chapter was, undesignedly, about death.
Not the death *of* the long poem, as Eli Mandel would have it, but death
in the long poem. *The Collected Works of Billy the Kid*, spoken, however
intermittently, by a dead subject, announces the dying of death in the
present tense. The silence that death incurs is present here, as is also
the linguistic ecstasy the dead subject achieves in his moment of undoing. Death and life, speech and silence, truth and untruth – all are
balanced with and against each other in a rhythm that strikes the vital
nerve of contestation (possibly annihilation), but a rhythm that also
comforts us with its familiar binary repetition. Yet, as *Billy the Kid* illustrates, the long poem never lets itself be entirely seduced by either
silence or words, death or life. Nor does it cradle the reader in a cosy
world of familiarity. Instead, it locates us in an unruly world where the
obvious, and often subliminal, pleasure of escaping from the rigours of
'law' is tempered, if not completely annulled, by its revealing to us the
impossibility of ever escaping from the aesthetic or ideological systems
that construct our reality as subjects and objects. The long poem's
processual unravelling, based as it is upon the undoing of its own comprising elements, whether thematic or formal, points to the aleatory
conditions that inform this 'new' genre. The contemporary long

poem borders on excess, an excess, however, that draws an elliptical figure.

In a similar vein, it goes without saying that I do not offer this study as the definitive reading of this genre, or, more specifically, of the long poem in Canada. It remains elliptical not only because of the necessary choices and limits a critical reader is faced with, but also because of the nature of its subject. If I were to begin again, I would, among other options, explore in a more concentrated and rigorous fashion the long poem's critique of the ideology of aesthetics and culture alongside its own emerging ideology. The long poem manifests itself to the reader, at least to this one, as the measure of the culture that it comes from and speaks to. It is a well-sustained (and therefore long) measure, yet a measure that remains indeterminable.

By questioning its legacies of epic, lyric, and narrative forms, it resides both inside and outside these inherited conditions. Its *generic* indeterminacy is nothing other than the sign of its *genetics*, the complex ways in which it relates to past traditions and to its present circumstances. It is the outcome of what I earlier referred to as a negative dialectics, an unfinished process of binary constructs. Inside and outside, within and beyond the limits of the genres it both employs and resists, the contemporary long poem offers us a 'long view' of the past it never inhabited and of the future it will never reach. This 'view' resolutely situates the long poem in the present; at the same time, and because of this, it endows it with the ability to deconstruct the normative values of the themes and forms that comprise it.

The long poem's aesthetic and ideological complicity is meant to engage the reader in its politicized and therefore political poetics. Its function is diacritical: we are invited to differentiate among the world-views and forms, more often than not contradictory, that constitute it as a 'new' genre. Moving away from the givenness of facticity through its self-reflexive gestures, disclosing the problematics of mastery hidden behind any sovereign genre, the long poem avoids reconciliation, shuns synthesis. In this respect, it does not embrace the Habermasian politics of consensus. Its contradictions and paradoxes do not swerve away from one master narrative in order to create another. Rather, it is produced within – we might even argue, intrudes upon – the very generic and cultural fissures it observes between the epic and the lyric, between its colonial predecessors and postcolonial instances, between referentiality and self-reflexivity.

Insofar as a literature speaks for a culture and its complexities, it is no coincidence that the literary evolution of the long poem took place at the same time that Canadian culture made significant gestures towards acknowledging the literatures produced by aboriginal people, writers of colour, women writers, and immigrant writers or those of ethnic origins other than English or French. In the 1970s and 1980s Canada not only had to regraph, legally and ideologically, the relationship between its two so-called 'heritage' peoples, but also began a series of accommodating gestures (the policy of multiculturalism is one such example) towards its 'other' minorities that were gradually to become of greater consequence. We could safely argue, I think, that the imperative to reconsider the Canadian literary canon was initiated by the same imperatives that demanded we review our concepts of nationalism, of the literary tradition, and of categories such as the literary and the popular. Many of these changes in the literary and pedagogical contexts have been informed as much by asking *different* questions as by a growing understanding of the need to thematize the questioning process itself. The recognition of what Barbara Godard calls 'a crisis of paradigms' (1987, 27) was coterminous with the changes in the climate of Canadian literature and criticism, more specifically the advent of theory. I am not suggesting an easy shift in writing and critical practices; as one might expect, the new directions Canadian writers and critics have taken have elicited various responses. As Godard puts it, '[t]hroughout the decade, critical theory in Canada has been on a see-saw between support for zero-degree writing – "minus Canadian" – and advocacy of contextually bound writing [– Canadian "plus"]' (47). Like the postmodern novel, which, as Linda Hutcheon has shown in *The Canadian Postmodern*, reflects the pulse of our current cultural uncertainty, the long poem of the 1970s and 1980s expresses similar concerns.

The instability of the long poem has, obviously, one stable manifestation, that is, its desire to thematize genre. This thematization of genre impinges upon our practices as readers of the meaning of genre and of its ability to signify in aesthetic terms the staple of our human condition: the double need for continuity and change. The long poem as a 'new' genre has evolved in ways that render problematic the linearity, cohesion, and sameness we have been taught to expect from tradition. While keeping at bay the ingredients that formulate patterns of recognition, it invites us to explore continuously why and how the forces that shape culture and literary tradition operate the way they do. Instead of relying on the sanctity of certainty, we are compelled as readers of the long poem to welcome the unreliability of recognition.

Yet the long poem does not accept ambiguity unequivocally. Far from being an apotropaic sign of cultural and political responsibility, its indeterminacy addresses what constitutes the political, what makes the literary. Working with logos as *langue* and *parole*, as epos and mythos, as the light and dark of reason, the long poem has an epochal function in the sense that its reflexivity measures the pulse of the specific time and place we find inscribed in it.

Thus, although self-referential, it does not rid itself of historical presuppositions. It deneutralizes, it brings back into motion, those axiomatic forces – aesthetic, ideological, political, historical – that we have long taken for granted. What it conceptualizes never loses its tangible relationship to reality; it still maintains the contingencies of consciousness that founded it. In this, the long poem does not propose a Babel of cultural, linguistic, and ideological indeterminacies; its intent is to make its readers apprehensive of the dangers of the well-established epistemological principles of liberal humanism. To borrow words from Barbara Johnson, it does this by engaging itself 'in a *critique* of value systems' rather than by elaborating 'a value system of its own' (17). Its indeterminacy marks its urgent agency as a 'new' genre: not to presume but to demonstrate.

Notes

1 AN ARCHAEOLOGY OF THE CANADIAN LONG POEM

1 See, for example, James F.G. Weldon, 'A "Heroic" Reading of Pratt's *Brébeuf and His Brethren*,' and Frank Davey's most recent reading of Pratt, 'Fort and Forest: Instability in the Symbolic Code in E.J. Pratt's *Brébeuf and His Brethren*.'

2 Frye does not argue, and nor do I, that the long poem was the most prominent form in nineteenth-century Canada. The Confederation poets, better known and more widely esteemed than practitioners of the long poem, wrote lyrics almost exclusively.

3 For further elaboration on the concept of supplement, see the discussion of Eli Mandel in chapter 3, especially 126 and 136.

4 On the relationship of colonial ideology and literary production, see 'Colonialism and Other Essays,' special issue of the *Oxford Literary Review*.

5 On this and other related issues with regard to this poem, see Kenneth Hughes, 'Oliver Goldsmith's *The Rising Village*'; W.J. Keith, '*The Rising Village* Again'; and K.P. Stich, '*The Rising Village, The Emigrant* and *Malcolm's Katie*: The Vanity of Progress.'

6 Unreadability refers to the impossibility of fully penetrating the opacity of language – the reader's inability fully to master the meaning of a text (whether written or cultural). Implicit in this are the inherent resistances to the reading act embedded in a text. In this respect, at the same time that a text is readable because of the common linguistic, generic, and cultural codes that it shares with its reader, it is also unreadable because of the questionable status of referential language. See Paul de Man's elaboration of this in *Allegories of Reading*, where he

states specifically that 'the assumption of readability, which is itself constitutive of language, cannot ... be taken for granted but is found to be aberrant. There can be no writing without reading, but all readings are in error because they assume their own readability. Everything written has to be read and every reading is susceptible of logical verification, but the logic that establishes the need for verification is itself unverifiable and therefore unfounded in its claim to truth' (202). For other elaborations on this, and other relevant issues, see also Barbara Johnson's 'Nothing Fails Like Success' and 'Rigorous Unreliability' in her *A World of Difference* 11–24, and J. Hillis Miller's *The Ethics of Reading*.

7 See Les McLeod, 'Canadian Post-Romanticism: The Context of Late Nineteenth-Century Canadian Poetry.'

8 My use of *chora* refers to the spatial, emotional, and linguistic locus within which a poet is firmly located, a locus the poet is not necessarily conscious of. The term *chora*, which literally means space, place, country, position, is to be found in Plato's *Timaeus* meaning a 'receptacle,' a mysterious formless being that receives all things ('mother' of all things). Julia Kristeva appropriated the term in 'The Semiotic *Chora* Ordering the Drives,' in *Revolution in Poetic Language* 25–30. Kristeva's appropriation is meant to remove from *chora* what Plato saw as 'incomprehensible' in what he called 'mother and receptacle.' The *chora* for Kristeva, although it 'precedes evidence, verisimilitude, spatiality and temporality,' is also part of 'the discourse of representation' (26). See also Jacques Derrida's critique of *chora* and its ontological essence in *Positions* 75 and 106, and n. 39.

9 See Bloom, especially p. 8; also Mandel's *The Family Romance: Critical Essays*, especially the essay 'The Long Poem: Journal and Origin,' perhaps Mandel's most complex essay/poem. Here, in his attempt to understand how 'The Long Poem Seeks to Define Itself and to Establish a Claim as a Canadian Form' (240), he also encounters the demons and benevolent ghosts of his ethnic, familial, and artistic past as he undergoes a journey to his ancestral origins in Russia.

10 Since I am dealing here with nineteenth-century Canada as a colonial text and Great Britain as an imperial text, my use of symbolism and semiosis is to some extent figurative. Yet the problematics of *reading* these cultural, and historical, *texts* does not permit us to forego the imperative of language. In this context, my use of these concepts is an appropriation of Kristeva's distinction between the categories of the symbolic and the semiotic. See her *Revolution in Poetic Language*. See

also Charles Sanders Peirce, *Collected Papers*, and Michael Riffaterre, *Semiotics of Poetry* and *Text Production*.

11 D.M.R. Bentley is the first Canadian critic to address the issue of ecology with regard to poetic form. See his 'A New Dimension: Notes on the Ecology of Canadian Poetry'; 'A Stretching Landscape: Notes on Some Formalistic Continuities in the Poetry of the Hinterland'; and 'The Mower and the Boneless Acrobat: Notes on the Stances of Baseland and Hinterland in Canadian Poetry.'

12 On the pragmatic function of genre see Adena Rosmarin, *The Power of Genre*.

13 According to Mikhail Bakhtin's 'Epic and Novel,' in *The Dialogic Imagination: Four Essays*, '[t]he field available for representing the world changes from genre to genre and from era to era as literature develops. It is organized in different ways and limited in space and time by different means. But this field is always specific' (27).

14 On problems relating to the construction, classification, and development of genres, I found especially useful the following studies: Paul Hernadi, *Beyond Genre: New Directions in Literary Classification*; Todorov, 'The Notion of Literature,' 'The Origin of Genre,' and *Les Genres du discours*; Christine Brooke-Rose, 'Historical Genres / Theoretical Genres: A Discussion of Todorov on the Fantastic'; Gérard Genette, 'Genres, "types", modes,' and *Introduction à l'architexte*; Karl Vietor, 'L'Histoire des genres littéraires'; Joseph P. Strelka, ed., *Theories of Literary Genres*; James H. Druff, 'Genre and Mode: The Formal Dynamics of Doubt'; Fredric Jameson, *The Political Unconscious: Narrative as a Socially Symbolic Act*; and Alastair Fowler, *Kinds of Literature: An Introduction to the Theory of Genres and Modes*.

15 In 'The Canadian Indian in Our Literature,' Dorothy Livesay says that Pratt's 'passion for documentation led him to study "The Jesuit Relations." This was well and good, but as a result Pratt's view of early Canadian history is reached through the eyes of those, priests, like Bréboeuf [*sic*], who labored to *change* the Indians' view of life and death' (11–12). Calling Pratt a 'Christian humanist' (12), Livesay continues to observe that *Brébeuf* 'would surely have been the greater had the poet offered a counterbalance to Bréboeuf [*sic*] – a more generous insight into the Indians' own plight as victims of a conquering race' (12). Quoted here from the Papers of Dorothy Livesay, Box 101, Folder 1.

16 I borrow the expression 'anthropomorphic narrative' from Jameson's discussion about 'traces of surface representation' in a narrative system

whose model is not yet sufficiently 'formalized'; see *The Political Uncon-scious* 122.

17 The term 'monologism,' together with my subsequent references to monologic genre and discourse, derives from Bakhtin's theories of dis-course and genre. More specifically, monologism stands in contrast to his concept of dialogism, which, in *The Dialogic Imagination*, is defined as that 'epistemological mode' whereby '[e]verything means, is under-stood, as a part of a greater whole – there is a constant interaction be-tween meanings, all of which have the potential of conditioning others' (Glossary 426). See also Morson's discussion of 'dialogue' and 'mono-logue,' in *Bakhtin: Essays and Dialogues on His Work*, edited by himself; for Bakhtin, Morson observes, '"dialogue" is a description of all lan-guage – in effect a redefinition of language ... In this sense of the word "dialogue," there can be no "monologue," because language is held to be dialogic universally and by definition. There is, however, a second sense of the word "dialogue" that does admit – in fact, de-mands – "monologue" as its opposite ... As Bakhtin outlines the oppo-sition, monologic utterances and situations are constructed so as to restrict or ignore this dialogic possibility' (83–4).

18 I am borrowing this phrase from Jacques Derrida's '*il n'y a pas de hors-texte*,' translated as '[t]here is nothing outside of the text [there is no outside-text]' (*Of Grammatology* 158).

19 This incident, in its linguistic and ideological ramifications, is echoed by the circumstances surrounding Red Rorty's death in Howard O'Ha-gan's *Tay John*.

20 On this point, see also Redekop's essay 52–3.

21 'Differance' is Derrida's concept, and neologism, deriving from the verb 'to differ' [*différer*], which, '[o]n the one hand,' he says, 'indicates difference as distinction, inequality, or discernibility; on the other, it expresses the interposition of delay, the interval of a *spacing* and *tem-poralizing* that puts off until "later" what is presently denied, the possi-ble that is presently impossible. Sometimes the *different* and sometimes the *deferred* correspond [in French] to the verb "to differ." This corre-lation, however, is not simply one between act and object, cause and effect, or primordial and derived. In the one case "to differ" signifies nonidentity; in the other case it signifies the order of the *same*. Yet there must be a common, although entirely differant [*différante*], root within the sphere that relates the two movements of differing to one another. We provisionally give the name *differance* to this *sameness* which is not *identical*: by the silent writing of its *a*, it has the desired

advantage of referring to differing, *both* as spacing/temporalizing and as the movement that structures every dissociation' (*Speech and Phenomena* 129–30).

22 Paul Denham also discusses her documentary poems in a similar context; see his 'Lyric and Documentary in the Poetry of Dorothy Livesay.'

23 See her unpublished talk, described in The Papers of Dorothy Livesay as 'On Dorothy Livesay's own 1930's poetry and its relation to social activism' Box 106, Folder 31.

24 Consider, in this context, Livesay's comments on Pratt in her review of Sandra Djwa's *E.J. Pratt*: 'Ned Pratt gives us a fascinating display of fireworks through language, erudition, dramatic tension, but even in his short lyrics he does not stir the sort of emotion created in reading Roberts' "Tantramar Re-visited" or "The Skater." Pratt uses fine words about love, hate, fear; but somehow they fail to create empathy between himself and the reader. His talents, I feel, lie in quite another direction' (1). She concludes her review by asking, 'Why is it that Pratt is more fascinating to the Canadian critics as a representative public figure than as a poet? I would suggest,' she replies, 'that this emphasis has been wrong, all along, and that Pratt saw himself, not as a lyric poet or a learned philosopher, but as bard, as the voice of the people, a story-teller par excellence' (2), Box 99, Folder 11.

25 On the differences between tradition and genealogy see Michel Foucault, *The Archaeology of Knowledge*.

2 A GENRE IN THE PRESENT TENSE

1 Jeff Henderson's 'John Gardner's *Jason and Medeia*: The Resurrection of a Genre' provides us with an example of just such a revision of the epic in modern poetry.

2 The two passages just quoted are printed in side-by-side columns in the original.

3 See Charles Olson, *The Special View of History*; *Poetry and Truth: The Beloit Lectures and Poems*; and *Additional Prose: A Bibliography on America, Proprioception, and Other Notes and Essays*.

4 Bernstein's problematic, yet rigorous, study in effect modifies Roy Harvey Pearce's discussion of the long poem in *The Continuity of American Poetry*. In his chapter, aptly entitled 'The Long View,' Pearce argues that since the American epic is an 'impossible task,' a genre that defeats its own intent primarily because of the lack of cultural myths

displaying epic ethos, its 'strategy is to make a poem which will create rather than celebrate a hero and which will make rather than recall the history that surrounds him.' Although freed from history, and therefore become a transcendent form, the American long poem as modern epic is, for Pearce, a 'fundamentally' American gesture (61), albeit not always supported in the same degree by many American long poems, for example, Hart Crane's *The Bridge*. It represents, however, the extent to which national ideology is both communicated by genre and creates a 'new' genre.

5 On the concept of the 'imaginary' see Anthony Wilden, 'Lacan and the Discourse of the Other,' in Lacan, *Speech and Language in Psychoanalysis* 174–5.

6 The distinction between *langage* and *parole* is to be found in Ferdinand de Saussure, *Course in General Linguistics*. In response to his question 'what is language [*langue*]?' de Saussure says that '[i]t is not to be confused with human speech [*langage*], of which it is only a definite part, though certainly an essential one. It is both a social product of the faculty of speech and a collection of necessary conventions that have been adopted by a social body to permit individuals to exercise that faculty. Taken as a whole, speech is many-sided and heterogeneous; straddling several areas simultaneously – physical, physiological, and psychological – it belongs both to the individual and to society; we cannot put it into any category of human facts, for we cannot discover its unity' (9). 'In order to separate from the whole of speech that part that belongs to language,' de Saussure focuses on the circuits of communication that 'execute' speech; 'execution,' he says, 'is always individual, and the individual is always its master: I shall call the executive side [of language] *speaking* [*parole*]' (13).

7 See, for example, Marjorie Perloff, *The Poetics of Indeterminacy: Rimbaud to Cage*, 'From Image to Action: The Return to Story in Postmodern Poetry,' and *The Dance of the Intellect: Studies in the Poetry of the Pound Tradition*.

8 On nostalgia and the lyric see also Paul de Man, 'Lyric and Modernity,' in *Blindness and Insight: Essays in the Rhetoric of Contemporary Criticism* 166–8, especially 168.

9 I refer here not to Barthes's earlier usage of the term in *Writing Degree Zero*, where *écriture* signifies writing style, thereby making it possible for us to speak of various *écritures* (bourgeois *écriture*, Marxist *écriture*, etc.), but rather to his later use of it in works like *The Pleasure of the Text*, *S/Z*, and *A Lover's Discourse*, where *écriture* relates to the *writerly*

(as opposed to the *readerly*) text, to what Barthes calls the text of *jouiss-ance* (bliss, as opposed to the text of pleasure). In this usage it suggests a writing that foregrounds language and how it comes into being – how it means – and that problematizes those value system that we normally take for granted.

10 See also de Man, *Allegories of Reading: Figural Language in Rousseau, Nietzsche, Rilke, and Proust.*

11 See also Douglas Barbour's insightful study of the anti-lyric.

12 Beginning with Ondaatje's anthology in 1979, the interest in the long poem gradually increased: Kroetsch's essay was written for the MLA Discussion Group on Canadian Literature in English (Houston 1979); I presented a paper on the long poem at the following year's MLA session (Chicago 1980); at the conference The Coast Is Only a Line, sponsored by Simon Fraser University (Burnaby 1981), Davey presented his first paper on the long poem; the Long-liners Conference sponsored by York University (see *Open Letter* 6. 2–3 [Summer-Fall 1985] for the proceedings) was the culmination of these events but not the end; in 1984 at Simon Fraser University, bpNichol, invited by Roy Miki, gave a 'marathon' reading from *The Martyrology*, and had a dialogue on the long poem with Bowering and Marlatt (see *Line* 6). See also Anne Archer's editorial statement in the long poem special issue of *Quarry*. For a more recent acknowledgment and discussion of the prominence of the long poetic form, see Laurie Ricou's chapter 'Poetry' in New, ed., *Literary History of Canada.*

13 See Fowler's discussion of conscious genres 52–3.

14 I am appropriating here Theodor Adorno's concept of 'negative dialectics,' a dialectics whereby no priority or privileging right is assigned to either part of a binary structure, thus avoiding reification. In this context 'negative dialectics' elides the sovereignty of a single genre and its assumed ideological import. See Adorno, *Negative Dialectics* and *Aesthetic Theory*.

15 In Hammon's essay, the objective of which is 'not to study so much the ideology "of the" text (in its "relationship" to the text) as the "ideological effect" of the text as a relationship inscribed in the text and constructed by it' (95), a 'semiotics of knowing' is characterized by 'strategies of manipulation, of evaluation, of the fixing of contracts, of persuasion and belief, of knowledge and misinformation, and so forth' (96).

16 On the serial poem, see also Sherman Paul, 'Serial Poems from Can-

ada' (a review of Ondaatje's *The Long Poem Anthology*), Alan Golding, 'George Oppen's Serial Poems,' and Mark Johnson, '"Passages": Cross-sections of the Universe'; as well, the special issue of *Boundary 2* on Jack Spicer includes a number of essays that address many issues relating to the serial poem.

17 I would like to thank Ron Smith, and especially Pauline Butling and Fred Wah, for the talks that helped me come up with this term. Whereas Wah, predictably, hears echoes of Olson's 'projective verse' behind the conceptive long poem, I hear the emphasis on concept – the conceptualization of the poetic image, the idea present conceptually and not necessarily translated into a visual metaphor.

18 On the complexity of poetic form as an aggregate structure see Edward Stankiewicz, 'The Centrifugal Structures of Modern Poetry.'

19 See Linda Hutcheon, *A Theory of Parody*.

20 See Juliusz Kleiner, 'The Role of Time in Literary Genres.' Kleiner argues that 'various types of literary works develop in conformity with ... different psychological attitudes. Consequently the theory of literary genres must, apart of [*sic*] other significant aspects, account for the time factor' (5).

3 LOCALITY IN THE LONG POEM

1 *Field Notes* is no longer a 'continuing poem.' Kroetsch's *Completed Field Notes* (*CFN*), a gathering of all his long poems, is meant to mark the end of this ongoing long poem. As he says, 'I like to believe that the sequence of poems, announced in medias res as continuing, is, in its acceptance of its own impossibilities, completed' (*CFN* 269).

2 The difference between dialogism and dialectics is spelled out by Bakhtin in *Problems of Dostoevsky's Poetics*. He says specifically that '[d]ialogic relationships are reducible neither to logical relationships nor to relationships oriented semantically toward their referential object' (183).

3 On the ability of nature to 'overcode' locality see Henri Lefebvre, *La Production de l'espace*, especially 24–6.

4 For the idea of nature as memory I am indebted to Lefebvre, *La Production de l'espace* 39–40.

5 This is reinforced by the dedication of *Completed Field Notes* to Ishtar. 'The finished book,' as Kroetsch says, 'is for that reader I call Ishtar, that undiscoverable and discovered reader towards whom one, always, writes' (*CFN* 270).

6 Olson's influence on the West Coast Canadian poets can be dated from the publication of Donald Allen's *New American Poetry* anthology in 1960. Also influential was the summer session course Olson taught at the University of British Columbia in 1963. That same summer, Robert Duncan, Robert Creeley, Philip Whalen, Denise Levertov, Allen Ginsberg, and Margaret Avison (the only Canadian) took part, together with Olson, in the Vancouver Poetry Conference.

7 Marlatt pointed out to me that what was printed as 'to imitate the flow of the rhythm' in *Broadside* was a misprint of 'to imitate the flow of the river.'

8 I quote from the Longspoon edition.

9 Unpublished interview with Marlatt 'on the West Coast' by Eleanor Wachtel, page 3 of manuscript. My thanks to Marlatt for providing me with a copy of the interview.

10 Chris Hall, in his essay 'Two Poems of Place: Williams's *Paterson* and Marlatt's *Steveston*,' also talks about Marlatt's 'research' methods, but he does so by relying on Levi-Strauss's anthropological model and calls *Steveston* 'a structuralist poem' (143).

11 For new readings of *Steveston* and other texts by Marlatt, see Marlatt, 'A Special Daphne Marlatt Feature,' a section in *Line* 13 (Spring 1989) that I co-edited with Shirley Neuman.

12 Mandel says in *Life Sentence* that '*Out of Place* will be designed by Ann' (93).

13 Hartman states that 'criticism is a genre, or a primary text' insofar as the critic is aware of employing a creative 'style.' A careful look at Ann Mandel's prose rhythms and use of imagery provides evidence of the extent to which, in the 'Preface,' she engages herself with language in a creative way.

14 See Andrew Suknaski, 'Emir Rodriguez Monegal, *Jorge Luis Borges: A Literary Biography*.' In this review of Borges's biography, Suknaski explores some important aspects of *Out of Place*, mainly that of doubleness.

15 Peter Stevens notices the same duplicity in his essay 'Poet as Critic as Prairie Poet.' See especially 68.

16 The structure and the devices Mandel uses in this passage could also be examined in the light of Gérard Genette's 'iterative narrative,' the 'type of narrative, where a single narrative utterance takes upon itself several occurrences together of the same event.' See *Narrative Discourse: An Essay in Method* 116.

17 On the different layers of narration in the present tense see the chapter entitled 'Voice' in Gérard Genette's *Narrative Discourse* 212–62.

18 Due to a misprint, 'signs' as the title of this poem does not appear in *Out of Place*. My thanks to Mandel for pointing this out to me.

4 THE SELF IN THE LONG POEM

1 See bpNichol, with Daphne Marlatt and George Bowering, 'A Conversation: "Syntax Equals the Body Structure"' 24. Roy Miki and others also participate in this 'Conversation.' See also Bowering, 'bpNichol on the Train,' 'Read the Way He Writes: A Festschrift for bpNichol' 15. Nichol refers directly to the utanikki in Book 5, Chain 3.

2 Most of Derrida's work is of great relevance to this issue; see especially his essay 'Language and Institutions of Philosophy' (1984); see also Richard Rorty, *Philosophy and the Mirror of Nature*.

3 Frank Davey and Roy Miki also discuss the primacy of language in relation to the concept of the self in the long poem. See Davey's 'Exegesis / Eggs à Jesus: *The Martyrology* as a Text in Crisis'; and Miki's 'The Lang Poem: The Cosmology of the Long Poem in Contemporary Canadian Poetry.'

4 All icon-like figures appearing in *The Martyrology* are drawings by Jerry Ofo.

5 On some of the functions of intertextuality in the long poem see Davey's 'Countertextuality in the Long Poem.'

6 The order of these beginnings changes in the revised edition of Book 1, further complicating the textuality of *The Martyrology*.

7 See Brian Henderson, 'Soul Rising out of the Body of Language: Presence, Process and Faith in *The Martyrology*'; see also Scobie's chapter '*The Martyrology*,' in his *bpNichol*.

8 On Stein's influence on Nichol, see Scobie, '*The Martyrology*,' in his *bpNichol* 9–15, 110–11.

9 See also Davey's treatment of this pronoun in 'Exegesis.'

10 See Lacan, 'Of the Subject of Certainty': 'For Descartes, in the initial *cogito* – ... – what the *I think* is directed towards, in so far as it lurches into the *I am*, is a real. But the true remains so much outside that Descartes then has to re-assure himself – of what, if not of an Other that is not deceptive, and which shall, into the bargain, guarantee by its very existence the bases of truth, guarantee him that there are in his own objective reason the necessary foundations for the very real, about whose existence he has just re-assured himself, to find the di-

mension of truth. I can do no more than suggest the extraordinary consequences that have stemmed from this handing back of truth into the hands of the Other, in this instance the perfect God, whose truth is the nub of the matter, since, whatever he might have meant, would always be *the* truth – even if he had said that two and two make five, it would have been true' (36).

11 See Scobie's discussion of Saint And, '*The Martyrology*,' in his *bpNichol* 115–18.

12 See Derrida, *Of Grammatology*, and Gregory Ulmer's *Applied Grammatology*.

13 See also Steve McCaffery, '*The Martyrology* as Paragram.'

14 These last five lines, according to Nichol, were 'the opening lines of the poem ... because I'd stumbled across this poem in a drawer that I could not remember writing ... I began out of that sense of trying, in that initial moment of dealing with one's own history of a writing' ('A Conversation' 23).

15 For a similar interpretation of these lines see Henderson, 'Soul Rising' 116.

16 In the first edition of Book 2 these lines appear in a slightly different version that makes Nichol's intent more obvious: '*father* i am one am many / as *ever* the need to be obsesses ...' (my emphases).

17 Book 5, Chain 11, is an excellent example of Nichol's 'pacing' through the alphabet.

18 See de Man, 'Autobiography as De-facement.'

19 The treatment of religion is an important part of the poem, demanding a study in itself.

20 My debts here are to Derrida's 'Signature Event Context,' in *Margins of Philosophy* and to *Signéponge/Signsponge*. See also Scobie's *Signature Event Cantext*.

21 Personal communication with Cooley, Winnipeg 1985

22 The section '*this is me: a retort*,' from which these references are taken, deals with the cover of the book. The ambiguity of the cover image is further accentuated in this poem by the referential subjects of 'I' and 'you,' which constantly shift from Cooley to Krafchenko.

23 Bakhtin, *The Dialogic Imagination* 65

24 I am quoting from Maurice Blanchot's essay 'Reading,' in his *The Gaze of Orpheus and Other Literary Essays* 92.

25 See Linda Hutcheon, *A Theory of Parody*; also Genette, *Palimpsestes: la littérature au second degré*.

26 In a typewritten page, included in his papers in the National Library,

Bowering records how H.D. found her way into his poem. The head-
ing, 'Dream of H.D.: diary, 12:38 p.m., Wed., Oct. 16, 1974,' is followed
by his record of the dream:

One of my dreams last night, I'm following H.D. to her apartment,
but I'm as usual too shy to talk to her. Then somehow later I'm sitting
inside her apartment in the dark and she is too, and trying not to
scare her, I softly announce that I'm there. She doesnt mind, and then
we start to talk, friendly. Old lady, and spry. One image is a new book
of hers, a thick paperback, 500 pages or so, & this I am fondling. It is
three books in one, three different sorts of things, prose & verse.
Later I look at it again & it is a larger-size hardback, with two photos
in it —— one is of a young H.D., & I dont remember that except
that she is pictured with a man. In the second she is lying down, snug-
gling a young light-brown complexioned woman; one sees there only
their faces & maybe shoulders. Then Jamie Reid [a member of the
Tish group of poets] appears in the dream. He is in a suit & tie, very
natty, with neat shortish hair. He is being very charming, half like a
businessman & half fey-hip show-business type. At one point H.D. and
I are in a large closet & Jamie is coming in to lay a strip of papery
linoleum on its floor. As he trippily turns to go out of the closet, I say,
'Jamie, you're ... charming!'

Following this, on a later date, 'Jan 22/82,' Bowering adds: 'This
dream of H.D., and others, are making their ways through the book I
have begun work on after years of imagining it. A book with the working title, Kerrisdale Elegies' (Box 28, Folder 3).

Among the various poets Bowering alludes to, Spicer is particularly
important because he translated Rilke's *Elegies* between 1950 and 1955;
see his 'Imaginary Elegies I–IV,' in *The Collected Books of Jack Spicer*, edited and with a commentary by Robin Blaser 333–9. Bowering, who has
shown his indebtedness to Spicer in *Allophanes*, said that Spicer facili-
tated his 'intrusion into the field of Rilke that had been staked out by
my many Rilke-loving friends, and to which I didn't feel real rights,
being hesitant about Rilke ... and not German.' Letter to the author,
January 1986. Cited with Bowering's permission.

27 Bowering said that he 'used basically 2 translations, and a bit of a third
... Not David Young,' but he couldn't recall which ones (letter to the
author). The translations I used are: J.B. Leishman and Stephen
Spender, *Rainer Maria Rilke: Prose and Poetry*; Stephen Mitchell, *The Se-*

lected Poetry of Rainer Maria Rilke; and A. Poulin, Jr, *Duino Elegies and the Sonnets to Orpheus*.

28 Bowering wrote that 'I wasn't interested in erasing Rilke so much as rewriting him. I have a funny relationship with him; although he is probably the most popular source for my poet companions in Vancouver, I have never been quite ready to trust him, his feyness, his rhapsody; I realize that he is right, he is onto something, and that he is a pre-Spicerian demonstration of the poet inspired or inspirated; but I have always been uneasy. I had to respond to that double feeling somehow' (letter to the author). Bowering's uneasiness about Rilke is manifested in the poem in more than one way, but a discussion of it falls outside the scope of this study. Whereas Bowering lets Rilke's signature stand, he hardly provides any clues for the poets' identities with regard to the French quotations in *Kerrisdale Elegies*. It is their language and tone that locate them in the context of French poetry. As Bowering said about them, 'Re the French quotations: well, they seem to me to do something – make connection? make correction, comment? on the surrounding text. They operate, it feels to me, the way quotations operate re the rest of the text in *Allophanes*. It is not exactly collage, because it reads on like poetic text, along the alonging poetic text that is there. They make sure that the writer is not running away with the poem ...' (letter to the author). The quotations are from: Baudelaire, 'La Prière d'un paine' (17); François Villon, 'Le Testament, CXIX' (30); Anne Hébert, 'Le Tombeau des rois' (61) (my thanks to Professor Stanley Dragland, University of Western Ontario, for this reference); Apollinaire, 'L'Ermite,' in *Alcools* (72); Michel Beaulieu, 'Rémission du corps enamouré,' in *Visages* (83) (my thanks to Bowering for this source); Mallarmé, 'Petit Air I' (99); Nerval, 'Vers dorés' (11); Laforgue, 'Complainte de l'oubli des morts' (123); I have failed to trace the source of the last quotation (131). See also Stanley Dragland's essay on the poem, 'The Bees of the Invisible.'

29 See Kristeva, *Semeiotiké: recherches pour une sémanalyse*; *Le Texte du roman: approche sémiologique d'une structure discursive transformationnelle*; and *Revolution in Poetic Language*. See also Michael Riffaterre, *Text Production*. For the history and development of the term intertextuality see Marc Angenot, 'L' "Intertextualité": enquête sur l'émergence et la diffusion d'un champ notionnel'; and 'L'Intertextualité: intertexte, autotexte, intratexte,' a special issue of *Texte* that includes Don Bruce's 'Bibliographie annotée: écrits sur l'intertextualité' 217–58.

30 See 'Linus,' *Oxford Classical Dictionary*.

31 The epigraph is from Kristeva's *Desire in Language: A Semiotic Approach to Literature and Art* 83.

5 OUTLAWED NARRATIVE: MICHAEL ONDAATJE

1 I am appropriating here Derrida's phrase 'white mythology' from 'White Mythology: Metaphor in the Text of Philosophy,' in *Margins of Philosophy*.
2 On the concept of literariness see de Man's title chapter in *The Resistance to Theory*.
3 Scobie's 'Postscript (1984),' added to his essay when reprinted in *Spider Blues*, shares to some degree my uneasiness about his reading of the poem. What this 'postscript' also reflects, however, is Scobie's development, as critic and as poet, from a modernist to a postmodernist perspective.
4 See Perry M. Nodelman, 'The Collected Photographs of Billy the Kid'; Dennis Lee, Savage Fields: *The Collected Works of Billy the Kid*.' See also Dennis Cooley, '"I Am Here on the Edge": Modern Hero / Postmodern Poetics in *The Collected Works of Billy the Kid*,' and J.M. Kertzer, 'On Death and Dying: *The Collected Works of Billy the Kid*.'
5 Dennis Lee argues that the poem is structured around 'six moments' that 'played no conscious part in the writing or editing; they are critical constructs devised after the fact' ('Savage Fields' 167).
6 Kertzer and Owens argue that the breakdown between friend and foe demonstrates the 'clear-cut pattern' of Billy's list. Their argument, I think, depends on the balance they expect to find between the opposites on a binary scale. If, however, they had approached this section from a generic point of view, they would have been sent, by the epic echo of Billy's list, to the epic model where conflict occurs not merely between friends and foes but also among friends or among foes.
7 Owens, too, acknowledges Angela's 'largeness,' but insists on seeing her in exclusively archetypal terms.
8 My reading of Billy as writer is close to, but not exactly identical with, Scobie's argument that Billy is both 'outlaw' and 'artist.' See his 'Two Authors in Search of a Character.'

Bibliography of Works Cited

Poetry Editions

Adams, Levi. *The Charivari; or Canadian Poetics: A Tale, After the Manner of Beppo* (1824). In *The Evolution of Canadian Literature in English: Beginnings to 1867.* Ed. Mary Jane Edwards. Toronto, Montreal: Holt, Rinehart and Winston 1973. 89–134

Atwood, Margaret. *The Journals of Susanna Moodie.* Toronto: Oxford 1970

Barbour, Douglas. *A Poem as Long as the Highway.* Kingston, Ont.: Quarry 1971

– *He & She &.* Ottawa: Golden Dog 1974

Blaser, Robin. *Image-Nations 1–12 & the Stadium of the Mirror.* London: Ferry 1974

Bowering, George. *Allophanes.* Toronto: Coach House 1976

– *Kerrisdale Elegies.* Toronto: Coach House 1984

Burwell, Adam Hood. *Talbot Road: A Poem* (1818). In 'The Poems of Adam Hood Burwell: Pioneer Poet of Canada.' Ed. and intro. Carl F. Klinck. *Western Ontario History Nuggets 30.* London, Ont.: Lawson Memorial Library, University of Western Ontario, May 1963. 4–17

Cary, Thomas. *Abram's Plains: A Poem* (1789). In Gnarowski 17–38

Cooley, Dennis. *Bloody Jack.* Winnipeg: Turnstone 1984

Crawford, Isabella Valancy. *Malcolm's Katie: A Love Story.* In *Collected Poems.* By Crawford. Ed. and intro. James Reaney. Toronto: U of Toronto P 1972. 193–236

Davey, Frank. *The Abbotsford Guide to India.* Victoria and Toronto: Porcépic 1986

– *King of Swords.* Vancouver: Talonbooks 1972

Garnet, Eldon. *Brébeuf: A Martyrdom of Jean De.* Erin, Ont.: Porcépic 1977

Gnarowski, Michael, ed. *Three Early Poems from Lower Canada.* Intros by

Gnarowski. Montreal: Lawrence M. Lande Foundation at the McLennan Library, McGill University 1969

Goldsmith, Oliver. *The Rising Village*. Ed. Michael Gnarowski. Montreal: Delta 1968

Gutteridge, Don. *God's Geography*. Ilderton, Ont.: Brick 1982

– *Tecumseh*. Toronto: Oberon 1976

Homer. *The Odyssey of Homer*. Trans. and intro. Richard Lattimore. New York: Harper and Row 1965

Howe, Joseph. *Acadia*. In *Poems and Essays*. Ed. and intro. M.G. Parks. Toronto: U of Toronto P 1973. 5–40

Jabès, Edmond. *The Book of Dialogue*. Trans. Rosemarie Waldrop. Middletown, Conn.: Wesleyan UP 1987

Jones, David. *The Anathémata: Fragments of an Attempted Writing*. New York: Viking 1965

Jones, D.G. *Kate, These Flowers ... (The Lampman Poems)*. In *Under the Thunder the Flowers Light Up the Earth*. Toronto: Coach House 1977

Kearns, Lionel. *Convergences*. Toronto: Coach House 1984

Kirby, William. *The U.E.: A Tale of Upper Canada* (1859). In Sinclair 81–114

Kiyooka, Roy. *The Fontainebleau Dream Machine*. Toronto: Coach House 1977

Kroetsch, Robert. *Completed Field Notes*. Toronto: McClelland and Stewart 1989

Lampman, Archibald. *The Story of an Affinity*. Ed. D.M.R. Bentley. London, Ont.: Canadian Poetry 1986

Livesay, Dorothy. *The Documentaries*. Toronto: Ryerson 1968

MacEwen, Gwendolyn. *Afterworlds*. Toronto: McClelland and Stewart 1987

– *The T.E. Lawrence Poems*. Oakville, Ont.: Mosaic/Valley 1982

MacKay, J. *Quebec Hill*. In Gnarowski 45–70

McLachlan, Alexander. *The Emigrant* (1861). In Sinclair 115–56

Mair, Charles. *Tecumseh*. In *Dreamland and Other Poems, Tecumseh: A Drama*. Ed. and intro. Norman Shrive. Toronto: U of Toronto P 1974

Mandel, Eli. *Life Sentence: Poems and Journals: 1976–1980*. Toronto and Victoria: Porcépic 1981

– *Out of Place*. 'Preface' and photographs Ann Mandel. Toronto and Victoria: Porcépic 1977

Marlatt, Daphne. *Steveston*. Photographs Robert Minden. Vancouver: Talonbooks 1974; rpt Edmonton: Longspoon 1984

Mouré, Erin. *WSW (West South West)*. Montreal: Véhicule 1989

Nichol, bp. *The Martyrology*. Books 1–6. Toronto: Coach House 1972–87

Ondaatje, Michael. *The Collected Works of Billy the Kid*. Toronto: Anansi 1970

–, ed. *The Long Poem Anthology*. Toronto: Coach House 1979

Pratt, E.J. *Complete Poems*. Ed. Sandra Djwa and R.G. Moyles. 2 parts. Toronto: U of Toronto P 1989

Reid, Monty. *The Alternate Guide*. Red Deer, Alta: Red Deer College P 1985

Rilke, Rainer Maria. *Duino Elegies and the Sonnets to Orpheus*. Trans. A. Poulin, Jr. Boston: Houghton Mifflin 1977

– *Rainer Maria Rilke: Prose and Poetry*. Trans. J.B. Leishman and Stephen Spender. Ed. Egon Schwarz. Foreword Howard Nemerov. New York: Continuum 1984

– *The Selected Poetry of Rainer Maria Rilke*. Trans. and ed. Stephen Mitchell. Intro. Robert Hass. New York: Vintage 1984

Sangster, Charles. *The St. Lawrence and the Saguenay* (1856). In Sinclair 43–80

Scobie, Stephen. *The Ballad of Isabel Gunn*. Kingston, Ont.: Quarry 1987

– *McAlmon's Chinese Opera*. Dunvegan, Ont.: Quadrant 1980

Sinclair, David, ed. *Nineteenth-Century Narrative Poems*. Intro. by Sinclair. Toronto: McClelland and Stewart 1972

Spicer, Jack. *The Collected Books of Jack Spicer*. Ed. and commentary Robin Blaser. Los Angeles: Black Sparrow 1975

Thesen, Sharon. *The Beginning of the Long Dash*. Toronto: Coach House 1987

Thomson, James. *The Seasons*. Ed. James Sambrook. New York: Oxford UP 1981

Tostevin, Lola Lemire. *Double Standards*. Edmonton: Longspoon 1985

– *Gyno-Text*. Toronto: Underwhich 1986

– *'sophie*. Toronto: Coach House 1988

Wah, Fred. *Breathin' My Name with a Sigh*. Vancouver: Talonbooks 1981

– *Music at the Heart of Thinking*. Red Deer, Alta: Red Deer College P 1987

Webb, Phyllis. *Hanging Fire*. Toronto: Coach House 1990

– *Naked Poems*. Vancouver: Periwinkle 1965

– *The Vision Tree: Selected Poems*. Ed. and intro. Sharon Thesen. Vancouver: Talonbooks 1982

Whitman, Walt. *Complete Poetry and Collected Prose*. New York: Library of America 1982

Whyte, Jon. *The Fells of Brightness*, Vol. 1, *Some Fittes and Starts*. Edmonton: Longspoon 1983

– *The Fells of Brightness*, Vol. 2, *Wenkchemna*. Edmonton: Longspoon 1985

– *Homage, Henry Kelsey*. Winnipeg: Turnstone 1981

Critical Works

ABBREVIATIONS

MLN Modern Language Notes
NLH New Literary History
PMLA Publications of the Modern Language Association of America

Adorno, Theodor W. *Aesthetic Theory.* Trans. C. Lenhardt. Ed. Gretel
  Adorno and Rolf Tiedemann. London and New York: Routledge and
  Kegan Paul 1984
– *Negative Dialectics.* Trans. E.B. Ashton. New York: Continuum 1983
Altieri, Charles. 'Motives in Metaphor: John Ashbery and the Modernist
  Long Poem.' In 'The Long Poem in the Twentieth Century' 653–87
Angenot, Marc. 'L'"Intertextualité": enquête sur l'émergence et la diffu-
  sion d'un champ notionnel.' *Revue des sciences humaines* 60.189 (Jan.–Mar.
  1983): 121–35
Archer, Anne. 'Introduction.' *Quarry* 35.1 (Winter 1986): 7–14
Arnason, David, Dennis Cooley, and Robert Enright. 'Interview with Eli
  Mandel, March 16/78.' In 'Prairie Poetry Issue' 70–89
Bakhtin, Mikhail. *The Dialogic Imagination: Four Essays.* Ed. Michael Hol-
  quist. Trans. Caryl Emerson and Michael Holquist. Austin: U of Texas P
  1981
– *Problems of Dostoevsky's Poetics.* Ed. and trans. Caryl Emerson. Intro.
  Wayne C. Booth. Minneapolis: U of Minnesota P 1984
Barbour, Douglas. *Daphne Marlatt.* Don Mills, Ont.: ECW forthcoming
– 'Lyric/Anti-Lyric: Some Notes about a Concept.' *Line* 3 (1984): 45–63
– 'The Phenomenological I: Daphne Marlatt's *Steveston.*' In *Figures in a
  Ground: Canadian Essays on Modern Literature Collected in Honor of Sheila
  Watson.* Ed. Diane Bessai and David Jackel. Saskatoon: Western Producer
  Prairie 1978. 174–88
Barthes, Roland. *A Lover's Discourse: Fragments.* Trans. Richard Howard.
  New York: Hill and Wang 1979
– *The Pleasure of the Text.* Trans. Richard Miller. Note Richard Howard.
  New York: Hill and Wang 1975
– 'Right in the Eyes.' In *The Responsibility of Forms: Critical Essays on Music,
  Art, and Representation.* Trans. Richard Miller. Pref. Richard Howard.
  New York: Hill and Wang 1985. 237–42
– *S/Z: An Essay.* Trans. Richard Miller. Pref. Richard Howard. New York:
  Hill and Wang 1974

– *Writing Degree Zero*. Trans. Annette Lavers and Colin Smith. London: Jonathan Cape 1967

Bayard, Caroline, and Jack David. 'George Bowering.' In *Out-Posts: Interviews, Poetry, Bibliographies and a Critical Introduction to 8 Major Modern Poets*. Erin, Ont.: Porcépic 1978. 77–997

Bentley, D.M.R. 'The Mower and the Boneless Acrobat: Notes on the Stances of Baseland and Hinterland in Canadian Poetry.' *Studies in Canadian Literature* 8.1 (1983): 5–48

– 'A New Dimension: Notes on the Ecology of Canadian Poetry.' *Canadian Poetry* 7 (Fall-Winter 1980): 1–20

– 'A Stretching Landscape: Notes on Some Formalistic Continuities in the Poetry of the Hinterland.' *Contemporary Verse II* 5 (Summer 1981): 6–18

Benveniste, Emile. *Problems in General Linguistics*. Trans. Mary Elizabeth Meek. Coral Gables, Fla: U of Miami P 1971

Bernstein, Michael André. *The Tale of the Tribe: Ezra Pound and the Modern Verse Epic*. Princeton: Princeton UP 1980

Bhabha, Homi. 'Representation and the Colonial Text: A Critical Exploration of Some Forms of Mimeticism.' In *The Theory of Reading*. Ed. Frank Gloversmith. Brighton, Sussex: Harvester P 1984. 93–121

Blanchot, Maurice. *The Gaze of Orpheus and Other Literary Essays*. Trans. Lydia Davis. Ed. P. Adams Sitney. Pref. Geoffrey Hartman. Barrytown, NY: Station Hill 1981

– *Le Livre à venir*. Paris: Gallimard 1959

– *The Writing of the Disaster*. Trans. Ann Smock. Lincoln and London: U of Nebraska P 1986

Blaser, Robin. 'The Fire.' *Caterpillar* 12 (1970): 15–23

– 'The Practice of Outside.' In *The Collected Works of Jack Spicer*. Ed. Blaser. Los Angeles: Black Sparrow 1975. 271–329

Blodgett, E.D. 'The Book, Its Discourse, and the Lyric: Notes on Robert Kroetsch's *Field Notes*.' In 'Robert Kroetsch: Reflections' 195–205

Bloom, Harold. *The Anxiety of Influence: A Theory of Poetry*. London, Oxford, New York: Oxford UP 1975

Bonanno, Giovanni, ed. *Canada Ieri e Oggi*. Bari, Italy: Schena 1986

Bouchard, Gilbert. Untitled interview with Daphne Marlatt. In *Gateway*, University of Alberta newspaper. 1 Oct. 1985. 7

Bowering, George. 'bpNichol on the Train.' In 'Read the Way He Writes' 7–20

– 'Dream of H.D.' George Bowering Collection. Literary Manuscripts Collection, National Library of Canada, Box 28, Folder 3

– Editorial. *Imago* 1 (1964): 2

- 'Given This Body: An Interview with Daphne Marlatt.' In special issue, 'Three Vancouver Writers: Interviews by George Bowering,' *Open Letter* 4.3 (Spring 1979): 32–88
- 'Look into Your Ear and Write: Allophanes.' In 'Statements by the Poets,' in Ondaatje, ed. 329–30
- and Daphne Marlatt. 'Keep Witnessing: A Review/Interview.' *Open Letter* 3.2 (Fall 1975): 26–38

Brooke-Rose, Christine. 'Historical Genres / Theoretical Genres: A Discussion of Todorov on the Fantastic.' *NLH* 8 (1977): 145–58
- *A Rhetoric of the Unreal: Studies in Narrative and Structure, Especially of the Fantastic*. Cambridge, London, New York: Cambridge UP 1981; rpt 1983

Brown, Russell. 'Seeds and Stones: Unhiding in Kroetsch's Poetry.' In 'Robert Kroetsch: Reflections' 154–75

Bruce, Don. 'Bibliographie annotée: écrits sur l'intertextualité.' In 'L'Intertextualité: intertexte, autotexte, intratexte' 217–58

Cameron, Sharon. *Lyric Time: Dickinson and the Limits of Genre*. Baltimore and London: Johns Hopkins UP 1979

Cobley, Evelyn. 'Mikhail Bakhtin's Place in Genre Theory.' *Genre* 21 (Fall 1988): 321–38

Cohen, Ralph. 'Innovation and Variation: Literary Change and Georgic Poetry.' In *Literature and History*. Ed. Cohen and Murray Krieger. Los Angeles: U of California P 1974. 3–34
- 'On the Interrelations of Eighteenth-Century Literary Forms.' In *New Approaches to Eighteenth-Century Literature*. Ed. Phillip Harth. New York: Columbia UP 1973. 33–78

Colie, Rosalie L. *The Resources of Kind: Genre-Theory in the Renaissance*. Ed. Barbara K. Lewalski. Berkeley: U of California P 1973

'Colonialism and Other Essays.' Special issue, *Oxford Literary Review* 9.1 (1987)

Cooley, Dennis. '"I Am Here on the Edge": Modern Hero / Postmodern Poetics in *The Collected Works of Billy the Kid*.' In Solecki 211–39
- *The Vernacular Muse: The Eye and Ear in Contemporary Literature*. Winnipeg: Turnstone 1987

Culler, Jonathan. 'Prolegomena to a Theory of Reading.' In *The Reader in the Text: Essays on Audience and Interpretation*. Ed. Susan R. Suleiman and Inge Crosman. Princeton: Princeton UP 1980. 46–66
- *The Pursuit of Signs: Semiotics, Literature, Deconstruction*. Ithaca, NY: Cornell UP 1981
- 'Reading Lyric.' In special issue, 'The Lesson of Paul de Man,' *Yale French Studies* 69 (1985): 98–106

Davey, Frank. 'Countertextuality in the Long Poem.' 'Long-liners Conference' 33–41

– 'E.J. Pratt: Apostle of Corporate Man.' In Davey, *Surviving the Paraphrase* 13–27

– 'E.J. Pratt: Rationalist Technician.' In Davey, *Surviving the Paraphrase* 29–45

– 'Exegesis / Eggs à Jesus: *The Martyrology* as a Text in Crisis.' In 'Read the Way He Writes' 169–81

– 'The Explorer in Western Literature.' In Davey, *Surviving the Paraphrase* 137–49

– 'Fort and Forest: Instability in the Symbolic Code in E.J. Pratt's *Brébeuf and His Brethren.*' In Davey, *Reading Canadian Reading* 167–79

– 'The Language of the Contemporary Canadian Long Poem.' In Davey, *Surviving the Paraphrase* 183–93

– *Reading Canadian Reading.* Winnipeg: Turnstone 1988

– 'Recontextualization in the Long Poem.' In Davey, *Reading Canadian Reading* 123–36

– *Surviving the Paraphrase.* Winnipeg: Turnstone 1983

de Man, Paul. *Allegories of Reading: Figural Language in Rousseau, Nietzsche, Rilke, and Proust.* New Haven and London: Yale UP 1979

– 'Autobiography as De-facement.' *MLN* 94.5 (Dec. 1979): 919–30

– *Blindness and Insight: Essays in the Rhetoric of Contemporary Criticism.* 2nd ed. rev. Intro. Wlad Godzich. Minneapolis: U of Minnesota P 1983

– 'Lyrical Voice in Contemporary Theory: Riffaterre and Jauss.' In Hošek and Parker 55–72

– *The Resistance to Theory.* Foreword Wlad Godzich. Minneapolis: U of Minnesota P 1986

– *The Rhetoric of Romanticism.* New York: Columbia UP 1984

Denham, Paul. 'Lyric and Documentary in the Poetry of Dorothy Livesay.' In Dorney et al. 87–106

Derrida, Jacques. *Dissemination.* Trans., intro., and notes Barbara Johnson. Chicago: U of Chicago P 1981

– *The Ear of the Other: Otobiography, Transference, Translation, Texts and Discussions with Jacques Derrida.* Ed. Christie V. McDonald. Trans. Peggy Kamuf. 'Otobiographies' trans. Avital Ronell. New York: Schocken 1985

– 'Language and Institutions of Philosophy.' *Recherches Sémiotiques / Semiotic Inquiry* 4.2 (June 1984): 91–154

– 'The Law of Genre.' *Critical Inquiry* 7.1 (Autumn 1980): 55–81

– *Margins of Philosophy.* Trans. and notes Alan Bass. Chicago: U of Chicago P 1982

- *Of Grammatology.* Trans. and pref. Gayatric Chakravorty Spivak. Baltimore and London: Johns Hopkins UP 1974
- *Positions.* Trans. and notes Alan Bass. Chicago: U of Chicago P 1981
- *Signéponge / Signsponge.* Trans. Richard Rand. New York: Columbia UP 1984
- *Speech and Phenomena and Other Essays on Husserl's Theory of Signs.* Trans. and intro. David B. Allison. Pref. Newton Garner. Evanston, Ill.: Northwestern UP 1973

de Saussure, Ferdinand. *Course in General Linguistics.* Ed. Charles Bally and Albert Sechehaye, with Albert Riedlinger. Trans. Wade Baskin. New York: McGraw-Hill 1959

Dewart, Edward Hartley. 'Introductory Essay.' In *Selections from Canadian Poets, 1864.* Ed. Dewart. Intro. Douglas Lochhead. Toronto: U of Toronto P 1973. ix–xix

Dickie, Margaret. *On the Modernist Long Poem.* Iowa City: U of Iowa P 1986

Djwa, Sandra. *E.J. Pratt: The Evolutionary Vision.* Montreal and London: McGill-Queen's UP 1974

Dorney, Lindsay, Gerald Noonan, and Paul Tiessen, eds. *A Public and Private Voice: Essays on the Life and Work of Dorothy Livesay.* Waterloo, Ont.: U of Waterloo P 1986

Dragland, Stanley. 'The Bees of the Invisible.' *Brick* 28 (Fall 1986): 14–25

Druff, James H. 'Genre and Mode: The Formal Dynamics of Doubt.' *Genre* 14.3 (Fall 1981): 295–307

Dubrow, Heather. *Genre.* London and New York: Methuen 1982

Dudek, Louis. 'Poet of the Machine.' In *E.J. Pratt.* Ed. David G. Pitt. Toronto: Ryerson 1969. 88–94

Eagleton, Terry. *Criticism and Ideology: A Study in Marxist Literary Theory.* London: Verso 1975; rpt 1984

Foucault, Michel. *The Archaeology of Knowledge.* Trans. A.M. Sheridan Smith. New York: Harper Colophon 1976

Fowler, Alastair. *Kinds of Literature: An Introduction to the Theory of Genres and Modes.* Cambridge, Mass.: Harvard UP 1982

Frame, Douglas. *The Myth of Return in Early Greek Epic.* New Haven and London: Yale UP 1978

Frye, Northrop. *Anatomy of Criticism: Four Essays.* Princeton: Princeton UP 1957
- 'Approaching the Lyric.' In Hošek and Parker 31–7
- 'Introduction.' *The Collected Poems of E.J. Pratt.* 2nd ed. Ed. Frye. Toronto: Macmillan of Canada 1962. xiii–xxviii
- 'The Narrative Tradition in English-Canadian Poetry' (1946). In *The Bush*

Garden: Essays on the Canadian Imagination. By Frye. Toronto: Anansi 1971. 144–55

Genette, Gérard. 'Genres, "types", modes.' *Poétique* 8.32 (1977): 389–421

– *Introduction à l'architexte.* Paris: Seuil 1979

– *Narrative Discourse: An Essay in Method.* Trans. Jane E. Lewin. Foreword Jonathan Culler. Ithaca: Cornell UP 1980

– *Palimpsestes: la littérature au second degré.* Paris: Seuil 1982

Godard, Barbara. 'Epi(pro)logue: In Pursuit of the Long Poem.' 'Long-liners Conference' 301–35

– 'Structuralism/Post-Structuralism: Language, Reality and Canadian Literature.' In *Future Indicative: Literary Theory and Canadian Literature.* Ed. and intro. John Moss. Ottawa: U of Ottawa P 1987

Golding, Alan. 'George Oppen's Serial Poems.' *Contemporary Literature* 29.2 (1988): 221–40

Goldsmith, Oliver. *The Autobiography of Oliver Goldsmith.* Intro. and notes Rev. Wilfred E. Myatt. Toronto: Ryerson 1943

Hall, Chris. 'Two Poems of Place: Williams's *Paterson* and Marlatt's *Steveston.*' *Canadian Review of American Studies* 15.2 (1982): 141–57

Hammon, Philippe. 'Text and Ideology: For a Poetics of the Norm.' *Style* 17.2 (Spring 1983): 95–119

Hardy, Barbara. *The Advantage of the Lyric: Essays on Feeling in Poetry.* London: Athlone 1977

Hartman, Geoffrey. *Criticism in the Wilderness: The Study of Literature Today.* New Haven and London: Yale UP 1980

Henderson, Brian. 'Soul Rising out of the Body of Language: Presence, Process and Faith in *The Martyrology.*' In 'Read the Way He Writes' 111–28

Henderson, Jeff. 'John Gardner's *Jason and Medeia*: The Resurrection of a Genre.' *Papers on Language and Literature* 22.1 (1986): 76–95

Hernadi, Paul. *Beyond Genre: New Directions in Literary Classification.* Ithaca and London: Cornell UP 1972

Herodotus. *The Histories.* Trans. and intro. Aubrey de Selincourt. Harmondsworth, Middlesex: Penguin 1954; rpt 1971

Herrnstein Smith, Barbara. 'Narrative Versions, Narrative Theories.' *Critical Inquiry* 7.1 (Autumn 1980): 213–36

Hošek, Chaviva, and Patricia Parker, eds. *Lyric Poetry: Beyond New Criticism.* Ithaca and London: Cornell UP 1985

Hughes, Kenneth. 'Oliver Goldsmith's *The Rising Village.*' *Canadian Poetry* 1 (1977): 27–43

Hutcheon, Linda. *The Canadian Postmodern: A Study of Contemporary English-Canadian Fiction.* Toronto: Oxford UP 1988

– *A Theory of Parody: The Teachings of Twentieth-Century Art Forms*. New York and London: Methuen 1985

'L'Intertextualité: intertexte, autotexte, intratexte.' Special issue, *Texte* 2 (1983)

Jameson, Fredric. *The Political Unconscious: Narrative as a Socially Symbolic Act*. Ithaca, NY: Cornell UP 1981

Johnson, Barbara. *A World of Difference*. Baltimore and London: Johns Hopkins UP 1987

Johnson, Mark. '"Passages": Cross-sections of the Universe.' *Ironwood* 11.2 (Fall 1983): 173–91

Keith, W.J. '*The Rising Village* Again.' *Canadian Poetry* 3 (1978): 1–13

Kertzer, J.M. 'On Death and Dying: *The Collected Works of Billy the Kid*.' *English Studies in Canada* 1 (Spring 1975): 86–96

Kierkegaard, Soren. *Repetition: An Essay in Experimental Psychology*. Trans. and intro. Walter Lowrie. Princeton: Princeton UP 1941

Kiyooka, Roy. 'The Fontainebleau Dream Machine.' In 'Statements by the Poets,' in Ondaatje, ed. 332

Kleiner, Juliusz. 'The Role of Time in Literary Genres.' *Zagadniena Rodzajow Literackich* 2 (1959): 5–12

Klinck, Carl F. 'Literary Activity in the Canadas (1812–1841).' In *Literary History of Canada: Canadian Literature in English*. Ed. Klinck. Toronto: U of Toronto P 1965. 125–62

– 'Thoughts on E.J. Pratt.' In *The E.J. Pratt Symposium*. Ed. Glen Clever. Ottawa: U of Ottawa P 1977. 9–13

Kristeva, Julia. *Desire in Language: A Semiotic Approach to Literature and Art*. Ed. Leon S. Roudiez. Trans. Thomas Gora, Alice Jardine, and Leon S. Roudiez. New York: Columbia UP 1980

– *Revolution in Poetic Language*. Trans. Margaret Waller. Intro. Leon S. Roudiez. New York: Columbia UP 1984

– *Semeiotiké: recherches pour une sémanalyse*. Paris: Seuil 1969

– *Le Texte du roman: approche sémiologique d'une structure discursive transformationnelle*. Paris and The Hague: Mouton 1970

Kroetsch, Robert. 'For Play and Entrance: The Contemporary Canadian Long Poem.' In *The Lovely Treachery of Words*. By Kroetsch. Toronto: Oxford UP 1989. 117–34

– 'Seed Catalogue.' In 'Statements by the Poets,' in Ondaatje, ed. 311–12

Lacan, Jacques. 'The Function of Language in Psychoanalysis.' In *Speech and Language in Psychoanalysis*. By Lacan. Trans. Anthony Wilden. Baltimore and London: Johns Hopkins UP 1968; rpt 1981. 1–87

– 'The Mirror Stage as Formative of the Function of the I.' *Ecrits: A Selec-*

tion. By Lacan. Trans. Alan Sheridan. New York and London: W.W. Norton 1977. 1–7

– 'Of the Subject of Certainty.' In *The Four Fundamental Concepts of Psycho-Analysis.* By Lacan. Ed. Jacques-Alain Miller. Trans. Alan Sheridan. Harmondsworth, Middlesex: Penguin 1979. 29–41

Lampman, Archibald. 'Two Canadian Poets: A Lecture, 1891.' In Smith, ed. 26–44

Lecker, Robert. 'Daphne Marlatt's Poetry.' *Canadian Literature* 76 (Spring 1978): 56–67

– *Robert Kroetsch.* Boston: Twayne 1986

Lee, Dennis. 'Savage Fields: *The Collected Works of Billy the Kid.*' In Solecki 166–84

Lefebvre, Henri. *La Production de l'espace.* Paris: Anthropos 1974

Lejeune, Philippe. *Lire Leiris: autobiographie et langage.* Paris: Klincksieck 1975

Lighthall, W.D. 'Introduction to *Songs of the Great Dominion 1889.*' In Smith, ed. 17–25

Livesay, Dorothy. 'The Canadian Documentary: An Overview.' In 'Long-liners Conference' 127–30

– 'The Canadian Indian in Our Literature.' Papers of Dorothy Livesay, Special Collections, Elizabeth Dafoe Library, University of Manitoba. Box 101, Folder 1

– 'The Documentary Poem: A Canadian Genre.' In Mandel, ed. 267–81

– Review of Djwa's *E.J. Pratt: The Evolutionary Vision.* Papers of Dorothy Livesay. Box 99, Folder 11

– *The Papers of Dorothy Livesay: A Research Tool.* Winnipeg: U of Manitoba 1986

'Long-liners Conference.' Special issue, *Open Letter* 6.2–3 (Summer–Fall 1985)

'The Long Poem in the Twentieth Century.' Special issue, *Genre* 11.4 (Winter 1978)

Lyotard, Jean-François. *The Postmodern Condition: A Report on Knowledge.* Trans. Geoff Bennington and Brian Massumi. Foreword Fredric Jameson. Minneapolis: U of Minnesota P 1984

McCaffery, Steve. '*The Martyrology* as Paragram.' In 'Read the Way He Writes' 191–206

McLeod, Les. 'Canadian Post-Romanticism: The Context of Late Nineteenth-Century Canadian Poetry.' *Canadian Poetry* 14 (1984): 1–37

Mandel, Eli. 'The Death of the Long Poem.' In 'Long-liners Conference' 11–23

– *A Family Romance: Critical Essays.* Winnipeg: Turnstone 1987

–, ed. *Contexts of Canadian Criticism*. Chicago and London: U of Chicago P 1971

Marlatt, Daphne. 'Excerpts from Journal Kept during the Summer of '63 Conference, Vancouver.' *Olson: The Journals of the Charles Olson Archives* 4 (Fall 1975): 76–85

– 'A Special Daphne Marlatt Feature.' Ed. Smaro Kamboureli and Shirley Neuman. *Line* 13 (Spring 1989)

Merchant, Paul. *The Epic*. London: Methuen 1971

Miki, Roy. 'The Lang Poem: The Cosmology of the Long Poem in Contemporary Canadian Poetry.' In 'Long-liners Conference' 71–84

Miller, James E., Jr. *The American Quest for a Supreme Fiction: Whitman's Legacy in the Personal Epic*. Chicago: U of Chicago P 1979

Miller, J. Hillis. *The Ethics of Reading*. New York: Columbia UP 1987

Morson, Gary Saul. *The Boundaries of Genre: Dostoevsky's 'Diary of a Writer' and the Tradition of Literary Utopia*. Austin: U of Texas P 1981

–, ed. *Bakhtin: Essays and Dialogues on His Work*. Chicago and London: U of Chicago P 1986

Nichol, bp. With Daphne Marlatt and George Bowering. 'A Conversation: "Syntax Equals the Body Structure."' Ed. Roy Miki. *Line* 6 (Fall 1985): 21–44

– 'Things I Don't Really Understand about Myself.' Shuffle text in 'Long-liners Conference' 3, 20, 25, 39, 49, 62, 69, 73, 80, 87, 95, 102, 108, 118, 132, 141, 148, 152, 156, 228, 258, 277, 285, 292, 308, 323

Neuman, S.C. (Shirley). *Gertrude Stein: Autobiography and the Problem of Narration*. Victoria: English Literary Studies, U of Victoria 1979

Nodelman, Perry M. 'The Collected Photographs of Billy the Kid.' *Canadian Literature* 87 (Winter 1980): 68–79

Olson, Charles. *Additional Prose: A Bibliography on America, Proprioception, and Other Notes and Essays*. Ed. George F. Butterick. Bolinas, Calif.: Four Seasons Foundation 1974

– *Poetry and Truth: The Beloit Lectures and Poems*. Ed. George F. Butterick. Bolinas, Calif.: Four Seasons Foundation 1971

– *The Special View of History*. Ed. and intro. Ann Charters. Berkeley: Oyez 1970

Ondaatje, Michael, ed. *The Long Poem Anthology*. Toronto: Coach House 1979

Owens, Judith. '"I Send You a Picture": Ondaatje's Portrait of Billy the Kid.' *Studies in Canadian Literature* 8.1 (1983): 117–39

Parry, Benita. 'Problems in Current Theories of Colonial Discourse.' In 'Colonialism and Other Essays' 27–58

Paul, Sherman. 'Serial Poems from Canada.' *North Dakota Quarterly* 50.2 (Spring 1982): 108–18

Pearce, Roy Harvey. *The Continuity of American Poetry*. Princeton: Princeton UP 1961

Peirce, Charles Sanders. *Collected Papers*. Cambridge, Mass.: Harvard UP 1960

Perloff, Marjorie. *The Dance of the Intellect: Studies in the Poetry of the Pound Tradition*. Cambridge and London: Cambridge UP 1985

– 'From Image to Action: The Return to Story in Postmodern Poetry.' *Contemporary Literature* 23.4 (Fall 1982): 411–27

– *The Poetics of Indeterminacy: Rimbaud to Cage*. Princeton: Princeton UP 1981

Plato. *Plato's Cosmology: The Timaeus of Plato*. Trans. and commentary Francis MacDonald Cornford. London: Routledge and Kegan Paul 1937; rpt 1966

– *The Republic of Plato*. Trans., intro., and notes Francis MacDonald Cornford. New York and London: Oxford UP 1945; rpt 1960

Poe, Edgar Allan. 'The Philosophy of Composition' and 'The Poetic Principle.' In *Literary Criticism of Edgar Allan Poe*. Ed. Robert L. Hough. Lincoln, Nebr.: U of Nebraska P 1965. 20–3; 33–56

'Prairie Poetry Issue.' Special Issue, *Essays on Canadian Writing* 18–19 (Summer-Fall 1980)

Rajan, Tilottama. 'Romanticism and the Death of Lyric Consciousness.' In Hošek and Parker 194–207

Rasula, Jed. 'Spicer's Orpheus and the Emancipation of Pronouns.' *Boundary 2* 6.1 (Fall 1977): 51–102

'Read the Way He Writes: A Festschrift for bpNichol.' *Open Letter* 6.5–6 (Summer-Fall 1986)

Redekop, Magdalene. 'Authority and the Margins of Escape in *Brébeuf and His Brethren*.' In 'Long-liners Conference' 45–60

Ricoeur, Paul. *Freud and Philosophy: An Essay on Interpretation*. New Haven and London: Yale UP 1970

Ricou, Laurie. 'Poetry.' In *Literary History of Canada, Volume IV: Canadian Literature in English*. 2nd ed. Ed. W.H. New. Toronto, Buffalo, London: U of Toronto P 1990. 3–45

Riddel, Joseph N. 'A Somewhat Polemical Introduction: The Elliptical Poem.' In 'The Long Poem in the Twentieth Century' 459–77

Riffaterre, Michael. *Semiotics of Poetry*. Bloomington: Indiana UP 1978

– *Text Production*. Trans. Terese Lyons. New York: Columbia UP 1983

'Robert Kroetsch: Reflections.' Special issue, *Open Letter* 5.8–9 (Summer-Fall 1984)

Rorty, Richard. *Philosophy and the Mirror of Nature*. Princeton: Princeton UP 1979

Rosenthal, M.L., and Sally M. Gall. *The Modern Poetic Sequence: The Genius of Modern Poetry*. New York and Oxford: Oxford UP 1983

Rosmarin, Adena. *The Power of Genre*. Minneapolis: U of Minnesota P 1985

Said, Edward W. *Beginnings: Intention and Method*. New York: Basic 1975

Scobie, Stephen. 'Amelia, or: Who Do You Think You Are? Documentary and Identity in Canadian Literature.' *Canadian Literature* 100 (Spring 1984): 264–85

– *bpNichol: What History Teaches*. Vancouver: Talonbooks 1984

– 'The Continuing Poem: Robert Kroetsch and bpNichol.' In Bonanno 243–52

– 'Postscript (1984)' to 'Two Authors in Search of a Character.' In Solecki 206–10

– *Signature Event Cantext*. Edmonton: NeWest 1989

– 'Two Authors in Search of a Character.' *Canadian Literature* 54 (Autumn 1972): 37–55

Sidney, Sir Philip. *An Apology for Poetry or the Defence of Poesy*. Ed. Geoffrey Shepherd. London: Thomas Nelson and Sons 1965

Smith, A.J.M. 'Introduction.' In Smith, ed. vii–xi

–, ed. *Masks of Poetry: Canadian Critics on Canadian Verse*. Toronto: McClelland and Stewart 1962

Solecki, Sam, ed. *Spider Blues: Essays on Michael Ondaatje*. Montreal: Véhicule 1985

Spicer, Jack. Special issue on Jack Spicer. *Boundary 2* 6.1 (Fall 1977)

Stein, Gertrude. 'Portraits and Repetition.' In *Lectures in America*. By Stein. Boston: Beacon Hill 1957

Stankiewicz, Edward. 'The Centrifugal Structures of Modern Poetry.' In *Sign, System and Function*. Ed. Jerzy Pelc, Thomas A. Sebeok, Edward Stankiewicz, Thomas E. Winner. Berlin, New York, Amsterdam: Mouton 1984

Starobinski, Jean. *L'Oeil vivant: essai*. Paris: Gallimard 1961

– 'The Style of Autobiography.' In *Autobiography: Essays Theoretical and Critical*. Ed. James Olney. Princeton: Princeton UP 1980. 73–83

Stevens, Peter. 'Out of the Silence and across the Distance: The Poetry of Dorothy Livesay.' *Queen's Quarterly* 78 (1971): 579–91

– 'Poet as Critic as Prairie Poet.' In 'Prairie Poetry Issue' 54–69

Stich, K.P. '*The Rising Village, The Emigrant* and *Malcolm's Katie*: The Vanity of Progress.' *Canadian Poetry* 7 (1980): 48–55

Stimpson, Katharine R. 'Charles Olson: Preliminary Images.' In special issue, 'Charles Olson: Essays, Reminiscences, Reviews' *Boundary 2* 6.1–2 (Fall 1973–Winter 1974): 151–72

Stock, Brian. 'Literary Discourse and the Social Historian.' *NLH* 8.2 (1977): 183–94

Strelka, Joseph P., ed. *Theories of Literary Genres*. University Park: Pennsylvania UP 1978

Suknaski, Andrew. 'Emir Rodriguez Monegal, *Jorge Luis Borges: A Literary Biography*.' *Brick* 9 (Spring 1980): 16–24

Thompson, Lee. 'A More Public Voice: Poet as Journalist.' In Dorney et al. 42–52

Todorov, Tzvetan. *Les Genres du discours*. Paris: Seuil 1978

– *Mikhail Bakhtin: The Dialogical Principle*. Trans. Wlad Godzich. Minneapolis: U of Minnesota P 1984

– 'The Notion of Literature.' *NLH* 5 (1973): 7–16

– 'The Origin of Genre.' *NLH* 8 (1977): 159–70

Ulmer, Gregory L. *Applied Grammatology: Post(e)-Pedagogy from Jacques Derrida to Joseph Beuys*. Baltimore and London: Johns Hopkins UP 1985

Van den Abbeele, Georges. 'Sightseers: The Tourist as Theorist.' *Diacritics* 10.4 (1980): 3–14

Vietor, Karl. 'L'Histoire des genres littéraires.' *Poétique* 8.32 (1977): 490–506

Wachtel, Eleanor. Unpublished interview with Daphne Marlatt. 6 pages. In Marlatt's possession

Watson, Sheila. 'The Mechanization of Death.' In Solecki 156–65

Weldon, James F.G. 'A "Heroic" Reading of Pratt's *Brébeuf and His Brethren*.' In Bonanno 253–88

Welsh, Andrew. *Roots of Lyric: Primitive Poetry and Modern Poetics*. Princeton: Princeton UP 1978

West, Paul. 'Ethos and Epic: Aspects of Contemporary Canadian Poetry.' In Mandel, ed. 206–15

White, Hayden. 'Getting out of History.' *Diacritics* 12.3 (1982): 2–13

Wilson, Milton. 'Recent Canadian Verse.' In Mandel, ed. 198–205

Wright, Ellea. 'Text and Tissue: Body Language.' An interview with Daphne Marlatt and Betsy Warland. *Broadside* 6.3 (Dec. 1984–Jan. 1985): 4–5

Wright, George T. 'The Lyric Present: Simple Present and Verbs in English Poems.' *PMLA* 89.3 (May 1974): 536–79

Index

Numbers in italic type indicate pages where a concept or term is defined.

THEORY / CULTURE SERIES